T0355257

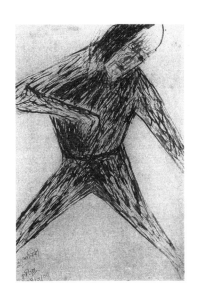

MEETING WITH
MUSSOLINI

MEETING WITH MUSSOLINI

Tagore's Tours in Italy

1925 and 1926

Kalyan Kundu

OXFORD
UNIVERSITY PRESS

OXFORD
UNIVERSITY PRESS

Oxford University Press is a department of the University of Oxford.
It furthers the University's objective of excellence in research, scholarship,
and education by publishing worldwide. Oxford is a registered trademark of
Oxford University Press in the UK and in certain other countries

Published in India by
Oxford University Press
YMCA Library Building, 1 Jai Singh Road, New Delhi 110 001, India

© Oxford University Press 2015

The moral rights of the authors have been asserted

First Edition published in 2015

ISBN-13: 978-0-19-945908-7
ISBN-10: 0-19-945908-8

Typeset in 10/13.3 Berling LT Std
by Excellent Laser Typesetters, Pitampura, Delhi 110 034
Printed in India by Rakmo Press, New Delhi 110 020

To
Daniele and Maya
for keeping my spirits alive in their own noisy way

Contents

Photographs

x PHOTOGRAPHS

Foreword

Krishna Kriplani, one of Tagore's most distinguished biographers, first quoted Tagore's words before his departure to Italy on 15 May 1926, saying, 'It is for me to study and not criticize from outside. I am glad of this opportunity to see for myself the work of one who is assuredly a great man and a movement that will certainly be remembered in history', and then commented that the idea that the Duce was 'a great man' was a delusion which Tagore temporarily shared with many shrewd and seasoned politicians of that time.[1] After Tagore's Italian tour when he met Romain Rolland in Villeneuve, Signora Salvadori in Zurich, Modigliani in Vienna, Firnande Luceir, wife of Gaetano Salvemini in Paris, and many others, he realized how the Italian propaganda machine had duped him and made him appear to be a defender of fascism. Tagore was able to apprehend Mussolini's sinister design and wrote a long letter to Charles Freer Andrews, which was later published in *The Manchester Guardian* on 5 August 1926, explaining his visit to Italy and condemning fascism in no uncertain terms. He especially wrote in that letter to *The Manchester Guardian*, 'It is absurd to imagine that I could ever support a movement [fascism] which ruthlessly suppresses freedom of expression, enforces observances that are against individual conscience, and walks through a bloodstained path of violence and stealthy crime.'[2] He also wrote to Romain Rolland, 'I have to pass through a purification ceremony for the defilement to which I submitted myself in Italy.'[3] But there were many in Europe and England, like the expatriate Salvemini, who were sarcastic in their treatment of Tagore and did not accept wholeheartedly what he said about Mussolini in *The Manchester Guardian*. In India also, many comments were published in a leading Bengali journal *Prabasi*, which were full of wild disbelief regarding Tagore's criticism of Mussolini and the reasons for it. Tagore remained ever indebted to Mussolini for his generous gift of a large number of classics in Italian to Visva-Bharati without realizing that it was to encourage and influence the poet to accept the Italian government's invitation to visit Italy—all part of Mussolini's heinous ploy. But the unfortunate part of the episode, which raised suspicion in the minds of many, came when Guglielmo Salvadori suggested to Tagore in a letter on 16 July 1926 that he return all these books to Mussolini, and Tagore ignored the suggestion.[4] Carlo Formichi, the prime mover of Tagore's Italian tour and a villain of the piece, was both adored and hated because of his knowledge of Sanskrit and Indian culture, and his allegiance towards Mussolini and fascism. But whether he had respect and regard for Tagore is a big question particularly when, firstly, after Tagore's first speech in Milan, Formichi referred to 'cheap sermons of love and peace' and said that this 'humanitarian sermon was absolutely out of place'.[5] And, secondly, Formichi sent a rejoinder to Tagore's letter to *The Manchester Guardian* criticizing Mussolini and fascism and made a determined attempt, with the help of concocted facts and lies, to show that Tagore had spoken in favour of Mussolini and his politics. What truly surprises me is that Mahatma Gandhi also visited Italy four years after Tagore's visit and lauded Mussolini's many economic and social reforms, but he was never targeted and besieged by criticism as was Tagore.[6] However, there is a single but very crucial difference between the two of them. Gandhi heeded Romain Rolland's advice and did not become a state guest of Mussolini, whereas Tagore accepted the offer to be a state guest, and this changed the attitude of the liberals towards both of them. However, Tagore redeemed himself considerably in his letter to *The Manchester Guardian*, and when Amartya Sen said in an interview for the Italian newspaper *La Voce Republicana* that 'in Italian Fascism there could have been the seeds of a new anti-imperialism'.[7] Dimmed by that illusion, Tagore accepted to be exhibited by the regime during a brief official visit in Italy.[8] But when Tagore decided to write a letter of gratitude to Mussolini four years after his visit to Italy in 1930 at Formichi's behest (whom Tagore met that year in America), it would have proved completely suicidal and Tagore would have remained beyond redemption. Thanks, however, to his son Rathindranath's advice, the letter was never sent.[9] However, Kalyan Kundu, quoting Mario Prayer and Sofori, maintains that the letter was actually sent, but there is no evidence yet to confirm whether or not Mussolini ever saw it.[10]

I have always thought that both Tagore's love for Italy and Mussolini and Jawaharlal Nehru's love for China and Zhou Enlae turned out to be their hamartia, which made them tragic heroes of that part of history which was related to the Italian and Chinese episodes in their lives.

Having this kind of attitude towards Tagore's Mussolini episode, when I chanced to read Kundu's latest manuscript 'Meeting with Mussolini: Tagore's Tours in Italy, 1925 and 1926', I was not only amazed by his deep, well-researched, and evaluative study of the subject, but also by his objectivity in discovering the truth and nothing but the truth about the whole episode. I have no hesitation in saying that there is no book on the Tagore–Mussolini episode like this one. It includes details such as an almost day-by-day record of Tagore's tours in Italy in 1925 and 1926 as well as news reports, interviews, etc., as much as he could gather from various sources. It incorporates detailed conversations between Tagore and all the main characters in this drama in which Mussolini is himself a major player.

There are references to Tagore's Italian tours in the biographies of Krishna Dutta and Andrew Robinson, Krishna Kriplani, and also Prabhat Mukhopadhyay. Understandably, there are no critical studies of this episode in those books. They all followed the conventional line. However, there are some important papers on the subject.[11]

Giuseppe Flora's article follows more or less the conventional tale, but it is a well-researched appraisal of the subject set against the European political context. Kundu mentions this in his introduction.

Kundu is the first scholar to place emphasis on the importance of the Italian news published in the Italian press in connection with Tagore's tours, particularly because of other scholars' constant and persistent blaming of Italian papers for publishing distorted news about Tagore during his tour in 1926. Kundu has made the Italian material an important part of the book so that the truth could be revealed.

Kundu says that he has no concrete evidence of what Tagore said in his interviews (especially at those times when Tagore's secretary was not present), but from the published reports, he found nothing offensive or any way of telling which part of Tagore's interviews had been edited on grounds of an anti-fascist element. But at the same time, we cannot forget that all the liberals and friends of Tagore—Romain Rolland, George Duhamel, J.G. Fraser, Forel, Bovet, and others—spoke with one voice when he met them after crossing over to Switzerland, about the garbled and distorted versions of his speeches and interviews which were being headlined by the Italian press to boost the fascist regime. It was only when Tagore was convinced that the Italian propaganda machine had made a dupe of him that he wrote the letter to Andrews. At the same time, it is difficult for me to believe that Kundu's conclusion, arrived at after a painstaking study of all the Italian material, is not worth considering.

Kundu also does not agree with the general perception of Carlo Formichi and Giuseppe Tucci as fascists trying to use Tagore for political ends. Kundu's purpose in his writing is to show Formichi and Tucci's actions in a newer light before imposing any indictment on these two very distinguished Orientalists. It is true that both the professors were fascists and they never hid that fact, but they had a high regard for Tagore that cannot be ignored. One thing we must remember, as explained by Kundu, is that Formichi came to know about Tagore through Kalidas Nag before Mussolini came to power (see the letter of 8 May in Chapter 1, 'Italian Tour, 1925'). He had a genuine admiration for Tagore's literary works and a passion for visiting India. In 1921, while touring Europe, Tagore was also searching for visiting professors for his university and Formichi's name was on the card. However, he failed to meet Formichi in 1921.

In 1925, when Tagore actually met Formichi, he invited him to join Visva-Bharati. So it was Tagore, concludes Kundu, who invited Formichi, not, as popularly believed, Mussolini, who sent Formichi to Tagore's university.

When Formichi failed to raise sufficient funds to buy Italian books and resources for Visva-Bharati (basically as a matter of prestige as other European visiting professors before him had donated books and resources to Visva-Bharati), he approached Mussolini for financial support. In 1926, Mussolini was passing through a difficult time in his political career. The murder of two prominent socialist activists had raised a hue and cry in the European left-wing press condemning fascist policies. Mussolini took the opportunity to divert political attention by inviting Tagore to Italy. He unhesitatingly accepted Formichi's proposal with unusual generosity.

Kundu's conclusion is that for Formichi and Tucci's safe existence they had to be loyal to Mussolini, and for that they had to play a dual role sometimes. This can be seen as their predicament, giving rise to some complex psychological tension, through which they passed at that time. I have no reason to disagree with this opinion except that the relation with Tagore was more of love, sometimes of disgust also, but at the end it was abiding respect and adoration for Tagore's creativity and scholarship.

Tagore's esteem for Mussolini was untarnished for a few more years. He even wanted to patch up the difference in 1930, four years after the incident, as mentioned earlier in this foreword. It was only after Italy invaded Abyssinia (now Ethiopia) that Tagore completely changed his opinion about Mussolini and wrote his poem 'Africa' on 10 February 1937, which was, as Sugata Bose explains, a searing and sarcastic criticism directed at the false universalist claims of an unnamed Europe (Italy). Even as the 'barbaric greed of the civilized' put on naked display their 'shameless inhumanity', church bells rang out in neighbourhoods across the ocean in the name of a benign God, 'children played in their mother's laps, and poets sang paeans to beauty'.[12]

I would like to end by saying that in Kundu I found a true Tagore scholar with a deep research-oriented mind. He has given a very objective and honest account of the Tagore–Mussolini episode, which still remains an enigmatic chapter in Tagore's life history.

13 January 2015   INDRA NATH CHOUDHURI

Notes

1. Krishna Kriplani, *Rabindranath Tagore: A Biography* (Calcutta: Visva-Bharati, 2012 [reprint]), p. 319.

2. Krishna Dutta and Andrew Robinson (eds), *Selected Letters of Rabindranath Tagore*, Letter no. 211 (Cambridge: Cambridge University Press, 1997), p. 333.

3. Ibid., Letter no. 209, p. 329.

4. Ibid., Letter no. 247, note 1, p. 394.

5. Mario Prayer, 'On Tagore', *Rabindra-Viksha*, vol. 39 (2001), p. 39; translated from Carlo Formichi, *India e Indiani* (Milan: Edizioni Alpes, 1929).

6. Bikash Chakravarti, '*Mussolini-ke Rabindranath*: 21 November 1930', *Chaturanga* (2009), pp. 105–18.

7. Giuseppe Flora, 'Rabindranath Tagore and Italy: Facing History and Politics', *Reclaiming a Cultural Icon* (Calcutta: Visva-Bharati, 2005), p. 281.

8. Ibid.

9. Dutta and Robinson, *Selected Letters of Rabindranath Tagore*, Letter no. 247, p. 394.

10. See Chapter 4, 'Post Tour', in this book.

11. Rathindranath Tagore, *On the Edges of Time* (Calcutta: Visva-Bharati, 1958), pp. 136–40; Prasanta Chandra Mahalanobis, 'Our Founder-President in Italy, 1926', Visva-Bharati Bulletin, *Visva-Bharati Quarterly* (October 1926); Nirmal Kumari Mahalanobis, *Kobir sange Europey* (Kolkata: Mitra and Ghosh, 1969); Formichi, *India e Indiani*, relevant section translated by Mario Prayer and published in *Rabindra-Viksha*; and Flora, 'Rabindranath Tagore and Italy'. Besides these, there are other articles, some in Italian and some in English, by Mario Prayer.

12. Sugata Bose, *Rabindranath Tagore and Asian Universalism* (2014), available at http://nsc.iseas.edu.sg/documents/conferences/Rabindranath%20Tagore%20and%20Asian%20Universalism.pdf, accessed 11 March 2015, pp. 1–28.

Prologue

Of the many countries Rabindranath Tagore visited in his lifetime, his sojourn in Italy in 1925 and 1926, especially the controversial tour in 1926 at the invitation of Benito Mussolini, has been a subject of great interest to Tagore scholars and researchers for mainly two reasons. Firstly, the ethics, ideologies, and beliefs of these two human beings were a world apart. Consequently, the acceptance of an invitation from a tyrant dictator by a great humanist baffled the international community of that time. Secondly, the high drama associated with this imperfect encounter aroused a great deal of media interest both within and outside Italy and also intrigued the scholars. The Tagore–Mussolini episode was largely debated in Indian, Italian, and the rest of the European media during the time of his tour and afterwards. The literature and newspaper reports on this subject—published in English, Italian, French, and Bengali—are not exiguous.

Rathindranath Tagore, Rabindranath's son, maintained a diary of his father's tours in Europe in 1920, 1925, and 1926. The uncut version of the diary of 1925 appeared in 2000 in *Rabindra-Viksha* (vol. 37), a bi-annual bulletin published from the research unit Rabindra Charcha Prakalpa of Rabindra Bhavan, Santiniketan. This diary can be considered an authentic record of Tagore's tour in 1925 as it is a real-time account and was not written from memory. Later, this account was incorporated in Rathindranath's book *On the Edges of Time*, published in 1958 from Kolkata. For the same reason, Prasanta Chandra Mahalanobis, who was Tagore's secretary on the 1926 tour, published an account in *Visva-Bharati Quarterly* immediately after the tour, which, though slightly abridged, was an equally veritable documentation. Mahalanobis's full account of the tour, once temporarily mislaid, but later recovered, was also published in *Rabindra-Viksha* (vol. 38) in 2000. These two articles are factually authentic, but not very critical. An analytical account of Tagore's visit to Italy was presented by Giuseppe Flora in a conference held in Toronto in 2005, later compiled in the conference volume titled *Rabindranath Tagore: Reclaiming Cultural Icon*, published from Visva-Bharati in 2009. Flora's article 'Rabindranath Tagore and Italy: Facing History and Politics' is a well-researched and critical study of the subject set within a European political context.

The authenticity of all these sources was further substantiated by news reports that appeared in the British and Indian press (both in English and Bengali) and articles and information that appeared in several journals during that period, of which *Prabasi* in Bengali and *The Modern Review* in English are worth mentioning.

In addition to the aforementioned material, the Rabindra Bhavan Archives has four important files labelled 'Formichi', 'Tucci', 'Mussolini', and 'Salvadori'. Each file includes letters and correspondences of Tagore with its marked writer. The fifth file marked 'Italy' includes general correspondences relating to Tagore's Italian tour. All these primary and other sources help us to frame the story of Tagore's Italian tours in 1925 and 1926.

The Italian sources relating to Tagore's visits to Italy are not deficient either. However, these are not easily accessible to non-

Italian readers unless transcribed faithfully into the reader's mother tongue. Gaetano Salvemini's article *'Tagore e Mussolini'* (Tagore and Mussolini) is quintessential. Salvemini was one of the many Italian expatriates who left the country in the early phase of fascist domination. He collected material for his article from various sources, but primarily from Italian newspapers, from personal communication with Elmhirst, and from Rolland's journal *Inde*. Salvemini was slightly sarcastic in his treatment of Tagore, but his frustration (and in this respect he is the typical expatriate) with Tagore is quite understandable. His article represents a typical study of the Tagore–Mussolini episode seen through the eyes of an expatriate. So far, Indian Tagore scholars have been critical along similar lines as Salvemini, though hardly anyone had read Salvemini's article in the original. Mario Prayer, another Italian Tagore scholar, published an expository essay *'Internazionalismo e nazionalismo culturale: Gli intellettuali bengalesi e l'Italia negli anni Venti e Trenta'* (Internationalism and Cultural Nationalism: Bengali Intellectuals and Italy in the Twenties and Thirties), published as a short monograph appended to the journal of the Department of Oriental Studies, Sapienza University of Rome, in 1996. This 113-page monograph devoted 19 pages to Tagore's Italian tour and took a rational approach to the subject of his visit and meeting with Mussolini, placing it in historical, political, and cultural contexts.

Another major and comprehensive Italian publication came out in 1929, three years after Tagore's Italian visit, entitled *India e Indiani* (India and Indians), published by Alps in Milan and written by Carlo Formichi. Although its title gives the sense that the book is an all-encompassing study of India and Indians, it is not: The greater part of the book deals with Formichi's own Indian experience and the details of Tagore's two Italian visits. It was written in Italian, and not many Indian scholars were aware of its existence until Mario Prayer translated the relevant section in two consecutive issues of *Rabindra-Viksha* (vols 39 and 40, 2001). As Formichi was Tagore's primary mover of his 1926 tour and was his interpreter throughout the poet's stay in Italy during that time, his account is a worthwhile document to analyse. But a section of Italian scholars suspect that Formichi's book was written for the Italians only and for one Italian in particular—Benito Mussolini—in order to justify his actions and to settle all controversies associated with Tagore's Italian tour once and for all. A copy of the book was found in Mussolini's private library.

Other than Italian and English publications on this subject, there is one important French publication, *Inde*, the diary in the form of a journal written by the French humanist and pacifist Romain Rolland. Keeping a journal was in vogue among French intellectuals and writers at that time. These journals are not strictly diaries, but scholarly writings of great depth, reflecting insights of the writer and his subject. Rolland's journal, dated 1915–43, was published posthumously in French in 1951. It includes diverse information and records of meetings with many Indians of all stature who Rolland came into contact with. However, in this assortment, reports of Rolland's meeting with two eminent Indians—Gandhi and Tagore—and accounts of their tours in Italy occupy a prominent place. The material for Rolland's account of Tagore's Italian tour was obtained directly from his conversations with the poet and also from his secretary Mahalanobis while they were staying in Villeneuve (Switzerland) immediately after the tour. The description of the events in the journal is more or less accurate, with some overly sensitive and slightly fabricated comments by its author. However, this journal is an important source in assessing the Tagore–Rolland perception, interaction, and exchange on the issue of Tagore's Italian visit. Unfortunately, there is no English translation of *Inde*, though a Bengali translation is available.

Finally, there is a Bengali publication written by Nirmal Kumari Mahalanobis—*Kobir sange Europey* (With the Poet in Europe). Mrs Mahalanobis, with her husband Prasanta Chandra Mahalanobis, was part of the entourage of the 1926 European tour. Her memoir, published in Kolkata in 1964, includes a delightful account of the Italian tour, but as it was written four decades later from memory, readers may find some information misleading.

Based on the information derived from the literature and essays discussed so far, Tagore scholars have summed up Tagore's visit to Italy in 1926 in the following way: Rabindranath Tagore's Italian visit of 1926 at the invitation of the government was the result of a heinous ploy by Mussolini. Following the assassination of two prominent socialist leaders, Amandola and Matteoti, in 1924, Mussolini's international image was at an all-time low. Hence, the dictator (Il Duce) wanted to divert the world's attention by inviting Tagore to Italy, expecting that Tagore would praise his fascist government. He dispatched two professors, Carlo Formichi and Giuseppe Tucci, to Santiniketan with a generous gift of books for Tagore's university library to encourage and influence him to accept the Italian government's invitation. Tagore, being unaware of Mussolini's plan and being ignorant of Italian politics, accepted the invitation in good faith, as he had responded before to other governments' invitations, and spent a fortnight in Italy as a guest of the Italian government. The Italian government gave a royal reception to Tagore and his entourage, and Tagore was overwhelmed by Mussolini's reception. His praise for Mussolini was reported in the Italian press with exuberance. As Tagore did not know the language, he did not realize that his speeches and interviews were distorted in favour of Mussolini and his regime. Scholars believe that all this may have been carefully manipulated by the two professors, especially Formichi, to please their 'Master'. The European press was baffled to read the poet's euphoric praise for Mussolini and his authority. However, after leaving Italy, he realized his mistake during his days as a guest of Romain Rolland and in the course of his meetings with some of the expatriates. Finally, Tagore saw sense and wrote a long letter to Charles Freer Andrews explaining the context of his Italian tour and how he had been trapped by Italian reporters, thus ending all speculation on the saga of his Italian sojourn.

As it stands, the story is very striking and apparently plausible. However, there are many questions that remain unanswered. A meticulous analysis of the evidence reveals discrepancies. In addition, some evidence raises further questions. For example: Did Mussolini actually send these two professors to Tagore's institution in order to bring Tagore to Italy to fulfil his mission to further his own ends? Was Tagore totally ignorant of Italian politics? Was Tagore really not aware before leaving India that he was going at Mussolini's invitation, which he apparently realized only after reaching Naples? Did Tagore really praise fascism or was this false propaganda on the Italian side? Did the Italian press publicize all aspects of Tagore's visit? Did Formichi really, and to what extent, manipulate the Italian press in favour of Mussolini? Was the visit planned as a chalked path to impress Tagore so that he could only see the best of the regime?

If we revisit Formichi's account in *India e Indiani* with an open mind and take into account the evidence provided, which has been overlooked by previous scholars, and furthermore take this into consideration alongside the policy of the fascist regime, we have to rethink Formichi and Tucci's action in a newer light before imposing any indictment on these two very distinguished Orientalists. The main object of the current study is to resolve some of these discrepancies and free ourselves from all kinds of aberrations.

Two decades ago, while I, along with two of my co-editors, was working on the reception of Tagore in Britain and going through the vast corpus of reportage published in the British print media, I was surprised and also fascinated by the abundance of reports on Tagore's Italian tours, especially in the months of May to September of 1926. Tagore visited 34 countries of the world, but such plentiful news was never before seen in the British press as that related to his tours in Italy. I was aware of the Tagore–Mussolini saga. However, when I read Tagore's historic letter to Andrews published in *The Manchester Guardian* on 5 August 1926 denouncing fascism and, two weeks later, Formichi's statement on the poet's tour in the same paper, I was intrigued. After completion of our project on Tagore in the British media and when our book *Imagining Tagore: Rabindranath and the British Press (1912–1941)* was published, I was drawn slowly to my next project—Tagore's tours in Italy.

My first approach was to go through all Italian news reports on Tagore available from that particular period (1925 and 1926) and transcribe these into English as accurately as possible to find out exactly what had been reported. This included his tour itineraries, the nature of receptions, summaries of his lectures and comments, and finally his interviews. A comprehensive analysis of the reports had not been done before. For materials, my first visit was to the British Library's Newspaper Division in London. I was not disappointed to find that the British Newspaper Library has only a

meagre collection of Italian newspapers of that period, but I found
a larger collection of newspaper clippings on the subject when visiting the Rabindra Bhavan Archives in Santiniketan, in files marked
'1925' and '1926'. During the poet's lifetime, the International Press
Cutting Bureau—a company based in London—was contracted
by the Tagore establishment to send all newspaper clippings on
Tagore published globally. Sadly, when I observed these clippings, I
found them to be in a delicate state due to lack of proper preserva-
tion and careful handling (these clippings are now preserved on
microfilm). Another disadvantage is that these clippings have no
page-numbering system, which is necessary for any reference work.
In spite of this, copies of the clippings provided useful material for
the primary phase of my research. Ultimately, my final destination
was the Biblioteca Nazionale Centrale di Roma (National Library
of Rome). After visiting it a number of times, I was able to collect
a good number of reports on Tagore's Italian tour. Eventually, those
news items were translated as faithfully as possible into English
by two of my competent translators. My slight knowledge of the
Italian language also helped in verifying the authenticity of these
translations.

In this space, let us quickly run through the nature and
character of the Italian newspapers in 1920s. These were mainly
provincial broadsheets. There was no national newspaper as such
like *The Times* or *The Telegraph* in Britain or the Indian *Times of
India*. However, *Corriere della Sera* (although the name suggests
an evening paper) was a morning daily newspaper published
from Milan and is still one of Italy's leading liberal newspapers. It
was the principal newspaper in terms of both circulation and influence since 1920, and was, and still is, circulated outside Italy. Other
broadsheet dailies were *Il Messaggero*, *Il Popolo d'Italia*, *Il Popolo
d'Roma*, and *La Tribuna* published from Rome; *Il Resto del Carlino*
from Bologna; *Il Gazzettino de Venezia* from Venice; *La Stampa*
from Turin; and so on. Some of these newspapers, such as *Corriere
della Sera*, *Il Messaggero*, and *Il Gazzettino de Venezia*, still exist in
their old glory. Before Mussolini's rise to power, each paper had its
own character and political colour. However, in Mussolini's time,
all papers lost their individual identities and were forced to express

fascist allegiance. Reports of Tagore's tour and special columns on Tagore were published in most of these newspapers.

During the course of this research, my contact with Clara Muzzarelli Formentini, the granddaughter of Professor Guglielmo Salvadori (1879–1953), another Italian émigré, is of significant importance. In Clara's private archive (*Archivio Salvadori Paleotti, Fermo, Italy*), there are rare images, original telegrams, and correspondences of Tagore and Salvadori. Some of these have been incorporated in this book. From a letter from this collection, I came to know that Salvadori, at one stage, wanted to send his son Max to Santiniketan. However, when Tagore received this proposition, Tucci was still in Santiniketan. Assuming that the presence of Max could incur some kind of aggravation and complication, Tagore politely declined the suggestion. In Clara's collection, there are two important papers, one being the article '*Il Poeta e l'Assassino*' (The Poet and the Murderer), written by Signora Giacinta Salvadori (1875–1960), published in *Corriere degli Italiani* without using her name: A copy of this was sent to Tagore earlier, before her meeting with the poet. Tagore acknowledged receipt of the article, but failed to decipher it as it was written in Italian. I am indebted to Clara as she also sent me a copy of the original article with an English translation, which I have included in the Appendix. Another important material in Clara's collection is the draft copy of the accounts of the meeting of Signora Salvadori and Tagore. This was Signora Salvadori's version of the meeting with Tagore and not the one that was published in *The Manchester Guardian* (7 August 1926).

In the Appendix, I have also included a transcript of a casual conversation on the subject 'On Death' between Tagore and Duke Scotti in Milan when the ailing poet was confined to his hotel. The poet's philosophical reflection on death has not been published anywhere before.

During his tour in Italy, Tagore delivered a total of four public lectures—one in 1925 and three in 1926. These are now included in the third volume of *The English Writings of Rabindranath Tagore*, edited by Sisir Kumar Das and published in 1996 by Sahitya Akademi, New Delhi, and are easily accessible to the English reading public. To avoid unnecessary repetition and due to the limitations of space, the lectures are not included here, except the lecture in Milan in 1925 due to its controversial aspect.

The political map of the world has changed considerably since Tagore's death. Czechoslovakia has been divided into two independent countries—Czech Republic and Slovakia; Yugoslavia has been broken into six provinces and two autonomous provinces; the Soviet Union has been fragmented into twelve constituent republics; India has been split into three independent countries—Pakistan, India, and Bangladesh; and so on. I have used old and undivided names of countries, where they appear in the text. Throughout the text, I have used the former names of the Indian cities such as Calcutta (Kolkata), Bombay (Mumbai), Madras (Chennai), Benares (Varanasi), and Dacca (Dhaka). When citing recent publications, the current names of the place of publication are used.

Via Milazzo was the name of the street where my wife and I stayed in a hotel during our third visit to the National Library of Rome. One evening when we were strolling around the neighbourhood, we were struck by the name of the street parallel to ours—via Marghera. It immediately flashed in our minds that House No. 43 on this street once belonged to Formichi. We did not spend much time exploring the house, adjacent to a hotel. We remembered that in this house, Kalidas Nag spent time with Formichi while holidaying in Rome. Tagore also spent an evening in 1926 here in the company of Formichi, his sister, and her children.

A mere coincidence indeed! But both of us were thrilled for a while.

London   KALYAN KUNDU
May 2015

Acknowledgements

My list of those to whom I am indebted for this project begins with the names of three Italian translators, Claudia Capencioni, Rosaria Ventura, and Clara Muzzarelli Formentini, who spent their valuable time painstakingly transcribing Italian news items and articles into English with a great deal of patience. Without their help, this work would never have seen the light of the day.

For archival and newspaper material, two names are very prominent, namely, Patrizia Calabresi, the Chief Librarian of the National Library of Rome, and Supriya Roy of Rabindra Bhavan. I gratefully acknowledge the much-needed help I received from them. I am equally thankful to Yvonne Widger, the archivist of the Dartington Hall Trust, who kindly allowed me to see the Elmhirst papers. My special thanks goes to Maria Rinaldin, my Venetian relation, who was from the very beginning enthusiastic about the concept of this book and was the first to post me all newspaper clippings from *Il Gazzettino de Venezia*.

I also acknowledge the contribution of those who enriched my manuscript with their suggestions, advice, and resources. Foremost among them is Mario Prayer of the University of Rome. Since becoming aware of his scholarship on this subject, I have been in constant touch with him by email almost from the beginning of this project. He helped me by providing articles, ideas, and opinions, all of which were invaluable.

In the preparation of the manuscript, I have received help from many of my friends. Debashish Raychaudhuri helped me with the manuscript in its early stages, which was followed by careful editing by Linda Edwards-Shea and Sandra Menzies. Others who helped me in preparing the manuscript and acquiring photographs are Don Holtum, John Debjit Kundu, Munna Vio in London, and Donata Duso in Italy. I express my sincere thanks to all of them.

I also place on record my unbound gratitude to Uma Das Gupta, former Professor, Social Science Division, Indian Statistical Institute, Kolkata, for her encouragement and support for this work and Indra Nath Choudhuri, former Secretary of Sahitya Akademi and the Academic Director of Indira Gandhi National Centre for the Arts, India, and currently the Tagore Professor of Napier University Edinburgh, for his invaluable suggestions on the manuscript and also for writing the foreword to this book.

I sincerely thank the editors at Oxford University Press who have worked diligently and tirelessly in looking after the quality of the production of this volume.

Last, but not the least, I owe a special debt to Devi Kundu, my wife, whose unfailing enthusiasm inspired me constantly throughout the course of this project.

I

Italian Tour, 1925

It was a cold but sunny winter morning on 19 January 1925 when the passenger liner *Giulio Ceaser* docked in Genoa's harbour. Originating in Buenos Aires, the liner sailed across the Atlantic towards Europe, finally ending its voyage in Italy. Among those disembarking from the ship that morning were two very distinguished passengers: the Indian Nobel Prize–winning poet Rabindranath Tagore and his English Secretary Leonard Elmhirst. This was Tagore's first visit to Italy at the age of 64. The people of Genoa, a small industrial hub on Italy's Ligurian coast, also famous as the birthplace of Giuseppe Mazzini, were not aware of their newly arrived guests and no reporters were present. The only people there to greet Tagore were his relatives and a couple of Italians.

Previously, Tagore had visited many countries of the East and the West and had toured Europe and America several times, but, surprisingly, not Italy, which had been dear to his heart since his teenage years. He seemed to regret the fact that he went to Italy rather late in his life: 'My wishes would have been fulfilled if I had reached you before I achieved fame. Then I could have known you more intimately as the English poets like Browning, Shelley, Keats or Byron did. I should have come to you in my youth.'[1] On a number of occasions, this note of regret was echoed in the lectures and interviews he gave during his Italian tour.

However, Tagore had had no opportunity to visit Italy in his youth, unlike his favourite poets. He did touch the Italian shore in 1878 when he was 17 while on his way to England for the first time. Italy was his first European experience, though it was only a fleeting acquaintance. In those days, most of the passenger liners bound for Europe terminated their route at the ports along Europe's southern coastline. One such port was Brindisi in Italy where passengers heading for England disembarked and then took an overland train through Italy and France to reach Calais. From Calais they would cross the English Channel to Southampton or Dover. A train would then take them to either Charing Cross or Victoria in London, and the young Tagore had taken this route to reach England in 1878. His initial impression of Italy was amusingly recorded in his letters written to his family and friends, later collected in a volume *Yerope Prabashir Patra* (Letters from a European Sojourner). He followed the same route to England during his second trip in 1890. However, his real chance to visit Italy came many years later, in 1925.

During 1920–1, Tagore toured extensively in the war-torn countries of Europe to promote his idea of the meeting of the East and the West in a common fellowship of learning and spiritual striving, with the hope of achieving peace. Visiting Italy was also on the cards. A letter from an Italian professor, Carlo Formichi, to the poet's son Rathindranath (8 May 1921) expressed such a proposition. Formichi wrote,

I dare say, your father's works are known and highly admired here by every cultivated person. We are all very happy to hear that he intends spending a week in Rome. I am sure it would be a great success. Let me know, please, as soon as you can, whether I may tell our Rector to announce and prepare everything for the lecture. Your father shall find here in Rome more sincere admirers than he can think of. Make me acquainted, please, with the day of your arrival and the hotel you will live in.[2]

Two days later, on 10 May 1921, Formichi also sent a cable from Rome to Zurich: 'Please wire me your arrival day and address at Florence—Carlo Formichi.'[3] Florence would have been the first stop on that tour. However, on this occasion, Tagore's Italian visit was abandoned due to some unforeseeable reason.

Although the poet had to wait another four years for a proper tour, he had been regularly featured in the Italian newspapers since 1913, when he had been awarded the Nobel Prize in Literature. Italian newspapers first reported on Tagore on 14 November 1913—the day after the announcement of the award. *Corriere della Sera* reported:

The Nobel Prize for an Indian Poet

A telegram from Stockholm announces that the Nobel Prize in Literature has been awarded to the Indian poet Rabindranath Tagore, who is very famous in India and the Eastern World.

Rabindranath Tagore was unknown in England and Europe until last year when he published a book of verse and religious hymns titled *Gitanjali* or *Poems*. These are rhythmical translations of his works, known for years by all Indian people, from Bengali into English biblical language. The famous Irish poet Yeats who wrote the preface of *Gitanjali* said: 'I don't know any man of my time who had written in English something which can be compared with these lyrics. Even in these literal translations in prose these are so exquisite in style and their content of thought.'

Rabindranath is a musician and his songs are sung in the West of India and everywhere the Bengali language is spoken.

He has translated poems by Shelley and Tennyson into Bengali and Sanskrit.[4]

This short, simple, and slightly inaccurate report was not unexpected. The Italians, like all other Europeans, were duly surprised at the decision of the Swedish Academy to award the highest literary prize to a figure totally unknown in 1913 Europe (except Britain). *Gitanjali* had not yet reached Italian shores. It was Giuseppe Tani who translated a selection of poems from *Gitanjali* and published them as *Canti votivi* (1914). With this handful of poems, Italian readers were first acquainted with Tagore and, at the same time, with the mind and spirit of modern India.

[...] We should lend ourselves to the mystical nature of these poems; the version translated into English prose has been done with great accuracy. [...] The poet himself set the music [...] and in so doing created a perfect beauty, true to the soul, inspired by the poetic sentiment which is the supreme aim of the music.

The Votive poems (*Canti Votivi*) are a trembling offer of a wandering human soul to the eternal divine soul of the universe. [...][5]

Later, several Italian translations from the English of Tagore's Bengali work appeared within a short space of time, and although two consecutive translations into two different languages may have diluted the nuances of the original text, the works were received well. In fact, between 1914 and 1925, the Carabba publishing house in Lanciano brought out 19 volumes of Tagore's work, all translated from English versions. These translations were mostly mystical in content, and so Italian readers formed an idea of Tagore that was akin to the medieval mystic figures of St. Francis of Assisi or Jacopone da Todi, but with a modernist frame of mind. Thus, before the poet's visit in 1925, Italian readers were familiar with his works, to the extent that one of his plays, *The Post Office*, was reportedly staged in a remote Italian village.

The Initial Plans for the Visit

Tagore's visit to Italy was initiated via two separate channels. In 1921, Kalidas Nag, a young friend of Tagore, came to Rome from Paris to spend his vacation.[6] He was then a research scholar working under Sylvian Lévi in Paris. In Rome, he came into contact with the university's professor of Sanskrit, Carlo Formichi, and through him, with two other Orientalists—Giovanni Vacca, who specialized in Chinese literature, and Giuseppe Tucci. Tucci was the deputy librarian at the Lower House of Parliament and professor-in-charge of Religions and Philosophies of India and the Far East at Rome University.[7] Formichi would invite Kalidas Nag to his home for leisurely tête-à-têtes on a wide range of topics including Italian and Indian politics, Sanskrit literature, and, invariably, Tagore's works and his forthcoming academic enterprise, the new university, Visva-Bharati. As a Sanskritist and scholar of Indology, Formichi had developed a passion for India—a passion to live on the banks of the Ganges. He was also aware of Tagore's literary stature. His personal experience after reading Tagore's *The Home and the World* is recorded with exuberance in a letter written to Kalidas Nag:

I devoured Tagore's *The Home and the World* kindly given to me by you. There is a splendid psychological analysis such as only Tagore is capable of. I am coming more and more to the persuasion that he is the greatest living man in the world, and I devotedly hope to come in contact with him before I die. You must prevail on him to get the promise that one day he will visit our Eternal Rome.[8]

Formichi's Indian dream never became a reality in spite of his interactions with many distinguished Indians. He came into contact with Vivekananda in London and met Prabhu Dutta Shastri in Bologna. He was also in touch with many Indians via several religious conferences, but nothing worked out for him. Finally, Nag inspired him to contact Tagore directly with the hope that he might help him fulfil his aspiration. Formichi liked the idea, but did not know how to achieve it. In the meantime, Nag's vacation was over and he returned to Paris.

Meanwhile, Tagore was in search of visiting professors from different European countries for his newly founded university, Visva-Bharati. Through Kalidas Nag, he came to know about Formichi. Nag was convinced that the erudite presence of Formichi would be a great benefit for Visva-Bharati and it was probably on Nag's advice that Rathindranath contacted Formichi expressing his father's intention of visiting Italy. Formichi's reply is already mentioned in the earlier paragraph. However, Tagore failed to go to Italy that year, and during the next two years there was no further development in this matter. In 1923, Nag visited Formichi again in Rome on his return to India. The prospect of Tagore's Italian tour again came up in their discussions, but without any concrete proposition.

Another channel opened up in 1923 when P.A. Waring and Melvin L. Brorby, two Englishmen, came to Calcutta from Italy to discuss an exchange programme of scholars between India and Italy. They sent a letter from Calcutta to Tagore's Santiniketan address, which read:

Today we are writing to Italy, to Dr. Assagioli, and to the student of whom we spoke, in exchange of men between Santiniketan and the University of Florence. We do hope that Amiya Babu[9] will be able to go for we feel that he shall carry much of the spirit of Santiniketan with him to those people who look for a word of inspiration from the East, and likewise a student from Florence imbued with the spirit of Dante, St Francis and Mazzini, will bring something of value to India. We are asking these men of Italy to write to you and talk the matter over and from what we know of their enthusiasm it seems most likely they will have good suggestions to offer.[10]

No copy of the reply to this letter could be found. Meanwhile, Waring and Brorby wrote another letter from Shillong on 1 September, which reads:

[...] Since talking with you [obviously they were able to establish a communication with the poet], we have written to Dr. Roberto Assagioli of Florence of whom we spoke to you, and he now writes what he has been able to do to further our plan. He has been to Rome where he has talked to Professor Formichi, professor of Sanskrit at the University, and found him most enthusiastic. Both of them made further investigations and now they believe that financial aid is forthcoming from the Italian Government. Arrangements will be made within the month of Sept. and then Dr. Assagioli will write to you and to us. [...]

The last paragraph of that letter mentions this:

[...] The men in Florence and in Rome of whom we spoke to you probably represent the best undercurrent of fine spirit in Italy today. It is these men who look forward to you coming to their country in 1924. Dr. Assagioli, writing for himself and for them says: 'If you see Doctor Tagore please assure him of my devotion and tell him that I and my friends are delighted at the prospect of having him with us.'[11]

No further correspondence on the subject was available in the archive.

In March 1924, Tagore began his tour in China and Japan. While in Japan, he received an unexpected invitation from the Government of Peru to attend the centenary celebration of the country's independence. The Peruvian government pledged to pay the poet 50,000 dollars as an honorarium for his lecture and his travel expenses. Tagore accepted the invitation. The Ambassador of Peru in Japan promptly finalized the paperwork for his trip. Elmhirst, the poet's secretary, who travelled with him, immediately informed Rathindranath in Santiniketan about the contract. Kalidas Nag was also a fellow traveller on that trip.

Meanwhile, Formichi met another close friend of Tagore, D.J. Irani, a lawyer with whom he also discussed further prospects of Tagore's visit to Italy (23 February 1924). He wrote to Kalidas Nag about the outcome of their meeting and also wrote to Tagore in a passionate letter on 9 March 1924:

Sir, May we trust that your friend Irani has just planted in our hearts the hope that you are coming to Italy? Let me know, please, every detail through Kalidas Nag. You have been in England, in France, in Germany, in Sweden, and your sense of justice will prompt you not to neglect any longer Italy who admires and loves you better than any other nation in the world. Do come only among us to persuade yourself of the truth of what I am saying. An entire nation has been waiting for you for a long time, and the dawn to the lark is less welcome than you will be welcome to all sons of Italy, among whom I humbly number myself.
Yours most respectfully.
Carlo Formichi.[12]

Nag received the letter in June. He wrote to Formichi:

I have received Irani's letter and yours on the same day, and I am trying to persuade Tagore to visit Italy this year. Meanwhile, our tour in the Far East brought a new engagement to us. The people of Latin America are going to celebrate the centenary year of their Republics in December. Tagore has accepted their invitation. [...] As we are expected for the centenary celebrations in early December, it will be necessary to leave Spain for South America in early November. Therefore, only one month, namely October, will be available for conference tours in Italy and Spain. The Spanish Government has already formally invited the poet to give lectures in Spain and to board a Spanish boat on his route to South America. What will Italy do on her side?[13]

Formichi had no idea how the Italian government would help. He knew that bringing Tagore to Italy would be an expensive project. Although Tagore did not take any fees, he travelled always with his entourage and 'although he abhors luxuries and values simple life more than anything else, he never even thinks of renouncing certain comforts, such as travelling by a car or in a reserved first-class compartment, and so on.'[14] Together, all these expenses would necessitate a large budget, and initially Formichi failed to raise the funds through private or government sources. He appealed to the Education Minister Alessandro Casati through his friend Professor Uberto Pestalozza, but that did not yield any result. So frustrated was Formichi that he almost decided to drop the entire idea of bringing Tagore to Italy when he met Guido Cagnola, an aristocrat from Milan. Cagnola was interested and, in turn, pursued the non-government organization Circolo Filologico Milanese (Milan Philology Circle) to issue an official invitation to Tagore to visit Italy. Simultaneously, a women's society from Turin and Angiolo Orvieto and Guido Biagi from Florence co-sponsored the trip in lieu of Tagore's lectures in those cities.

The government of Spain was also interested in the poet visiting their country. Initially, the tour was planned in such a way that Tagore would tour first in Spain and Italy, followed by a trip to Latin America to join Peru's celebration, but this plan was eventually abandoned. The poet did not visit Spain at all. Finally on 20 August 1924, a cable was sent to Milan—'Shall visit Italy on my way back from South America next winter'—confirming Tagore's Italian tour.

Tagore left Calcutta on 19 September 1924 for Peru, going via Cherbourg in France on 18 October. However, he never made it to Peru, becoming seriously ill after reaching Argentina and having to call off the trip on his physicians' advice. Victoria Ocampo took it upon herself to nurse the ailing poet until he pulled through. Finally, when the poet was well enough to sail, he left Argentina for Europe. Rathindranath informed Formichi in a letter that the liner *Giulio Ceaser* would sail from Buenos Aires with the poet and his secretary on board on 3 January 1925.

Genoa

Tagore and Elmhirst left Latin America for Europe. Illness and the strain of the journey left the poet exhausted. 'I am heading for Italy. But it doesn't seem to be the best time for me to take such a journey. [...] I don't seem to have left with the energy needed to start a new acquaintance. I seem to lack the extra energy that is needed while visiting a new country,' he wrote to Kalidas Nag from the *Giulio Ceaser*.[15] The founder-director of Circolo Filologico Milanese, Duke Tommaso Gallarati Scotti, wrote to Rathindranath informing him about the possible date of the poet's arrival in Italy.[16] Rathindranath was in London during that time.[17] The letter, written in French, informed the poet's son that his father was due to reach Genoa around 19 January and accommodation was arranged for him at the Eden Park Hotel, where Formichi would also be present.

Formichi also wrote to Tagore from Rome on 12 January:

Dear Sir, I advise you to go directly to the Eden Park Hotel where rooms have been reserved. You are expected on Sunday morning, the 18th.

I shall leave for Genoa as soon as I receive a hint from you telling me the day and the hour you want me to call on you at the Hotel. Better to do so than try to meet at the station. It is indifferent therefore at what station you alight.

Please, wire me just two words; that I may prepare everything for my departure. Looking forward to the great pleasure of making your personal acquaintance. I remain, Carlo Formichi.[18]

At the dock of Genoa, 19 January 1925. Back row, standing
from the left: Leonard Elmhirst, Pratima Devi, and Suren Kar.
Front row: Rabindranath Tagore and granddaughter Nandini.
Source: Rabindra Bhavan.

The liner *Giulio Ceaser* first docked at Barcelona in Spain. There,
an Italian admirer of the poet, Madame Clelia Zannoni-Chauvet,
informed him that a warm welcome awaited him in Italy. Madame
Chauvet had translated some of Tagore's poems into Italian, and she
took him around Barcelona for a brief sightseeing tour.

Finally, Tagore and Elmhirst disembarked at Genoa on 19
January. Amongst those present at the port to welcome the poet
were his son's family, the artist Suren Kar, Alberto Poggi, an Italian
physician interested in Indology, and Formichi. Duke Scotti was
not there to receive his guest at the jetty, as he was occupied in
organizing the poet's welcome in Milan. He had sent his representative Dr Zanussi to Genoa to discuss the poet's itinerary. Tagore
and Formichi met each other for the first time. As planned earlier,
Tagore and his family checked in at the Eden Park Hotel. The 20
January issue of *Corriere della Sera* reported the news of the poet's
arrival in Genoa:

Tagore in Italy

Genoa, 19 January
Today from Buenos Aires arrived the *Giulio Casare* [*sic*], carrying one long-desired guest onto Italian soil: Rabindranath Tagore. He is the Indian poet. Europe and America have already heard his serene voice of wisdom, which is different from what they hear today; a religious voice which preaches peace and not violence, fraternity and not fight, contemplation and work but not frantic activity generating evil.

In Italy, the philosophy and poetry of Tagore are now fairly well known outside those people who study and understand the spirit of the eternal East. The poet of *Gitanjali* and *Gardener*; the author of the philosophy of *Sadhana—The Realisation of Life* is known to us and affectionately appreciated by us. Today the news of his presence and his words will spread through the wider circle of the public; his teachings will be given attention with gratitude by European intellectuals.

It took a long time and much shifting of plans for the poet of glorious India to come to Italy. The initiative came from two learned Orientalists, Professor Formichi of Rome University and Guido Cagnola of Milan, who worked out the plan to make it possible. As a result Tagore has come to Genoa today, and over the next few days he will attend several meetings and deliver a special lecture in Milan on Thursday as a guest of our Philological Circle.

What the Poet Sees within Us

He came from South America, where he had committed to several lectures, but he was attacked by influenza and had to cancel all engagements. After convalescing, he came to Italy to keep his promise to his Milanese friends. He arrived a little tired, but eager to communicate with an unknown public for which he felt a natural bond.

Although Tagore possesses a vast knowledge of Western culture he will yet find in Italy the same sensibility as found in the East. He told a few friends he met on the first day: 'You Italians are very happy because your civilisation is influenced by diverse centres and, what is more important, is not overcome by only one centre'. He doesn't like big cities, tentacled,—grasping nature and naturalness, 'Sturdiness'—he said today—'is not strength.' Some of these concepts have been mentioned in an article recently published from his school at Bolpur, known as 'Scianti-Nikketan' [*sic*]—meaning refuge of peace. In one of his articles *City and Village* he mentioned the return of civilization to nature; in another symbolic drama *Red Oleander* he described the beauty of rural life as opposed to the demoniacal surroundings of the underground mines.

But Tagore is not a social agitator; he just wants to be a poet. In fact, he is very much disturbed on hearing that some English sources spread the rumour that he went to America for political propaganda. He also keeps himself aloof from the agitations in his own country. He tries to communicate with people on the basis of truth and the faith that he believes universal. His faith, in substance, is based on the traditional religious thought of India, of Brahma and Buddha, and in some essential points identified in Christian ideas. He believes a poet is a natural interpreter of the universal yearning of man for the good and the god. The sweet imaginations in his poems have already echoed in many hearts.

The Charm of the Man

Today, being tired, he didn't speak much but had a limited conversation with those close to him. He has within him a kind of shyness which prevents him talking freely on first contact. Considering his splendid prophetic figure, gentle look, flowing beard, and his solemn traditional Indian dress (from which he never separates himself), the charm of his figure exerts an impression everywhere.

Dr. Elmhirst, who is from America and one of the teachers at his university in Bolpur as well as his secretary, came with Tagore. His son and daughter-in-law also came to Genoa to meet him. He was talking with pleasure of his journey and the kindness he received from the members of the Italian steamer, especially when he was identified and the purpose of his journey revealed.

On Wednesday he will be arriving in Milan. On the same day the president of Circolo Filologico (Philological Circle), Duke Gallarati Scotti, will give a reception in his honour; in the evening Tagore will be present to watch *La Traviata*, to be performed in his honour at La Scala. On Thursday he will deliver a lecture at the Philological Circle and, the day after, at the Teatro del Popolo, where he will meet opera students and their teachers. His plays, even though a delicate poetry, must be appreciated by the people for their simplicity of sentiment and optimism of hope.

During his stay in Milan in the Azzurra Hall, there will be a staging of one of his plays, probably *The Post Office*. From Milan Tagore will proceed to Turin, where another committee will receive him. After Turin he will go to Florence, where he will again deliver a lecture, this time to the Leonardo da Vinci Society.

So, while making himself known in several Italian cities, the Indian poet will come to know this country to which he is attracted by the inextinguishable flame of poetry. He wants everybody to understand him and not admire him. The first fleeting contact with him makes a deep impression of purity, ancient simplicity and goodness.

G. Caprin[19]

Rathindranath was apprehensive about his father's health and withheld the news of his arrival from the media on purpose. He shared his concern with Formichi. Though a tentative tour schedule was published in some of the newspapers, he did not like the idea of his father beginning the busy tour so immediately.

Despite confidentiality, the news of the poet's arrival spread all over the city. In the evening, the university president came to pay the poet a visit at the hotel and to welcome him to the city of Mazzini. The conversation could not continue longer due to the language barrier, and after a short while, he left.

The next morning, on 20 January, some university staff showed Tagore around the city by car. The poet did not like the idea, but obliged them, and soon he felt tired and so retreated to his hotel.

In the afternoon, a large number of visitors came to meet Tagore. One of them had set his poem to music and performed it in front of him. Formichi later wrote in his memoir that he never expected so much enthusiasm from a mundane business centre like Genoa. In the evening, the poet and his party politely excused themselves from the visitors to retire early on the grounds of catching the early morning train to Milan.

Formichi asked the poet to write a short goodwill message for Italy before leaving Genoa. Tagore wrote:

In the far-away East, where I have always lived, I knew since my early youth how beautiful Italy was, the beloved country of the poets. It had always been my dream to be able one day to come to her door and offer my homage. Finally I have reached there, and I am sure that I shall go back to my country with my heart filled by her sun and her love. I am here to have the honour to be acknowledged by her as one of the poets who love her, and to whom she has granted the favour of a gracious smile.[20]

According to Formichi, the goodwill message in English was published in some of the Italian dailies, although there is no evidence of its publication in any of the papers in our collection.

The poet himself was not entirely confident about his health. He wrote to Rothenstein before leaving Genoa: '[...] I have just arrived in Italy. I hope I have strength enough to be able to respond to the reception awaiting me in this country. If I were not tied by my promise [to visit Italy] I should have gone straight back to India [...]'.[21] Throughout his journey from Genoa to Milan, Tagore and Formichi discussed a range of topics. At one stage, Tagore wanted to know about the current political situation in Italy. Formichi informed Tagore that Italy had deteriorated in the post-War period, but that peace and order had been restored without major bloodshed owing to the intervention of the 'extraordinary man' [Mussolini]. But, of course, Mussolini enjoyed the support of the king and the majority of the people. The conversation about politics did not continue further, probably because Formichi did not want to talk freely on such topics with the newly acquainted poet.

Milan

On 21 January at about 12.30 in the afternoon, the poet and his entourage reached Milan, along with Formichi and Alberto Poggi. Present at the Milan railway station to receive the poet were the Duke and Duchess Scotti, Guido Cagnola, and other members of the Circolo Filologico reception committee and representatives of the press and media. After an initial exchange of greetings, the poet and his retinue left the station to check in at the Hotel Cavour. *Il Popolo d'Italia* carried a brief news item describing the arrival of the poet in Milan.

Rabindranath Tagore's Arrival in Milan

The Indian poet Rabindranath Tagore arrived in Milan from Genoa by a direct train at 12.30 pm.

A small group of his admirers and curious people welcomed him at the railway station. Among them were the Duke and Duchess Gallarati Scotti, Sabatino Lopez, Professor Pizzagalli, Piero Preda, Gualtiero Tumati and his wife, the Honourable Cagnola, the composer Gatti, Mrs Meyer Camperio, Professor Pestalozza and Professor Mantegazza.

The mystical poet was greeted by loud applause as the train arrived at the railway station.

Rabindranath Tagore appeared to be a little tired after the journey. He thanked the Duchess Gallarati Scotti with moving words when she offered him a bouquet of white flowers. After he was introduced to a few people, he walked towards the exit.

Our colleague Gasparini welcomed the poet on behalf of the press. The great Indian thinker replied with a few kind words and then got into a car with his niece Nannica [sic, Granddaughter Nandini] who was carried in her mother's arms.

The son of the famous bard, Aren Tagore [sic, Rathin Tagore], and an Indian painter Essen Kar [sic, Suren Kar], who travelled with the poet, got into another car.

The distinguished guests are staying at the Cavour Hotel.

* * *

Today, as previously announced, Rabindranath Tagore will give a speech in English at the Philological Circle of Milan at 5 pm. The Indian poet will be introduced by Carlo Formichi, a professor from the University of Rome.[22]

On the same afternoon, in the presence of distinguished citizens, artists, and intellectuals of the city, the poet was received at the duke's palace. Duke Scotti addressed the assembly. This was followed by a visit to La Scala to see Verdi's opera *La Traviata*, conducted by Toscanini. Company Commander Piero Prada and Madam Edrige Zoeplitz, wife of the president of the Banca Commerciale Italiana, escorted the poet and the party to the theatre by motorcar. The poet shared the royal box with the duke and, as soon as the audience in the theatre saw him, they greeted him with cheers. A detailed article entitled 'Tagore' was published on the same day in *Corriere della Sera*.

Tagore

'Thou hast made me known to friends whom I know not. Thou hast given me seats in homes not my own. Thou hast brought the distant near and made a brother of the stranger.

I am uneasy at heart when I have to leave my accustomed shelter; I forget that there abides the old in the new, and that there also thou abidest.

Through birth and death, in this world or in others, wherever thou leadest me it is thou, the same, the one companion of my endless life who ever linkest my heart with bonds of joy to the unfamiliar.

When one knows thee, then alien there is none, then no door is shut. Oh, grant me my prayer that I may never lose the bliss of the touch of the one in the play of the many.'

This poem of fraternity is one of the great gifts offered to God in the pages of *Gitanjali* and is undoubtedly reflected in the cordial smile of Rabindranath Tagore when he, amidst the mass of humanity, extends a hand of friendship in a spirit of curiosity and with a feeling of intimacy. Today he is in Milan, yesterday he was elsewhere, tomorrow he will be elsewhere again. He has travelled in Japan, England, the United States and now he is travelling in Italy. He is visiting the greatest place that God can offer to the poets, thinkers and philosophers of the world. He speaks with serenity but is alert to his listeners, just as he often speaks to his audience at his school in Bolpur where he teaches.

Rabindranath Tagore belongs to a family in which thinkers and poets are born. Today two of the Tagores are artists; one of his brothers is considered a great philosopher. His father, in his own way, is also a mystic and a poet. 'Once while he was in a boat upon a river'—told by an Indian to Yeats—'he fell into contemplation because of the beauty of the landscape, and the rowers waited for eight hours before they could continue their journey.' Rabindranath himself composes his music from his lyrics. He is so popular that his songs are sung by people from India to Burma wherever Bengali is understood. At nineteen he wrote his novel and his plays were later performed in Calcutta. *Chitra*, symbolising the valour and love of a woman, has been performed without scenery.

In 1912 [*sic*] he received the Nobel Prize and became famous in Europe. He then translated into English a single volume *Song Offerings* (*Gitanjali*) which reveals him as an exquisite and spiritual poet. His fame then grew and his works, primarily those translated [into English], were retranslated rapidly into Italian, as had happened elsewhere [in Europe].

With his rising fame, naturally his works were also discussed. When a writer comes into fashion, stirs up the drawing room with feminine enthusiasm, a little harm occurs to that writer; but his work is above any fashion and survives—it will not be wrecked like toys.

Rabindranath Tagore, one of the finest voices from the rising Asia, sends greetings to us in the West as fresh as an eternal dew-drop. He is not only a harmonious sound from the ancient India which we have learnt to venerate and love, but also a poetry from a distant land, a poetry similar to a big stream heading for a river where you sail slowly amidst mist in a fantasy world combined with old religion and myth which are the most beautiful in the world. Rather he himself is this harmonious echo. No doubt ancient India is within him, but the flower of originality lies in the lively transformation of an ancient spirituality into a modern sensibility; his intelligence seems to be more western than oriental. He takes inspiration from the history of his great country. There is no one influential person of letters who will find in him any trace of pharisaism (whereas there is pharisaism in all traditions and religions). He who has read his book *Sadhana*, a collection of lectures Tagore gave to the students of his school at Bolpur, will find several comments from *Upanishad* about the fusion of the spirit of the past with the spirit of the present. He says 'How the ancient spirit of India revealed in *Upanishad* is so vital to today's life.' Even those who have a strong fascination in reasoning find his lyrics very passionate. Admirably, the poet wrote in his own words about the free mind. 'Man is not conditioned as the messenger of the King of the Universe behind the shadow of the throne, abandoning his liberty. His material being and the physical part of his body may be subjected to the dominion of the King but as far as his mind is concerned he can ignore the domination of the King. In this respect when his body gains entry to the kingdom, his mind is waiting outside for an invitation. That invitation comes to us as love and when he receives that invitation he is admitted to the kingdom of God.'

According to him the wisdom of India is the understanding of 'When the physical and mental barriers are separated from nature, when a man becomes not the man of the universe, we face enormous difficulties; sometimes there are no solutions and then we try all sorts of artificial means to overcome those difficulties.' But the wisdom of India, according to him—the interpreter of the pantheistic *Upanishad*—is that the man of the universe is the man in God. This concept prevails also in Christianity, which is why he feels the greatness of Christianity. We find a reflection of this wisdom in the morning prayer of Bolpur School, *Pita nohsi.* 'You are our father. We recognise you as our own father. Don't strike us. Let us pray sincerely to you. Oh Lord and Father don't give us gifts but give us what is good. We pray before you lying prostrate to give us blessings and goodness.'

Understanding the man of the Universe is the basis of this Bengali poet; it gives rise to a greater aversion to nationalism and the aversion is absolute. This great idea of fraternity (in the particular way the poet thinks) is not acceptable to Westerners because it alters their national values. Thus it is true that Western civilization is organized nationalistically (which does not mean nationally), thereby creating an imbalance and, as a result, suffering greatly. This nationalistic trait suppresses the spirit and creates a threat as a fatal power. His eastern poetry, influenced by the English poets, may be influenced by their horror of big industrial enterprises—similar feelings one can find in candid Ruskin.

* * *

But Tagore is a poet.

Yes, he is always, above all, a poet. In his intoxicating *Gardener* love sings the sweetest, most melancholy and passionate songs. Those are beautiful. 'When the two sisters go to fetch water […].' They have moments of love, fresh and most intense. Those are songs that profoundly touch our nostalgia: those are songs of life lived and life to be lived. 'I look in her for something that I don't find, and I find what I don't look for'— emotions are veiled in melancholy; desires are illuminated like lamps in the dark with their flames bent by the perfume-laden wind (a rare, discordant sign of folly). Love, great love, painful and beautiful with the disappointment which does not kill the dream but lives in the memory. […] And Tagore's women are so noble and beautiful 'O woman, you are not merely the handiwork of God, but also of men, they are ever endowing you with beauty from their hearts […].' But let us listen to the dramatic symbol of *Chitra*, the daughter of the king of Manipur, who through divine grace received physical beauty and the power of seduction to win the heart of Arjun; she ultimately discovers that she is more than a beautiful face. 'I am Chitra, no goddess to be worshipped, nor yet the object of common pity to be brushed aside, like a moth, with indifference. If you deign to keep me by your side in the path of danger and daring, if you allow me to share the great duties of your life, then you will know my true self.'

A Day of Tagore in Milan

Yesterday at 12.30 pm [21 January 1925] Rabindranath Tagore arrived in Milan from Genoa. He was accompanied by his son, daughter-in-law, nephew,[23] faithful secretary Elmhirst and Professor Formichi, one of the main organisers of the poet's first trip to Italy. At the station Tagore was cordially welcomed, even by people who were not familiar with his work. The reception party included all Tagore's good friends in Milan, including Duke Tommaso Gallarati Scotti, Dr. G. Cagnola, Professor Rebora, Gualtiero Tumiati, and Sabatino Lopez. He was offered flowers by some of the ladies, including Duchess Gallarati Scotti and Mrs. Toeplitz. A Milanese journalist separately welcomed him and the poet in his soft moving voice expressed his gratitude. His figure, like a benign prophet in Indian garments, attracted more eyes and camera lenses. The group then proceeded to the Hotel Cavour.

In the afternoon Tagore was introduced for the first time to a circle of intellectuals, hosted by Duke Gallarati Scotti at his palace. The natural courtesy of the aristocratic Indian poet matched the spiritual aristocracy of the location. Tagore was a little tired from the journey and his recent malady, yet he cordially accepted the tribute offered to him by the ladies, gentlemen and men of letters present in the audience. A group of children gave him a bouquet of flowers. The children were told that one of the Three Wise Men had appeared in front of them. The smile of the noble old man confirms this illusion. Even his poetry sometimes fails to arouse such a fairy-tale atmosphere.

Yesterday evening the Poet went to see the performance of *La Traviata* at La Scala. He arrived with his family before the performance started and took his place with his son next to Duke Gallarati Scotti. Other members of the party sat next to Commander Piero Preda. With the appearance of the old man, with his tall noble figure and conspicuous costume, there was a movement of curiosity inside the hall which was already full of spectators. There was a thunder of applause. Tagore was amazed and emotional for a while, expressed his thanks and took his seat. He sat motionless and absorbed while the auditorium plunged into darkness and the first soft notes of *Traviata* rose from the orchestra, invisible like a perfume. Tagore followed the whole performance with rapt attention, visually captured by the novelty and charm of the place, which was new to him. During the entire performance nothing distracted him or interrupted his attention.

We asked what his impression of the performance was. He spoke hesitantly 'My senses do not reach far enough to analyse and understand this kind of music. All I realised is its elegance, strength and poetry. It gave me the impression of a sweet song, naive, that flows near me like a murmur of a gurgling stream from which lifts the sounds of freshness and mirth. My soul feels all these with a great pleasure and perceives this song with a new joy and an unexpected sweetness.' He was asked what he thought about La Scala's environment and about the staging. Tagore answered that he was dazzled. 'I am finally convinced' he added, 'that the worldwide fame of this theatre is fully deserved. The lyrics of the operatic masterpieces sung at La Scala are more elegant and perfectly appreciated.'

* * *

It was announced today [22 January] that at 5 pm Tagore would give a lecture in English at Circolo Filologico, who organised his trip to Milan. The gist of his speech will be translated into Italian at the beginning.

Also, tomorrow morning [23 January] at Teatre del Popolo he will meet a group of students. A choir of children will sing songs from Bach and Martini. Then, as announced before, Tagore will be present to watch the performance of his play *Letter of the King* (*The Post Office*) in the Sala Azzurra.[24]

On the following day (22 January), a meeting was organized by the poet's admirers in the hotel and a local committee was formed. The main agenda of the meeting was to discuss the possibility of an exchange programme of scholars and intellectuals between India and Italy. Formichi, Duke Scotti, Guido Cagnola, Piero Prada, Ballini, the editor Mondadori, Alberto Poggi, and a few others were present as members of this committee. It was decided that the committee would find the necessary funds to send an Italian professor to teach Italian literature at Visva-Bharati on a two-year contract. Visva-Bharati would also provide exchange opportunities for Italian students and scholars to study aspects of Indology or similar subjects, and an Italian chair would be established in Santiniketan. Eighteen months later, Visva-Bharati received a veritable library and a professor with grants from the Italian government. This meeting was the initiation of that process.

In the evening, the poet addressed a full house at the lecture hall of Circolo Filologico Milanese. After initial formalities, Formichi introduced the poet with the following words:

[…] We offer our thanks to you for accepting our invitation, thanks for coming to Italy, to a country where so many admire and love you. They love you not because you have found a new weapon of war, nor a new medicine to avert death temporarily, nor a better source of satisfaction for our senses, nor even a means to increase man's control over Nature's forces. They love you because you have built in everyone's heart an abode of peace, a Santiniketan; they love you because of the joy you have given their spirit through the sublime expression of your sublime thoughts on God, death, life and love.

Speech, your venerable *Rigveda* says, is composed of four parts which are known to the seers. However, they keep three quarters hidden from circulation, so that people speak only a fourth of the speech potential:

catvâri vâk parimitâ padâni
tâni vidur brâhmanâ manîshianh
guhâ trîni nihitâ nengayanti
turîyam vâco manushyâ vadanti. […]

[…] Unlike those ancient bards, you have revealed the secret and circulated the remaining three quarters of speech among men. You have found words which are the worthiest expression of great mysteries, and made it possible to get glances of immortality. […]

[…] Master, do not hesitate to give the people of Milan your good message, your words of peace and human solidarity. We shall listen as if to the trumpets of prophecy; each one of us exhorts you as an *udgatar* [priest], the chanting priest sacrificing the Soma would do:

Lead me from untruth to truth,
Lead me from darkness to light,
Lead me from death to immortality. […][25]

Amidst applause, Tagore began his first address of the tour.

My friends, I have been waiting for this moment. My friend Professor Formichi had asked me to tell him what would be my subject this evening. I said I did not know, for you must realise that I am not a speaker. I am nothing better than a poet; when I speak, I speak with my surroundings and not to my surroundings. Now, when I see your kind faces, they speak to my heart. Your voice has reached me and now that I am to speak to you my voice will blend with it. I have waited for this inspiration. But how unfortunate I am that I do not know your beautiful language, neither do you know mine. Yet when the heart wishes to pay its debt, it must have some coin with the stamp of its own realm upon it, and that is our mother tongue. We can only express the deepest things we feel through the language we have learnt from our mothers, but since the language cannot be made a medium for the commerce of thought, of sentiment between you and myself I have reluctantly to use the English language, which you know is neither yours nor mine. Therefore at the outset I ask you to forgive me, those of you who do know this language as also those of you who do not know it, because my English is a foreigner's English.

Now I know what I am going to speak of; it will be an answer to the question as to what was the urging that brought me to you across the sea. In our language we have these words, *Jagrata Devata*, the Divinity which is fully awake. For the soul of the individual the Divine is not active everywhere. Where men's consciousness is illumined with love, God acts through our spirit. The shrine of the wakeful Divinity is there where the atmosphere of faith and devotion has been created by the meeting of generations of true worshippers. So our pilgrims in India are attracted to these places where, according to them, the Divine Spirit is active through the religious life and activity of the devotees.

Sometime in 1912 I felt a great desire to take my pilgrimage to the shrine of humanity, where the human mind was fully awake, with all its lamps lighted, there to meet face to face the eternal in man. I had a deep longing for this, for it had occurred to me that this present age was dominated by the European mind, only because that mind was fully awake. You all know how the Spirit of the great Asia is going through an age-long slumber in the depth of night where a few lonely watchers try to read the stars and wait for the sign of the rising sun across the darkness. So I had the intention to come to Europe to see the human spirit in the full blaze of its power and beauty. Then it was that I took that voyage of pilgrimage to Europe, leaving for a moment my own work at Santiniketan and the children I loved.

But that was not my first voyage to Europe. In the year 1878, when I was a boy, barely seventeen, I was taken by my brother to the shores of Europe. It will be difficult for you to realise what visions we had in the East, in those days, of this great continent of Europe. It was a dream to me, and when I was told that I was actually going to realise this dream, I was so excited that I could hardly sleep for nights and nights. Though I was young and though my knowledge of English was very insufficient, yet I had heard of her great poets and the heroes of Europe, the Europe of literature, so full of the love of freedom and of humanity. Italy was my first introduction to Europe.

In those days the steamer stopped at Brindisi and I still remember that night, it was midnight under a full moon, when my brother came to my cabin and said that we had arrived at the port. I came rushing on deck and shall never forget the marvellous beauty of that shore, enveloped in the silent mystery of the moonlight, and the sight of Europe asleep like a maiden dreaming of beauty and peace. It was fortunate for me that Brindisi was a small town, a quiet place which is still perhaps not so aggressively different from those scenes to which I had been accustomed from my childhood. I felt sure that its heart was open to me, to welcome a boy poet, who though young, was even in those days a dreamer. I was greatly elated, I left the steamer that night and slept in what I supposed in these days of progress would be termed a third rate hotel having no electric light or other conveniences. I felt that I was in the arms of this great mother Europe and my heart was satisfied.

The next day I woke and my Indian friend and my brother took me into an orchard close by. We wandered into the garden without giving any notice and what delight I had in the limpid sunlight, in the hospitality of leaf and fruit and flower; there was an Italian girl there, who reminded me of our Indian maidens, with eyes dark like bees, which have the power to explore the secret honey cells of love in the lotus of our hearts. (You know, with us the lotus is the emblem of the heart[.]) So I was delighted to find the same glances on a strange shore that have always fascinated me from my childhood. She was a simple girl with a coloured handkerchief round her head and a complexion not too white. That is, it was not a want of complexion. I wish to be forgiven when I say that complexion of whiteness is the complexion of the desert, it is not the complexion of life. Hers was like that of a bunch of grapes, for the sun with its warm kisses had imparted to the beauty of her face a tender bloom. I need not dwell at length upon the feeling I experienced. It is enough to say that I was of an impressionable age, I was 17, and I had come to the land of beauty, the land of rest and joy, which even at that time inspired my mind with the idea that one day I should claim its love for me. With me it was a case of love at first sight, but for those with me this was but a fleeting moment, so that I was not free to stay, but had to accompany my brother, who wanted me to take my lessons in English.

Being a truant boy I had always refused to take lessons. I was a problem to my elders, so they had decided that they would bring me to England where I should be compelled to learn English. This, they thought, would give me the stamp of respectability. England is a great country, and I pay my homage to the greatness of her people, but for an Indian boy, such as I was, to be left there alone in the depth of winter when the birds were silent and the sun so miserly with its gifts of warmth and light, what a terrible ordeal it was, those few months! I was homesick and extremely shy. I was frightened of the great people who stared at me. I was forced to live in a house facing Regent's Park, so that I would gaze with a feeling of bewilderment at its naked leaflessness, through the mists, the fogs, and the drizzle. However, I was young, too young to enter the spirit of England at that time, and I merely glanced at things whilst my home-sick heart was always longing for its own nest across the sea.

After a few months' stay I went back home to India. But I dare not here give a recital of idle days to those of you who are young and students, and for whom the example of a strenuous life of usefulness, would perhaps be more beneficial. I avoided all kinds of educational training that could give me any sort of standardised culture, stamped with a university degree. I dreamt, I wrote verses, stories and plays. I lived in solitude on the banks of the Ganges and I hardly knew anything of movements and counter-movements in the great world. When, all of a sudden whilst I was in the midst of my creative work came the call to come out of my seclusion to seek life in the heart of the crowd. I did not know what I could do. I had a love for children, so that I called them round me, in order to rescue them from the prison house of the educational department, and find for them that atmosphere of sympathy and love and freedom which they needed more than their elders. I chose a beautiful and secluded spot where in collaboration with Mother Nature it was possible to go on training these boys in a spirit of wisdom and love.

When I was still busy doing service to children I do not know what possessed me all of a sudden. From some faraway sky came the call of pilgrimage to me. We are born as pilgrims, pilgrims of this great green earth. A voice questioned me: 'Have you been to the sacred shrine where the Divine Spirit reveals itself in the thoughts and dreams and deeds of Man?' I thought possibly it was in Europe where I must seek it and know the full meaning of my birth as a human being in this world. And I did come to Europe. I had grown up in the meanwhile and learnt much of the history of man. I had sighed with the great poet Wordsworth who became sad when he saw what man had done to man. We too have suffered at the hands of men, not the tigers and snakes, not the elemental forces of nature, but man. Man is ever the greatest enemy of man. I had felt and known it, but all the same there was hope, deep in my heart, that I should find some place, some temple, where the immortal spirit of man dwelt hidden like the sun behind clouds. My friends, when I see Europe from outside, when I know how she is racked with unrest, how the spirit of suspicion and jealousy and greed has overspread all these beautiful countries, I feel a sense of despair hovering over me. When I first travelled from Italy to Calais I saw the beautiful scenery on both sides of the railways, I said these men are able to love their soil and what a great power is this love! How they have beautified the whole continent of Europe. I must know, I said to myself, these men who have been able for generations to pour out their love over the soil to which they have been born, and through this gift of love, what a great power has come out of this mute gift of earth. The earth is overwhelmed by it, not because of man's greed and passion, nor because he is fond of power and wealth, but because of this life-giving shower of heart that he has poured around him. How he has struggled to eradicate the dismal ugliness of barrenness from the inert, how, step by step, he has fought and defeated evils in everything that was hostile in his surroundings.

But why this dark misery lowering over her? What has happened? How has Europe suffered today, how widespread is the menace of the doom in her sky? What is the reason? It is a lack of love which makes everything barren, ugly and forbidding. The love for her own soil and children will no longer suffice for her. When destiny offered to her a limited problem to solve, Europe did more or less satisfactorily solve it. Her answer was patriotism, nationalism, that is to say love for that and those to which she happened to be related. According to the degree of truth of this love she reaped her harvest to welfare. But today through the help of science the whole world has been given to her for a problem. How to answer in the fullness of truth she has yet to learn. Because the problem is vast the wrong answer is fraught with danger. A great fact has been laid bare to you, according to your dealing with it you will attain the fulfilment of your destiny. If you do not have the strength to accept it in the right spirit your humanity will rapidly degenerate, your love of freedom, love of justice, love of truth, love of beauty will wither at the root and you will be rejected […] God. Do you realise how the mark of ugliness is everywhere apparent, in your cities, in your commerce, the same monotonous dreadful mask, so that nowhere is there a living expression of the spirit of love? When we see how this demon of greed smothered the beauty of our own Ganges, one of the beauty spots of the earth, how this demon of greed has established a stronghold of petrifying death, we realise how all this ugliness comes from a want of love.

Love can be patient. Beauty is matured and moulded by patience. Your great artists knew it in the days when they could gladly modulate all the riches of their leisure into some tiny detail of beauty. The greedy man can never do this. He has no patience for beauty. Factories are the triumph of ugliness, no one has the patience to try and give them the touch of grace, and so everywhere in God's world today we are faced with what is called progress, a progress towards ugliness, towards the whirlpool of passion which is greed and never creative of great work. Can you call to mind any great voice speaking out of the human heart in these modern days? We are proud of science. We offer to it our homage in return for its gifts which are now bequeathed to posterity. In this field of Science you have touched the eternal in the material world, in the world of extension. Our sages have said 'The Infinite has to be known and realised. For man the Infinite is the only true source of happiness.' Europe has touched the Infinite in the domain of external Nature. I do not cry down the material world. I fully realise that it is the nurse and the cradle of the Spirit. By achieving the Infinite in the heart of material world you have made this world more hospitable than it was. But merely becoming rich in fact does not give us the right to own it. The great science, which you have discovered, still awaits your meriting through what you have gained; outwardly you may become successful, but you may miss greatness all the same. Because you have strenuously cultivated your mind in Europe, because of your accuracy of observation and the development of your reasoning faculties, these discoveries you have deserved.

But discoveries have to be realised by the complete humanity; only then is truth honoured. The knowing has to be perfectly brought under the control of the being. It is not the domain of science to deal with our being yet this is the highest truth in the human world and therefore all other truths have to be brought into harmony with it at any cost. Truth when not properly treated comes back to us to destroy us. Your very science is becoming your destroyer. If you have earned a thunderbolt for yourself, you must possess the right arm of a god to be safe. In your mind you have failed to cultivate these qualities which would give full sovereign right over science and therefore you have no peace. You cry for peace but you only build another machine, some new combination. Quiet may be imposed from outside for some time, but peace comes from the spirit, it comes from the power of sympathy, the power of self-sacrifice and not from the power of organisation. I have great faith in humanity. Like the sun it can be clouded but never extinguished. I admit that at this time when the human races have met together as never before, the baser elements are predominant. The powerful are exulting at the number of their victims. They take the name of science to cultivate the superstition that they have certain physical signs indicating their eternal right to rule, as the explosive power of the earthquake once might have claimed its never-ending sway over the destiny of this earth. But they in their turn will be disappointed. Theirs is the cry of a past that is already doomed, a past that has depended upon geographical and racial boundaries, that has thrived upon the exclusive spirit of national individualism, a past that is gone. Only those races will prosper who, for the sake of their perfection and permanent safety, are ready to cultivate that spiritual magnanimity of mind which is able to realise the soul of man in the heart of all races. For this is the truth of Man, and only truth can save us and give us peace, and nothing else. We are waiting for a time when the spirit of the age must be translated into human truth and I have come to your door seeking the voice of humanity, which must sound its challenge and overcome the noise of the greedy crowd of slave drivers. Perhaps it is already sounding in whispers behind closed doors, till it burst forth in a thundering cry of judgement and the vulgar shout of brute force is silenced in awe.[26]

At the end Formichi, summarized the content of Tagore's lecture in Italian.

A more or less comprehensive report of the speech was published in the 23 January issue of *Corriere della Sera*.

Journey into Europe's Ideology
Tagore's Lecture at the Philological Circle in Milan

Nothing can invoke the spirit of the East more than what happened in the hall of the Philological Circle. Long before the time fixed for Tagore's lecture, the hall was full of our Western crowd. When the poet appeared, solemn and gentle, and took his chair, immediately a religious atmosphere succeeded, humming stopped, and there was formed an air of a different spirit and thought—the thought which is recurrent in his writings, the essential aim of art and love. The dense audience felt immediately the presence of someone in front of them who has the power to communicate with others, even when speaking in a foreign language. The ancient nobility in his appearance and the benign smile in his paternal glance immediately impressed the public, opening their hearts.

After prolonged warm applause Professor Formichi introduced the poet with a passionate eloquence, expressing the pleasure of the people of Milan to hear, for the first time in Italy, one of the few poets of universal fame living in the world today: a poet, teacher, educator and seer. We love him, Formichi said, because this person, simply by using the power of poetry, created a spirit similar to that found in his great school of Santiniketan, an abode of peace. The *Rigveda* says a speech consists of four parts of which Brahman keeps three parts secret; but Tagore, in his poems and mostly in prayer, shows it whole. We are fortunate, Formichi concluded after another round of applause, that we shall hear the message of peace and solidarity for the first time in Milan, a city of vibrant life, always ready to receive all great operas and all great ideas.

Then the poet started speaking with his sweet and gentle voice. The serenity emanated from the face, and the sober movement of his hands added to the majestic and passionate eloquence. Sometimes the words were very slow and sounded like singing and prayer. Even those people who didn't understand the meaning of some of the English words guessed the sense of it.

Pilgrimage of Conscience

Tagore regretted that he had to speak in a foreign language to the audience for whom it was also a foreign language. Only the mother tongue allows the total expression of ourselves. He also apologised for not saying exactly what would be the theme of his speech. I am not an orator, he said, but only a poet, but I want to tell you, he added, why I came to your door crossing the seas. An ancient Indian saying asserts that divinity is fully awake. God is awake in the conscience of man. How the pilgrims of his country go from sanctuaries to sanctuaries; like them he loves wandering among those sanctuaries where the conscience prevails. For India, Europe is that continent which is entirely awake while Asia is still sleeping. There [in Asia] within the darkness where many are sleeping, only seers discover the light. Then to see the awakened Europe he had heard a voice which reached him in his peaceful Asian abode.

This was not his first pilgrimage to Europe. From his memory Tagore described his first journey to Europe when he was only 17 years old. His father sent him to England to educate him in the English way. Europe at that time appeared to an Indian young man as a dream world, as it was the land of poets, of ideals and of freedom. His first contact with Europe was in the port of Brindisi. It was a moonlit night and Europe appeared to him not as a harsh land of action but like a 'young maiden who dreams in sleeping'. Happily, the day after, he went into a garden where he saw flowers and fruits and also a young Italian girl with brunette hair and 'with eyes of bees', just like the young girls of his own country. Indians represent the heart with the lotus flower and the eyes with bees caressing flowers. Tagore confessed, apologising to the ladies in the audience, that he is attracted more to the sun-tanned complexion than the white. To him, white is the colour of the desert whereas sun-browned faces are radiant. Duty forced him to leave Brindisi and go to England. Although he pays homage to

England, his first months in London in a boarding house were tormented by homesickness. Afterwards he returned to the eastern shore of his own country, not to avoid his studies but to find some inspiration. He engaged himself in dreaming and writing, ignoring the tumultuous world around him; he found a refuge where he started educating children amidst God and nature.

The Power of Love

From this refuge he again received a call for a new pilgrimage. From Wordsworth he learned about man's cruelty towards men: 'neither tigers nor lions nor natural calamities of the world have done so much harm as man has done to his fellow man.' Tagore came to see the awakened Europe with its immortal spirit. During his first journey from Italy to England he saw happy countries and prosperous lands, and he thought that such beauty is the work of love because it was created by men who love their land. Today, however, he sees Europe tormented by jealousies and greed, and he feels a sense of despair. 'Today,' Tagore said, and his voice expressed a real anguish, 'you are suffering. The shade of misery spreads over Europe. You were great when you used to love. Now you suffer because you don't love anymore.' The lack of love doesn't allow you to create beautiful things. The monotonous mask of a commercial civilization fails to express the spirit of love. Beauty is born by patience and the greedy spirit does not have it. Where is there now a voice which can interpret the whole of humanity?

Yes, there is science. Even we Indians can feel it and admire it. It has touched the bounds of eternity but only in the material world, which is finite. Europe has made the world materially habitable. It is great, strong and powerful. But what does it do with this power? Science is an impersonal power. 'Your very science is becoming a destroyer.' Europeans sometimes appear to be children playing with pistols [this example was not in Tagore's text]. From one side they are invoking peace and from the other they are looking for new ways of destruction. 'Peace comes from the spirit, born from the power of the heart and not from organisation. But we must not despair. There were also great events resulting from science and organisation. The meeting of all races in the paths of the world is now more inclusive. Initially this meeting might have produced more evil than good because races met each other and then started to hate each other. But this evil cannot persist. This knowledge must bring back love.' Tagore ended his lecture confessing his firm faith in the destiny of man and, quoting a line from *Upanishad*, he said that the God who is awaking close to us takes us

to the light. The lecture was followed by long applause, showing the gratitude of the audience. The poet stood there overwhelmed, joining hands in
prayer. There was more applause when Professor Formichi summed up the
lecture in Italian with precision and warmth. The public were still expressing their joy as the poet made his exit onto the street.

While leaving the hall, a member from the audience commented
that he has experienced meeting a real Brahman as Marco Polo praised
Brahmans and their spiritual purity when he wrote: 'Let me tell you that
these are true Brahmans, they are the best men and the most loyal people,
and they would not tell a lie for anything in this world.'[27]

Reports of Tagore's lecture in Milan also appeared in other
newspapers. *Corriere della Sera* published a special article entitled
'Rabindranath Tagore' by Margherita Sarfatti, a Jewish-Italian journalist, art critic, and socialite in its 24 January issue covering three
columns with a photograph of the poet. Regrettably, the condition
of the microfilm is too bad to decipher.

According to Formichi, Tagore's speech upset some fascists.
Some newspapers published unfavourable comments about the
poet. 'Factories are the triumph of ugliness'; 'We are faced with
what is called progress, a progress towards ugliness, towards the
whirlpool of passion which is greed and never creative of great
work'; and 'In order to exercise supreme control over science, one
has to practise certain virtues which you [in Europe] never did. This
is why peace eludes you'—such statements angered militants. In
addition, the spiritual note in Tagore's speech on humanism failed
to impress those Italians who were struggling hard to overcome
their economic and social decadence. The newspapers in our collection do not carry any harsh negative statement about Tagore's
speech (although harsh criticism may have been published in some
fascist tabloids which were financially sponsored by the regime,
but which disappeared after the war). Formichi has not mentioned
the name of any newspaper in this regard. But there must have
been some criticism and commotion reaching even the shores of
America. Sudhindra Bose of Iowa University observed that '[...]
within the present Fascist government which is operating without check of an intelligent Italian public opinion, international

altruism as preached by Tagore cannot live [...].'[28] One extreme suggestion appearing in a New York newspaper claimed that Tagore had to leave Italy in a hurry because the fascist government did not like his opinions. Tagore was not aware of such comments in the Italian newspapers during his stay in Italy.

Tagore was received on 23 January at the Teatro del Popolo in Milan. The Teatro del Popolo was established in 1911 by Sociatá Umanitaria (Humanitarian Society) to provide the working classes with the opportunity to participate in the cultural activities of Milan. The welcome was arranged by the president of the theatre, Piero Preda, who was an industrialist and also a poet. Children presented the poet with a bouquet of flowers. The president read out the following greeting which is preserved in the Formichi File at the Tagore Archives in Santiniketan.

Teatro del Popolo

Milano 23 Gennuie, 1925

To you Magnificent Poet of Goodness, the true religion of all men of all faiths and lands, the Theatre of the People of Milan want you to understand how touched and grateful we are for your visit, and we send you our best thanks.

Do please accept this expression of true devotion and immense love.

The President
Piero Preda

This was followed by choral songs performed by children; the poet then gave this address:

Friends, I thank you from my heart for the gifts you are offering me today, namely, flowers and these children singing. When I am with children, I turn into a child myself, and believe that behind my old man's appearance they will discover the youth in my poet's heart. I have been falsely reputed as a wise man, a prophet, but I am and want to be only a poet. As such I do not speak from an elevated platform, but step down among the children to be their friend, their poet, and not their guide. Meanwhile, I am delighted as I realize that, despite the language barrier, you have understood me, you offer your friendship to me and accept me as your poet.[29]

An elaborate report of the reception at Teatro del Popolo came out on the 24 January issue of *Corriere della Sera*.

Tagore among Children

Yesterday morning about 3000 children were gathered in the Teatro del Popolo (Peoples' Theatre), some along with their mothers, a few fathers (as it was a working day) and many teachers. They came to welcome the Indian poet. They all knew one thing about Tagore: that the poet believes kindness is beauty and beauty is kindness. They realised this through their instinct. Think of Garibaldi's charm. Although he was not a poet but a warrior, yet he could touch the soul of the crowd because he was not a warrior only. He could stop and listen to the birds singing at the same time as dreaming of fighting the last human battle. There is something in Tagore's bright look and in his magnificent white hair that reminds some of the popular noble heroes of our people—although more feminine and old.

The organizers of the solemn ceremony—Piero Preda together with Sabatino Lopez and Master Gatti, who are the promoters of the new fortune of the Teatro del Popolo—invited a large number of young people to the huge theatre. It was a simple ceremony in the morning. The young girls and boys of the *Fa Mi* choir sang in harmony the ancient music of Martini and Pieraccini, a Bach hymn and a chorus from Mrs Oddone's work, directed by Master Perlasea. During the performance Tagore was present on the stage; he sat in front of a table decorated with little bunches of violets. He was absorbed and intent. The young boys and girls then offered him bouquets of white and red roses.

After the ceremonial welcome by the children and their teachers, Tagore delivered a brief message in a slow melodious voice. Professor Formichi faithfully translated it into Italian. The theatre was a loud buzzing of bees that stopped and turned into an affectionate and respectful silence.

'Friends,' the poet said, 'I thank you heartily. You, the children, have given me the best of presents—flowers and songs. I would like to be known as the poet of youth and I hope you, my dear children, will realise that within an old man there is always hidden youthfulness, as it is in my case. This youthfulness is immortal in a poet's heart. I am rejuvenated by seeing children. I love children and out of my contemplation I founded a school where children learn to love Nature and God. You will hear people saying about me that I am a wise person and a prophet: do not believe it. I am only a poet and I am not interested in fame but in your love.'

Amidst new songs and endless applause, the children of Milan promised friendship to this poet of humanity and compassion.[30]

On the afternoon of 23 January, the poet gave an hour-long
portrait sitting with the famous painter Rietti at the Duke's palace.
During the evening the poet fell ill again—he became too ill to
watch the performance of his play *The Post Office* (*L'ufficio postale*)
at the Azzurra Hall. Instead, he was kept under the observation
of two physicians, Dr Achille Aliprandi and Dr Giuseppe Betti,
who advised him to take complete rest. All remaining programmes
were cancelled.

What was the audience reaction after watching the play *The
Post Office*? *Corriere della Sera* published the following review in the
'Theatre and Entertainment' column on 24 January.

Azzurra Hall
The King's Letter (*The Post Office*)
A Two-Act Play by Rabindranath Tagore

This play does not bloom on the very old trunk of Indian Theatre. It seems
a sweet and sad Western imagination under the veil of beautiful oriental
shades, with a delicate plot. The scent of the poetic sadness of the play
probably imposes upon us a different reaction to that of the emotion it
imposes upon the audience for whom the play has been written. Kim,
the child created by Kipling, as well as the dear little child Amal, whom
Tagore describes dreaming with a pathetic smile while approaching death,
is certainly remote from our culture but curiously more exotic. We, the
Westerners, find within Amal an ailing little child who looks at the colour-
ful life and passers-by through the window of the room he cannot leave.
He imagines far-away countries, never-ending streets, having adventures
near beautiful silver springs with clear water; lingering in a flower garden;
playing in the shade of vast ancient woods. This dying child, using other
people's words to incorporate his own ideas, imagines a life which he cannot have and becomes excited with an ardent desire! He wants to receive a
letter from the King delivered from the new Post Office, built close to his
home, on top of which there is a golden flag waving. He is unaware that
his premonition will never happen as the King has no time to remember
him. However, the boy feels that the most powerful of all people will
communicate with him. The constant mention of this letter, footfalls, the

opening of doors and the approach of the nameless shadow reminds the audience of the coming of death as in Maeterlinck's *The Intruder*.

Amal thinks that the King will write to him and has no doubt about this. But does Amal know anything about the greatness of the King or his own insignificance? In his heart, there is love and faith. Next to him, his adoptive father nods his head knowing that the child will die and that the King is a far-away presence, unaware of the child's existence. The village chieftain, haughty and irascible, becomes vexed at the thought that a little boy dares to think about the King so confidently. He jokes cruelly with the sick child giving him a blank page, saying sneeringly that it is the royal letter he has been waiting for and that the King will soon come and eat the rough food that Amal's family can offer. Only an old crazy man, loved by the children because he encourages all kinds of their fantasies, reassures Amal's desire. Suddenly the desire works a miracle. The King sends his herald to announce his arrival with his doctor to cure the child. Amal's ardour is so strong that his dream becomes real to others as well. The child is happy, closes his eyes and falls asleep forever. 'But,' the herald says, 'when the King calls him, he will wake up.' The majestic guest who has written the letter to the child, who will come and call, who has sent his herald to precede him, who also sent his doctor to cure all diseases, is Death. This is the letter a human eye cannot read which we all receive one day. Nevertheless, when it arrives, not all of us will be smiling and serene, like little Amal.

The above interpretation of Tagore's imagination is realised by us although there may be some other meanings. It is full of charm, thought-provoking, dressed in a pale dark luminosity. We can reach the meaning of the words but the mystical sense within it escapes us. We believe his imagination is rich in symbols, whose cipher keys we do not know. Perhaps the room where the sick child is confined represents the prison of life; the places the child knows without having ever seen them may be the memories of his previous life; the long far-away roads he thinks about are the path through which the human soul makes its journey, out of obedience to the law of changes, finally reaching the great palace of infinite silence and returning to God. There is the end of the dream, lost like a wave within an ocean.

This play must therefore have a message that we cannot decipher fully as it is not clearly addressed to us. We lack the confidence necessary to understand it. Nevertheless, although we cannot read the great words and, far from understanding it, we see only the white page as the village chieftain does. A few symbols seem to be meaningful to us too. The play tells us that Death is also great and graceful. It shows us that those who have simple hearts can explain more about life by offering fine examples than the scholars can. It shows that an innocent smile can disarm the evil and bring goodness. There is no novelty in expressing these truths and that is why we are less impressed. In Amal there is a childishness that does not belong to the child's soul only but also to the poet's art. It seems that the poet has written this story of a child for children. He becomes a child with them and for them, for a while. The characters surrounding Amal are just outlined and not complete. They are sketchy, such as the character of Gaffer, the old man, who knows many beautiful stories to tell the children; he is the shade of a character and could have been more magnificent and artistic. On the whole, *The Post Office*, in spite of some deficiencies, pleases us with some disappointments. Its clear simplicity is its major beauty. The underlying kindness within the story touches all human beings; even an incomparable sadness like a child's death consoles us with a kind of serene compassion.

The young Marichette Valentini, without losing her childish charm, her playful and innocent grace, showed rare ease and accuracy in her acting. She expressed Amal's dreams and death whilst avoiding the traits of a precocious child. On the contrary: her spontaneity, abandon and tenderness were very convincing and fascinated the audience, who repeatedly and warmly applauded the play, especially Marichette Valentini and other members of the cast, although they were not very confident. Mrs. Beryl Tumiati made the Indian costumes with taste and authenticity.

Rabindranath Tagore should have been present but could not attend the show because of his sudden indisposition. However, his family attended.

Tonight's show is *John, the disciple*. On Sunday, *The King's Letter* will be staged again in the morning.[31]

Incidentally, the first production of *The Post Office* in the West was in English and performed by a professional group of the Abbey Theatre in Dublin in 1913. The original play *Dakghar* in Bengali was staged four years later in Calcutta. Many Western reviewers criticized the extensive use of symbolism in Tagore's plays, saying that it was a hindrance to the general audience in appreciating the beauty of his work. In spite of that, *The Post Office* is one of Tagore's plays that has been produced several times in different countries, in many languages, and, in some cases, with interesting innovations. In many productions, the central character, the boy

Amal, was successfully played by teenage girl actors like Lilian Jago (in Dublin) and Marichette Valentini (in Italy).

Between 24 and 28 January, Tagore was confined to bed in his hotel. The Milanese public was regularly informed about the poet's health through the medical bulletins issued by Dr Betti. The bulletin on 25 January read as follows:

> Milan, 25th January
> The poet Rabindranath Tagore, who is convalescing from a light influenza fever, needs absolute physical and mental rest on account of his weak general condition.
> Professor Dr. Giuseppe Betti[32]

Corriere della Sera (26 January 1925) also published news of the poet's illness:

Tagore Indisposed

Since last Friday, our city's important guest, Rabindranath Tagore, has been ill. As a result he could not attend the performance of his play *A Letter to the King* (*The Post Office*) at the Azzurra Hall. He is suffering from a bad type of influenza. For the whole of Saturday the poet was in bed and still he is in bed.

Yesterday the poet was supposed to visit Turin but the visit was eventually postponed. He is now in the Hotel Cavour, surrounded by his family. As advised by Dr. Pasquale [Achille?] Aliprandi the hundreds of well-wishers who are eager to know the poet's health are requested not to see the poet. The doctor thinks this influenza is not serious. There is no possibility of any kind of complications. He is very exhausted due to his work over the last few days.[33]

Il Gazzettino di Venezia (27 January 1925) published Tagore's brief tour itinerary in Venice in the first section of its report, but concluded the same article with the news of the poet's illness.

Tagore in Venice

The intellectual public of Venice will listen to the great Indian poet Sir Rabindranath Tagore who has accepted an invitation from the

Presidency of the Venetian University to deliver a lecture. The poet, who has been in Milan and Turin, will be in Venice on the first day of February when a reception has been arranged in his honour, which will be worthy of the poet's lofty spiritual personality and the embodiment of Eastern thought and culture.

Tagore will speak to the audience at the St. Fantin Hall of the University of Venice which will certainly not be large enough to accommodate all those people who aspire to hear him talking about the art and sentiment of a civilization far from us and different from ours.

Tagore Indisposed

News has come from a Milanese newspaper that the venerable poet who was supposed to visit Turin on Sunday was forced to postpone the visit because he caught cold and is now suffering from exhaustion. He has been in bed at the Hotel Cavour since Saturday afternoon.[34]

Finally, the news of the cancellation of all Tagore's engagements and his return to India appeared in *Corriere della Sera* in its 27 January issue, with an interesting note of his intention to buy a villa in Lombardia.

The Poet Tagore Is Returning to India: To Buy a Villa in Lombardia

The condition of Tagore's health is getting better but the poet is worried about his weakness which prevents him from giving public lectures. For this reason he has decided to leave Italy and come back again next summer when the weather will be more like that of his own country. Then he can stay much longer and fulfil his mission.

On Thursday the poet will be leaving Milan for Venice where he will stay until Monday and receive those people who want to see him. However, he will not repeat his lecture in Milan. On Monday he will embark on a Lloyds steamer where cabins are already booked for him and his family to take him to India.

Tagore's returning to Italy is so sure that he has entrusted one of his friends to buy a villa on the lake at Lombardia[35] where he wants to stay for a long time.[36]

The poet himself was very upset by the constant interruption of his life by this bout of influenza. He wrote to Rothenstein on 27 January:

What I did fear has happened. I have fallen ill. I almost feel guilty that it should have been so—for I have been met with such an outburst of welcome that it grieves my heart not to be able to respond to it in an adequate manner. Twice I have been able to appear before the public and the enthusiasm of the people has made me feel humble—I only wish I could do something for them to deserve this. But I have not even the strength to leave my bed and appear before them to say how grateful I am. I am sailing back to India on the next Monday. But I am sure to come back to Italy either next autumn or in the following spring [...].[37]

On 28 January, Tagore received a few visitors for a brief period in his hotel. They included some representatives of the Società Pro Cultura Femminile (Women's Cultural Society) based in Turin. The poet had been due to visit Turin on 27 January and address the society, but the event was cancelled. Hence, the members of the society paid the poet a visit and presented him with an elegantly bound edition of Dante's *Divina Commedia*.

In the meantime, letters and telegrams were pouring in from Turin, Florence, and Rome, where receptions had been arranged for the poet and news of a recovery from his ailment were anxiously awaited. However, the physicians did not want to take any chances.

The cancellation of all the poet's engagements caused a little embarrassment to Tagore's tour organizers, especially Formichi. Although the sponsors in Milan bore the major part of the tour expenses, sponsors from Turin and Florence also made a substantial contribution. As promised by Formichi, these societies were expecting a visit or a lecture from the poet. Tagore also felt that his illness caused a great deal of disappointment and embarrassment for many. Before leaving Milan, he expressed his wish to return to Italy in a poem. This was immediately translated into Italian by Formichi and sent out for publication in some newspapers. *Corriere della Sera* published this poem on 29 January.

Tagore's Greetings to Italy

Before leaving Milan, Rabindranath Tagore offered the President of Circolo Filologico a poem about Italy. This poem of greetings is translated by Professor Formichi from the original Bengali into Italian, and is published in the Italian press as follows:

To Italy

I said to thee: 'O Queen,
Like many other lovers, who have brought their gifts to thy feet,
I have come, as a lark at the gate of thy Dawn, only to sing to thee
and then to go.'
From thy window thou speakest to me through thy veil:
'Now it is winter, my sky is dark, my garden without flowers.'
I said to thee: 'O Queen,
I have brought my reed from the eastern shore
Waiting to play to the light of the dark eyes,
Open to me thy veil.'

Thou saidst in answer, 'Go back my impatient poet,
For I have not yet decked myself in colours,
In the sweet month of May, when I sit on my flower throne,
I shall ask thee to my side.'

I said to thee: 'O Queen,
My journey has borne rich fruit in thy words of hope:
Floated on the breeze of spring the magic of the call to me
will burst in flowers in our faraway forest.
I shall seek back my path to thy window
On some sunny day, drunken with the fragrance of roses
and humming with bees' wings.'
Today, while I take my leave and go back, I sing:
'Victory to thee!'[38]

The poem inspired some major and minor poets in Italy; some translated it in verse, some composed a new poem containing Italy's reply to her lover.[39] At one extreme, beautiful though the verse may be, some saw in it a malign reference to the Italian elections to be held in the spring: Those opposed to fascism were hoping for an unfavourable outcome for the government. However, Tagore was completely unaware of the impending elections as well as of the fascists' anger after his speech at the philology circle.[40]

During his illness in Milan, the poet was not allowed to meet any visitors other than representative members of a few selective societies and some close friends. Formichi and the Duchess and Duke Scotti were amongst those who used to visit him regularly. The poet enjoyed their company and various subjects were discussed amongst them, one of which, 'On Death', is appended at the end of this book.

Venice

On 29 January, the poet and his party took the 2 pm train to Venice. Before boarding the train, the Latin professor Felice Roemorino gave a farewell speech in Latin at the station. The poet responded by saying:

The first welcome of hospitality in this country has come to me from Milan, whence it was proposed I should begin my tour in Italy. The very few days I have been able to spend here were made so overflowingly full with the generosity of kindness, that they have brought Italy close to me and given me a feeling that I have known her for long.

It is a rare privilege for a stranger to find the heart of a great country open to him, without having wearily to wait and repeatedly to knock at the gate. How I have deserved this honour I know not, but I know how to appreciate it and cherish it in my memory.

I take my farewell of Milan with an inner assurance, that I shall find my seat ready in a warm corner of her heart when I come back, which will be before long, if my own wish be realised.[41]

A group of Fascist militia requested a signed photograph of the poet for Mussolini as a present. Throughout the journey to Venice, at every station, people thronged to get a glimpse of the poet. There were large groups of students to greet the poet at Vicenza and Padua stations, shouting in chorus '*Viva il Poeta Indiano, Viva Tagore, Viva il poeta dell'amore e della pace*'. The train reached Venice at

7.45 pm. *Il Gazzettino di Venezia* published the following report on 29 January.

Tagore in Venice

According to Milanese newspapers Rabindranath Tagore will leave Milan today to come to Venice for a short time before going back to his country. The departure date has been brought forward as his health has been shaken by discomforts and the variations of the climate.

Venice, the oasis of poets, is getting ready to receive this venerable figure of poet, philosopher and apostle with due honour.

Tagore—who doesn't know him?

His fame spread throughout Europe in 1913 when he received the Nobel Prize for his *Gitanjali* (*Song Offerings*), translated by himself from his Indian mother tongue into English. His subsequent works include other poetry collections and novels such as *The Gardener*, Votive collection, *The Lover's Gift*, *Sadhana* and dramas such as *Chitra*, *The Post Office*, *The King of the Dark Chamber* and essays on education and politics.

The sweet soul of the gentle poet emerges from his entire work; he sings the song of life, which is beautiful, and he speaks of love. He brings to us a reflection of the light from his own country Bengal, which is strange to us like a will-o'-the-wisp in a dead land, painted in the colours of the rainbow that reflects from the sky like a mirror.

Tagore was born in 1861 near Calcutta within a rich noble family of Bengal merchants. His grandfather, Prince Dwarkanath Tagore, in association with Ram Mohan Ray, founded 'Brahmo-Samaj' in 1828 which aimed to fight idolatry and to support the spiritual worship of Brahma, the Creator of the universe, without images, sacrifices and rites.

In 1841 the poet's father Maharishi (the Great Saint) Devendranath Tagore became the leader of 'Brahmo-Samaj' and after his death it was taken over by Dwijendranath, Rabindranath's brother, who was also a philosopher and a thinker. Rabindranath is also associated with the 'Samaj'. The Samaj draws its inspiration from one of the sacred books of India *Upanishad*. He is deeply religious and convinced of his faith.

He began his education in his own country and afterwards continued in England, where he came to know about the West and its rush to war; he detested its insatiable thirst for blood.

On the quiet banks of the River Ganges, where he lives with his family, he used to study the simple and humble life of the poor and wrote songs in fresh in a serene language. He does not write in Sanskrit, the cultured language of priests and well-educated people (like Latin for us), but he uses Bengali, a popular language in his country, spoken by more than forty million Indians.

He composes music from his lyrics, his people know and love them so that, wherever in India Bengali is understood, the poet is well-known.

When he was 40 years old, his wife, a young daughter and a son died. This terrible incident shattered his life, but instead of retreating into himself like a hermit, this opened up a new and vast horizon. He turned to the earth and the whole of humanity, embraced them with his unique great love and his idea of God. His soul is like a very sensitive string, stretched to the infinite, vibrating with every breath of wind, melting in a sweet harmony.

'The joy of man', he says, 'does not come from need or desire, but comes from the action, from the love for God and for the service of humanity. It should be neither tiring nor tormenting but of peace, goodness and joy'.

Rabindranath Tagore came to old Europe watching the horror of recent slaughter. He moves around the restless countries with calm and serenity. His tall figure rises above the uproaring crowds and they are impressed with his nobility.

'Peace, Goodness and Joy'—'The infinite personality of man, the *Upanishad* says, may be accomplished only by the grand harmony of all human races'—'Let's love our brothers'—that's the Biblical teaching he preaches.

Venice today will greet the poet with her lovely smile and will offer him her most beautiful treasure.

* * *

Tagore will come to Venice tonight at 7.30 pm and he will stay here until Monday, when he and his family will board a Lloyds steamship. He will go back to India as he needs rest. He is exhausted by the journey throughout Europe and the change of climate. He will come back to Italy next summer.

There is a rumour that he bought a villa near a lake in Lombardia.

In Venice he will not give a lecture but will greet various people.[42]

The same newspaper published the following report the next day (30 January 1925).

Tagore Arrived in Venice

Yesterday evening at 7.45 pm, the Indian poet Rabindranath Tagore came to Venice on the non-stop 187 train from Milan. According to a vague telegram, sent before his departure from the capital of Lombardy (Milan), he would arrive at 6.50 pm. So, from that time, at the St. Lucia station there assembled the Royal Commissary Comm. Fornaciari and the Co. Bianchini, the Head of the Govt. Dept of the Town Council, Dr. Cav. Mattarucco, the Headmaster, Professor Dusso; Cav. Calo of Lloyd Triestino, Dr. Lorenzetti and Mr. Nobili from Venice University (where the poet is supposed to deliver the same lecture given to the Philological Society of Milan, provided his health permits) and Countess Valmarana and Mrs. Piccoli.

Along with the dignitaries a large number of spectators waited in the hall near the exit gates. When the train from Milan arrived at the station after a considerable delay, it was announced by the staff that Tagore was in the last coach of the train, then all the authorities including the station master Cav. Mingolla and the Commissar of P.S. Dr. Bolognesi rushed towards the tail end of the train.

The Poet's Charm

When the small oriental group got off the train, they were immediately surrounded by the crowd. Tagore got off the train supported by his companions and then received the first delicate gift of Venice, a bouquet of red carnations offered by Countess Valmarana. The poet in a sweet musical voice thanked her saying 'I am so glad to see you.'

The dignitaries gathered around his high and majestic figure which did not seem to be shaken by his recent illness. After introductions the poet departed. He was escorted by his daughter-in law, his adopted granddaughter and his followers, among whom were three Indians with olive complexions, Dr. Elmhirst, his agricultural consultant from Santiniketan University and Professor Formichi.

Tagore walked between two rows of spectators. It is incredible to see the charm which this man exercises over a crowd which is ignorant of his soul and thought. Tall and slim, he wore a long tobacco-coloured coat covering light-coloured trousers; the silvery locks of his hair escaped rebelliously from under his round and high red velvet cap and the white, flowing beard descended onto his wide chest. His gaze, behind the glasses hanging on his aquiline nose, darted around in a lively manner; his dark and restless eyes looked with dignified indifference as he moved through the European crowd under that famous roof [of the station].

Every now and again he smiled, speaking to Cav. Calo of Lloyd Triestino and Mrs. Piccoli, who walked close to him, in English.

Among the people who were waiting for him at the exit gates there was a girl who pushed through the crowd to the front to glimpse Tagore; she offered him one white and one red flower.

She offered the flowers with a gesture of anxious admiration and Tagore took the gift with a smile. He kept those flowers in his hand all the way from the station to the Grand Hotel whilst riding on the council launch *Loredana*.

Venice's Wish

On the way Professor Formichi, the eminent Orientalist, told us with nervous awe about the man and the poet. To see and speak to Tagore, he said, is to live completely within Indian philosophy. Italy is the last European country he is visiting!

In Milan his welcome was triumphant, worthy of him and his genius: but the climate was very dangerous for him. He was taken ill with influenza before leaving for Turin and the physicians Dr. Aliprandi and Dr. Betti advised him to leave immediately for India on the first available steamer, which was *Cracovia* leaving on Monday for Bombay.

Tagore was happy to know that he has to return [to India] but Venice is the city that he has always yearned to see. He was telegraphed from Naples advising him to go to Venice as the balmy weather there is more favourable. But the doctors' prescriptions are absolute—leave the country immediately.

—Will he be able to take rest in Venice?

—Sure, no official engagements, no conferences, as everyone agrees. He will receive only one or two persons in private.

While his launch was passing the 'Fri-era', Tagore raised his head to watch the outline of the Rialto Bridge in the flickering lights of the evening.

He arrived at the Grand Hotel at dinner time and passed almost unnoticed. His suite at the Grand Hotel was reserved on the second floor with its windows facing the Grand Canal.

Tagore checked into the hotel with his entourage and his luggage (twenty suitcases) and thanked everyone for the reception given to him; he apologised for his short stay in Italy caused by his poor health and immediately expressed his desire to take rest.

The Poet's Salute to Italy

MILAN 29—before leaving Milan, Rabindranath Tagore offered the president of Circolo Filologico a brief valedictory poem about Italy. Professor Formichi has translated the poem from the original Bengali.[43]

The report was concluded with the same poem.

In Venice, the poet was under the medical supervision of Jona, who was also the president of the University of Venice. Though he cancelled all meetings and engagements, he allowed the poet to go for a sightseeing tour of Venice. On 30 January, Tagore was shown the Grand Canal and the lagoons from a motor boat. On 31 January, *Il Gazzettino di Venezia* published the following article by Marco Egidio Allegri.

The Science of Love and the Love for Science
An Interview with Rabindranath Tagore

Yesterday, I approached the Indian poet Rabindranath Tagore, the most welcome guest in our city. I wanted to meet him in order to reveal his philosophical side, which is less known to our readers. Everyone speaks about his poetry and philosophy which are admired by scholars but these are often confused by young men and women with theosophy.

Tagore is a poet of wonderful spontaneity and his creativity is absolutely splendid. His company is very much enjoyed and loved by many such as the eminent orientalist Formichi. Furthermore, thanks to his vast fame, he has attracted wide public attention; however, he could not go in glory to the whole of his public.

How I Approached the Poet

Yesterday it was not easy among so many people to ask to see Tagore and to have his autograph, or to seek advice from him or to ask for the immense honour of interviewing him.

At 3.30 pm the poet returned from a trip on a launch and was a little tired.

After a brief conversation with the famous Orientalist Professor Formichi, with my colleague accompanying me, we gave up any hope of seeing the poet.

Then I took a notepad and wrote a few words in Sanskrit 'Oh! [Om] tat sat…' Oh! You know, that is how my note began, and then the author of 'Sadhana' received me immediately.

It is superfluous to describe such a famous person whose name is printed in reviews; all the newspapers have mentioned the enormous charm of his deep black eyes.

—I would like to project Tagore more as a philosopher than as a poet—I began.

—It is possible that each work of mine—said the Master—has a philosophical centre but excuse me if that philosophy does not enter your conscience. I am a contradiction of knowledge.

His slow words, spoken with priestly gestures revealing wisdom, came to me like an echo from a papyrus. Wonderfully, a mystical apparition was created around the poet and the sage.

—If you speak to me about philosophy I can't give you an answer because I don't imagine it is an absolute science.

—So, philosophy is more love for science than science for love.

—I didn't do a special study to answer that; but as a poet I have had to face Life's problems and I have formed an opinion: love is a means that the poet has at its mercy.

Love Must Have an Aim in Itself

Love must have an aim in itself. In truth, I tell you, love belongs to the poet. If it belongs to science it will die in captivity.

—If love is followed for its own sake then whatever way one follows, love follows, and that may be across philosophy, poetry, music, art, rhythm, sound, life and joy.

It has infinite and wonderful aspects. But it must be expressed from one's inner and essential nature, and not from one's knowledge. It is written in the *Upanishad* (a religious Hindu text): Knowledge, power and action are our own inner nature, they do not originate from the outside world.

In the West people are greedy for things which belong to the external world.

So, the West believes knowledge is that which is closer and more fundamental to men.

So, men in the West are in pursuit of knowledge.

But, perfection comes, instead, from within.

Tagore then revealed to us something new about his poetry-philosophy. A man shares his self and his knowledge at the same time but prefers the self.

God and Sin

Then the poet told me how some Chinese philosophers, some time ago, asked him two questions: What is God?—what is his idea about God and how does he understood sin?

'My idea of God,'—he said, 'is different from biblical and Christian ideas. God is living and exists in all things, but manifests differently in different things. Each being is God in power and in germ, but he must reveal himself.'

I am God and so you are—said Vedas. Tagore is a pantheist.

He explained sin to me as 'Maya', the ignorance that covers the essential nature of a being, so man is driven to sin.

Sin is not the violation of love but a desire to destroy 'ahimsa' [non-violence]—said the Indian poet.

I feel sin in this world but my self is divine. That is in relation to the being and to the things of the external world. The more my self is intimately linked to beings and things—the purer I feel.

This reminds me of Saint Paul when he said: 'I live in everything and everything lives in me.'

The Tradition of Medieval India

—On the concept of God and sin, 'I associate,' the Poet said, 'with the Indian Medieval tradition which understands the divinity in man, or, divinity in the shape of man. The divinity in man.'

And here Tagore was not silent. He spoke with the elation which in him generates beauty, rhythm, music, art.

—My pride is in my music!

He then discussed his musical compositions and melodies.

—Do you compose the words or the music first?

—Simultaneously—said Rabindranath Tagore.

Then he spoke about Venice. It is a limpid and transparent city like Beneras. A city which reveals its profound character. A city where history and life are both perfectly visible.

—Beneras reveals its mystical, religious and philosophical nature. Venice reveals its nature through life and art. Its splendid domination over the sea—The Queen of the Adriatic.

The voice of the famous Indian was a magic sound like ripples of water in which was felt the whole harmony of life, the fullness of being.

We did not know whether Buddha or Christ spoke like him, but his rhythm is certainly deep and sublime. The glorious words flowing from that ascetic figure whose boundaries of love and radiance extend to all humanity.

Marco Egidio Allegri

Greetings from the Roman Orientalists

Rome 30 (according to the telegram)—The students of oriental studies at Rome University sent Rabindranath Tagore the following telegram containing greetings:

'The Sanskrit students of Rome University are sorry for missing the opportunity of listening, meeting and honouring the Great man who embodies the highest ideal for which India has been glorified for centuries; we find that Italian youth are concerned by the indisposition of the poet. They bow to the master saying "Gurave-nama" (honour to the Master). They pray for his return.'

A Day of Tagore

It was agreed that only a few Venetians would meet the poet Tagore. He stopped at our city on his way back to the distant country India, whose tropical climate is necessary for him to restore his health, which has been shaken by the harsh European winter. Yesterday only a few people crossed the threshold of his suite on the second floor of the Grand Hotel by the Grand Canal, where the poet stayed after his arrival from Milan.

He arrived in the evening, so the incomparable charm of the city was hidden from him under the cover of the darkness. The enchantment of the waterways and the flickering shadows of reflected lights which he watched from his window affected him deeply.

The Enchantment of the Song

Late at night there arose from the Grand Canal an Italian song, sung by a female voice on a Gondola passing the Grand Hotel. Tagore listened to the rhythm. It was different to that of his oriental soul. Then he remembered his presence with his friend Professor Formichi on that evening at La Scala, the great opera theatre of the West, where Toscanini conducted 'La Traviata' in his honour. He immediately told his friends and journalists—he feels the beauty of European Music but still doesn't entirely understand it.

The Venetian panorama was gradually immersed in the night, the sound of music gradually faded away, and the smiling poet told Formichi— 'In Venice, this song is worth more than that spectacular song of Milan.'

Yesterday morning the President of Venice University, Professor Giuseppe Jona, went to see Tagore. He was privileged to see him and determine his physical condition. Professor Jona observed that, although his condition has been lowered and is not as bad as in Milan, he is still weak, so he has recommended that the poet reduces the number of his appointments.

The poet stayed the whole morning in the Hotel with his son, daughter-in-law, the Indian painter Kar and Dr. Elmhirst, who is an Agriculture graduate from an American University and who has spent many years in India, at Santiniketan, where Tagore founded his school. There he is the Head and a venerated teacher who has travelled through Bengal's villages, introducing modern methods of agriculture. Now Dr. Elmhirst, after the Poet's return to India, will prepare to leave the Master for good.

Besides Professor Formichi, who arranged the poet's trip to Italy and who published some translations of his poems from the original Bengali text, the group included another European person, a Swedish governess who looks after the adopted young daughter of his son and daughter-in-law.

It is well known that Tagore is primarily a vegetarian and abstemious. However, he doesn't dislike European cuisine in moderation and he sometimes partakes of the hotel's breakfast in good humour.

A Tour in a Launch

At 2.30 pm Tagore took the Community launch for a brief tour in Venice's canals. His constant interest and admiration were expressed through his lively and searching look. He sat at the back of the cabin. The tall figure of the poet-philosopher with his priestly composure and permanently interlocked hands in his lap missed nothing. Accompanying him in the launch were Dr. Lorenzetti, Dr. Nobili and the Countess Pia di Valmarana, whose company was very pleasant to the poet. Due to inclement weather he didn't get out of the launch, and so the trip was curtailed at the jetty at St. Marco and Fondamenta Nuove. The trip to the Armenian monastery at St. Lazzaro was postponed. However, someone on the bridge of Fondamenta Nuove spotted the famous guest and greeted him pleasantly. At 4.30 pm the launch, from which Tagore didn't get down, returned to the Grand Hotel. Today the poet will probably visit Murano.[44]

On 31 January, the poet and his group were shown around the famous glass factories of Murano and the lace works of Burano Island. Count Alessandro Marcello, an intellectual and a member of the ancient aristocratic family of Venice, presented Nandini, the poet's granddaughter, with an exquisite piece of lace. Among the few privileged people who could meet the poet at the hotel were Marcello, Allegri, and Corona, whose company the poet enjoyed. However, the poet liked most the company of Countess Pia of Valmarana because of her sharp intellect and charm.

Brindisi

On 2 February, the poet and his party set out for Brindisi from where they were to board the ship for Bombay. *Corriere della Sera* published the news on 3 February:

Tagore Is Making His Journey towards Home
The Poet's Farewell to Venice

Tagore left this evening. Yesterday evening he had received the Royal Commissioner Fornaciari and a representative from the Athenaeum of Venice, Professor Bordiga, who on behalf of the Institute of Venice offered Tagore a copy of a study on his work by Enrico Castelnuovo, the late Director of our Business School. Tagore sincerely thanked him and said: 'There was a time when Italy's door was open for the exchange between the East and the West. I hope Italy will be an intermediary for such exchange again. I wish this exchange will not be of materials only but mostly of a spiritual exchange. I also wish the many chasms which divide us will be filled up in a friendly atmosphere of understanding so that civilizations of the north and the south will meet as one unique civilisation.'

'When journeys were difficult,' the poet continued, 'messengers from the West approached the people of the South with the spiritual preparation necessary for the understanding of their people. This was exemplified by your own Marco Polo who loved the people of the East and was loved by them in return. Today the long journey is thought of as a picnic where the passengers are travelling by rail as tourists. When they go to India they stay in luxurious hotels but never knock at the doors of the houses to find out the true character of the people. That is the cause of incomprehension leading to misunderstanding and dissension.'

'Just to heal this dissension,' Tagore added, 'I founded a school that aspires to a fusion between East and West, or better between India and the East. India is unique for its character, morality and interest.' 'My work,' he concluded, 'and my school are not for the good of India alone, but for the good of humanity. I named the school "universal voice", the voice which comes from India to be heard by the rest of the world and especially in Europe where a major sum of the spiritual gift will be donated.'

This evening the steamer *Cracovia* where the poet will embark is moored at Zattere. There was a crowd of curious people surrounding the steamer. On the wharf there were about two hundred students from a primary school. At 4.30 pm Tagore was on a launch approaching the jetty at Ognissanti. On landing he was presented with bouquets of flowers by Mrs Piccoli, Countess Valmarana, Miss Elsa Jesurum. Among the dignitaries present there were the Royal Commissar, representatives from the city's cultural clubs, and members of the Armenian community. Finally, the poet went aboard the Cracovia where the rest of the passengers were waiting for him. The Commander Captain Quarantotto directed him towards the lounge, which was already full of flowers. A pupil offered him another bouquet and said a few words. Tagore thanked him saying 'This is not a farewell. This is an invitation and if I do not come back here in another season I shall leave this world with a great regret.' Then the steamer weighed anchor for Brindisi.[45]

The news of the poet's arrival at Brindisi spread like a fire. In the morning, there was a huge crowd at the jetty. A group of girls took flowers, grapes, and oranges for the poet and remarked in jest that these were from the garden he had visited when he was 17! Indeed, his speeches in Milan had their echoes throughout Italy. A commander of the Italian navy offered to take the poet on a motorboat ride, which he politely refused. However, after a while, the poet and his entourage travelled around the town under cover in a horse-drawn carriage. Perhaps, the poet wanted to see any changes from the old Brindisi he had seen when he was 17. Soon people came to know of the trip: The clever driver, tipped off by a photographer, stopped the coach in front of the local museum. The photographer and the curator of the museum, along with a few important people, appeared as if from nowhere. The poet was given a welcome in Italian and the curator presented the poet with a Roman vase, which is still preserved at the Rabindra Bhavan Museum in Santiniketan.

After returning to Bombay, Tagore said in an interview to the *Free Press of India*:

[…] During this trip, my first halt in Italy was at Milan. There I was given a very cordial welcome which was very encouraging. Their geniality touched me. Italy always fascinates me. I believe that poets from all other countries consider Italy their second home. I would like to be a part of that league and would like to draw inspiration from Italy like my predecessors. I have promised the people of Milan that I shall return to them as soon as I am well. I have decided to return to Italy when I recover to take rest at some beautiful spot amidst nature and also to take the opportunity to come in contact with the lively spirit of the western mind. […][46]

Tagore's Italian tour had originally been planned to take 25 days. He was to sail from Genoa for his return journey to India. Regrettably, his illness had upset the entire schedule: He had to cut short his visit after 15 days and leave for India from the port of Brindisi. In those fifteen days, he gave only one lecture during the first six days of his stay. The rest of the nine days he was ill, either confined to bed or too tired to meet the public. He was only allowed to meet some of his very close friends and, with the permission of his physician, visited just a few places of interest. Although the tour organizers had to face a lot of embarrassment for the cancellation of appointments, they accepted the unforeseen situation with sympathy. The poet was equally apologetic and repeatedly expressed his wish to return to Italy and the Italian people in good health during the summer months. He kept his word, yet, ironically, his second Italian visit gave rise to a serious international backlash. Before unfolding that episode, we need to look at the rise of Mussolini in the history of Italy and the politics of the time.

Notes and References

1. Nirmal Kumari Mahalanobis, *Kobir sange Europey* (Kolkata: Mitra and Ghosh, 1969), pp. 39–40.

2. Formichi File, Rabindra Bhavan, Santiniketan.

3. Ibid.

4. *Corriere della Sera*, 14 November 1913, p3c2.

5. 'Canti Votivi (premio Nobel. trad. e note di Giuseppe Tani)— Rabindranath Tagore', *Rassegna Contemporanea*, vol. VII (10 January 1914), pp. 21–9.

6. According to Nag's own recollection, he met Formichi between the end of August and early September, which is a little ambiguous as Tagore was aware of Formichi's scholarship through Nag in an early week of May 1921. My guess is Nag visited Formichi during the Easter holidays, which would be at the end of March or at the beginning of April 1921.

7. Carlo Formichi, 'On Tagore', tr. Mario Prayer, *Rabindra-Viksha*, vol. 39 (2001), p. 48.

8. Mario Prayer, 'Internazionalismo e nazionalismo culturale: Gli intellettuali bengalesi e l'Italia negli anni Venti e Trenta', *Rivita degli Studi Orientali*, vol. LXIX (1996), p. 18.

9. Amiya Chakrabarty (1901–1986), a distinguished poet of the post-Tagore generation, and a writer and critic, accompanied Tagore as his secretary in the 1930 European tour.

10. Italy File.

11. Ibid.

12. Formichi File.

13. Ibid.

14. Formichi, 'On Tagore', p. 32.

15. Kalidas Nag, *Surer Guru Rabindranath o Gurudever Patrabali* (Kolkata: Papirus, 1986), p. 181.

16. Italy File.

17. Rathindranath was in London at that time, and his wife Pratima was staying with her daughter at Paris with the family of Andrée Karpelés. Receiving the news of his father's arrival from Scotti, he and his family came to the dock of Genoa to receive his father.

18. Formichi File.

19. *Corriere della Sera*, 20 January 1925, p2c2.

20. Formichi, 'On Tagore', p. 34.

21. Mary Lago (ed.), *Imperfect Encounter: Letters of William Rothenstein and Rabindranath Tagore 1911–1941* (Cambridge: Harvard University Press, 1972), p. 311.

22. *Il Popolo d'Italia*, 22 January 1925, p4c4.

23. Suren Kar was not Tagore's nephew—the reporter has confused him with Suren Tagore, the poet's nephew.

24. *Corriere della Sera*, 22 January 1925, p3c1–4.

25. Formichi, 'On Tagore', p. 36.

26. This is the original lecture typed dated '22 January, Milan' with some ink corrections. It is still preserved in the 'Italian Adventure' folder at Dartington Hall Trust Archive. The lecture was published later with the title 'Voice of Humanity' in *Visva-Bharati Quarterly*, vol. III, part 1 (1925), pp. 1–10. There are some minor alterations in the published version from the typed copy.

27. *Corriere della Sera*, 23 January 1925, p3c3–4.

28. Sudhindra Bose in *Forward* (22 July 1925); cited from Prabhat Kumar Mukhopadhyay, *Rabindra Jibani o Rabindra Sahitya Prabeshak*, vol. 3 (Calcutta: Visva-Bharati, 1952), p. 211. However, Bose was contradicted by Sudhir Kumar Lahiri in his article published in the same journal, *Forward*, and was later cited by A.C. in his 'Notes' in *The Modern Review* (August 1925), pp. 251–3, which stated that,

What seems to me most extraordinary is that Mr. Sudhindra Bose should have completely ignored the numerous enthusiastic and friendly notices that appeared in the Indian press, some of the most influential among the papers vying with one another in the warmth of their admiration for Rabindranath. I was on a short visit to some of the Italian cities at the time Dr. Tagore was in Italy and I was an eye-witness to the enthusiastic ovation that all classes of people, men and women, rich and poor, old and young, accorded to him. In fact most of the important newspapers of Genoa, Milan, Rome, Naples, Venice etc. welcomed Tagore in leading articles and followed his movement with the greatest interest.

29. Formichi, 'On Tagore', p. 40.

30. *Corriere della Sera*, 24 January 1925, p3c5.

31. Ibid., p3c4.

32. Formichi, 'On Tagore', p. 41.

33. *Corriere della Sera*, 26 January 1925, p3c5.

34. *Il Gazzettino di Venezia*, 27 January 1925, p5c2.

35. Ketaki Kushari Dyson, *In Your Blossoming Flower Garden: Rabindranath Tagore and Victoria Ocampo*, Letter no. 17 (New Delhi: Sahitya Akademi, 1988), p. 403. Buying a villa was another of the poet's

dreams that never materialized. He wrote to Victoria Ocampo about his plan: 'Leonard is working with our friends here to find a suitable place for me. I shall be very happy indeed to have my European nest in this delightful country which is so friendly to me.'

36. *Corriere della Sera*, 27 January 1925, p6c4.

37. Lago, *Imperfect Encounter*, p. 312.

38. The original Bengali poem 'Italia' is included in his book of verse *Purabi*. The Italian translation was published in *Corriere della Sera*, 29 January 1925, p3c2. The present English translation of Tagore was published in *Visva-Bharati Quarterly*, April 1925. Formichi's own English translation of this poem, published in *Rabindra-Viksha*, vol. 39 (2001), p. 42, is slightly different from the *Visva-Bharati Quarterly* version.

39. Formichi, 'On Tagore', p. 42.

40. Ibid.

41. 'Farewell to Milan', *Visva-Bharati Quarterly* (April 1925), p. 80.

42. *Il Gazzettino di Venezia*, 29 January 1925, p4c3.

43. Ibid., 30 January 1925, p4c4/5.

44. Ibid., 31 January 1925, p4c3.

45. *Corriere della Sera*, 3 February 1925, p3c4.

46. *Visva-Bharati Quarterly* (July 1925), p. 124.

2

The Rise of Mussolini

The fascist dictator Benito Amilcare Andrea Mussolini was born on 29 July 1883 in Dovia di Predappio, a village in the Romagna district of northern Italy. The nearest town was Forli, 16 kilometres north of the village. Benito's mother, Rosa, was a primary-school teacher and a conservative Catholic, and his father, Alessandro, was a blacksmith who spent most of his time in the Socialist Party's local office, where he passed his time reading books and pamphlets on past revolutions and revolutionary ideas. Sometimes he invited his friends to his house and they read together from Marx's *Das Kapital* or discussed the lives of Machiavelli or Mazzini. And so, from childhood, Mussolini grew up in an environment of socialist ideals.

Alessandro often took Benito to Socialist Party meetings. Their house was a safe haven for political ruffians hunted by the police. Against this backdrop, Benito, his brother Arnaldo, and sister Edvige began their lives.

From his early childhood, Mussolini was an ill-tempered, whimsical, aggressive, and brutal child, who had a penchant for the odd fight or two. He assumed a dominating role amongst his friends and became the leader of the gang, habitually becoming involved in fights over petty squabbles. If he was even slightly provoked for no reason or humiliated, he took his revenge. He was a bully at school. This habitual belligerent behaviour often impeded his normal schooling; as a result he could not settle in one school for too long, once even being removed from a school over a knifing incident.

At the age of 17, Mussolini liked to think of himself as a Don Juan, and used to visit the red-light areas in Forli. In spite of this, Mussolini was intelligent enough to complete his schooling. His early life did not give any indication that in the last 25 years of his life, he would control the destiny of Italy.

He was a good trombone player in school. Another quality that helped him in his later years was his sharp memory and oratory powers. He could quote from Dante; paragraph after paragraph virtually from memory. He was also a voracious reader; he read everything he could lay his hands on.

At the age of 18, Mussolini got his first job as a substitute teacher in a primary school in Gualtieri. At that time, his inclination was growing towards international socialism. He identified himself as a socialist, became a member of the local Socialist Party in Gualtieri, and started writing for left-wing magazines. He was harbouring a faint ambition of becoming an editor and journalist, and was also practising public oration. He once gave a lecture on Garibaldi, uninterrupted for 90 minutes. Like Hitler, he would present his subject convincingly, dramatically, and, if necessary, with a touch of false information.

In 1902, compulsory military training for youth was introduced in Italy. An unwillingness to enter military service, combined with his interest in travelling, led Mussolini to leave for Switzerland, using the excuse that a job was waiting for him there. Despite his father being behind bars and his mother struggling to make ends meet, she bought him his ticket to Switzerland even though he had no job there. In those days, Swiss factories and industries employed cheap Italian labourers. His only income came from day labouring in chocolate factories or helping out in butchers' shops, and most of his nights were spent sleeping rough in cardboard boxes with other vagrants, though on one rare occasion, he spent the night under the portico of the Grand Pont in Lausanne.

Even in such adverse conditions, Mussolini was in contact with the socialists in Lausanne, and, from time to time, published articles in their pamphlets. When he was working as a day labourer in the construction industry, he quickly became the secretary of the Builders' Union. As a result of his excellent public-speaking skills, he was able to start a commotion against the factory owners. Ultimately, he was arrested in 1903 and handed over to the Italian police.

Mussolini himself spread the news of a meeting with Lenin in Switzerland, but he denied this later when he severed all connections with the socialists. Whether he met Lenin or not, in Switzerland, he did come into contact with an intellectual socialist, Angelica Balabanoff, who tutored him in classical European socialist literature. Later on when he became the editor of the national daily L'Avanti, he came to depend on her in many ways.

Mussolini was an atheist. His early years were very much influenced by Marx. He believed that 'Marx was the greatest of all theorists of socialism'.[1] According to Mussolini, Marx was a man who stressed the values of materialism, personal egoism, and economic determinism—the writer who first pointed out the fallacy of class cooperation, who rescued socialism from the Christian philanthropists and made it scientific. Mussolini always carried a nickel medal engraved with Marx's head.

From 1904 to 1906, he moved around from France, Germany, Austria, and back to Switzerland. He learnt languages, occasionally writing in these countries' socialist papers. Finally, he returned home and enlisted in military service in 1905, where he continued to serve for the next 18 months.

In 1908, Mussolini was again involved in active politics in Oneglia. He took charge of editing a socialist periodical La Lima and found that the paper was an ideal platform for expressing his extreme leftist ideas:

—Jesus of history was an ignorant Jew […] and who was a pigmy compared to Buddha.[2]

—Christianity in particular was vitiated by preaching the senseless virtues of resignation and cowardice.[3]

—The proletariat and the bourgeoisie had nothing in common: 'one of the two must disappear' and this could only be achieved by a major catastrophe that would lead to the dictatorship of the proletariat. A bloody social revolution was necessary.[4]

Reading the ideas Mussolini gradually expressed through these papers, it becomes evident that a future dictator was in the making.

In 1909, Mussolini married Rachele, the daughter of his father's mistress. That was his second marriage. Rachele had no intellectual pursuits of her own. They started their family life in a one-room apartment and passed their days in dire poverty, although Mussolini cared little about their circumstances.

While he was working as a secretary to a trade union in Trent, he was given the opportunity of editing a local daily, *Il Popolo*, which he joined as a sub-editor. During this time, Mussolini also started writing a novel, *The Cardinal's Mistress*, which was serialized in the paper's weekly supplement, *La Vita Trentina*, from January to May 1910. The novel was bitterly anticlerical. It was published as a book and translated into other languages after 1928. Though he was associated with this paper for only three months, he diligently learnt the techniques of popularizing the paper, such as reporting an incident with enough dramatic detail to draw the readers' attention or spicing reports with false stories that never happened.

Up to that point, the socialist Mussolini was thinking of journalism and political editorship as a profession. At one time, the Forlie socialist club invited him to edit a four-page weekly magazine: Mussolini chose to call the magazine *La Lotta di Classe* (The Class Struggle). Within a year, its circulation doubled. Incidentally, by the time Mussolini became a dictator, all his writings on socialism had been destroyed.

In 1910, he went to Milan to join the annual socialist convention and made his first appearance on a national platform. In Italy, at that time, the socialists were a centre-left minority party controlled by a section of intellectuals. The main points of his address were: 'armed revolution is the only way for the world's proletariats'; 'Italy does not need reformists'; 'when the entire product of the nation is controlled by a handful of people, then *trade union, co-operative, democracy*—all these words do not make any sense'; 'the reformists are moving towards a parliamentary democracy but that will not work out'; and so on.

However, Mussolini was not well rehearsed for the convention. His address appeared incoherent and ridiculous at some points; moreover, his rustic appearance and shabby dress made him something of a laughing stock. This annoyed him and, as a result, he was determined to sever his connection with the socialists and make his own revolutionary party based on his own ideas. In 1911, when Giolitti attacked Libya, Mussolini criticized the attack as an imperialistic war and vehemently opposed the action, even though in later years he was himself to become imperialistic and strongly nationalistic, launching attacks against Mediterranean countries and Abyssinia (now Ethiopia). However, back then, he stood against the attack on Libya, and to obstruct the movements of Giolitti's soldiers, his followers tore up the tram and railway tracks. Shops and trading centres were vandalized and looted by Mussolini's hooligans. The police quickly took control of the situation and Mussolini was arrested, thereby gaining national prominence.

On leaving prison, Mussolini was surprised to find his popularity had risen considerably. He began to consolidate his preparations for the next annual socialist convention and to establish his leadership. He decided his future line of action: His first priority would be to regain the party's confidence and then slowly to rid it of reformists, ultimately transforming the party into a revolutionary one. His plan worked out well, as evidenced by the following year's party convention where the majority of the socialist members, including a tiny minority of Marxists, pledged their support to his proposed revolutionary party.

Four months after the socialist convention, Mussolini received an unexpected offer of editorship of the esteemed socialist paper *L'Avanti*. It was an unusual stroke of luck for a 28-year-old journalist like Mussolini to be entrusted with such an important responsibility.

Although *L'Avanti* was a national daily, its circulation was falling. After taking charge of the paper, Mussolini immediately terminated the contracts of the existing staff and columnists and appointed fresh people from his own circles. Balabanoff was appointed as his deputy editor. The readership of the paper was now aimed at the working class, peasants, and people from the lower strata of society, and not the intellectuals who Mussolini was uncomfortable with. By using the language of the commoners and dealing with their problems, *L'Avanti* regained its popularity and its readership almost doubled within a year. In the 1913 election, about a million people voted for the Italian Socialist Party, which seized 53 seats in the Lower House. The increased circulation of *L'Avanti* contributed to that success. Younger readers found the paper inspirational.

Meanwhile, the First World War broke out. Initially, the anti-militarist, anti-imperialist, and anti-nationalist Mussolini vehemently opposed Italy's involvement in the War. However, his party became divided on the War issue and Mussolini was also beginning to change his political strategy. On 18 October 1915, without properly consulting his party activists, he suddenly declared a change of policy. He explained that in the present crisis in Europe, Italy should not stay neutral. He asked the party to unite, support, and approve the participation of Italy in the War. The party members were astounded by this unexpected turn of events: He was labelled a treacherous, disloyal member and eventually expelled from the party. Mussolini had to sever all connections in his longstanding association with the socialists forever. Simultaneously, he lost the editorship of *L'Avanti*. A new anti-socialist Mussolini was born.

Within two weeks of losing the editorship of *L'Avanti*, Mussolini promptly brought out a new daily newspaper, *Il Popolo d'Italia*. It was funded through subsidies from countries including France and Russia to encourage Italy's involvement in the War, on the side of the allies. The first edition of the paper was published on 15 November 1914. In this issue, Mussolini first published his nationalistic message: 'We are all Italians today. From now on our key slogan will be Viva Italia.' Afterwards, Mussolini joined the War and was transformed into an aggressive nationalist.

In October 1914, a new political party—Fasci d'azione rivoluzi-
onaria internazionalista—was born in Milan under the leadership of
two nationalists, both of whom were also, like Mussolini, expelled
from the Socialist Party. In Italian politics, the word *'fascio'* (a
bundle) has a special connotation: In ancient Rome, someone had
to walk holding a lictor's rod (a bundle or fascicle of birch rods
which were tied tightly together) in front of the magistrate, symbolizing the power and strength of unity. This symbol had a romantic
effect in Mussolini's mind. Within two months of the initiation of
this new party, Mussolini was invited to take charge. However, his
enlisting in the army interrupted his initial rapid organizing activities. During the War, he was promoted to corporal and retired with
injuries sustained by a grenade. By the time he returned from Allied
service in the War, he was fully convinced that socialism as a doctrine had largely been a failure.

It has now been revealed that in 1917, Mussolini received a
£100 weekly wage from MI5, the British Security Service, for work
as an agent. This help was authorized by Sir Samuel Hoare.[5] Thus,
with financial support from various quarters, he founded his Fasci
di Combattimento (Combat Squad), which was officially launched
as a political party on 23 February 1919 in Milan.

A new political movement was initiated. The first aim of the
party was to put pressure on the existing government by means of
his group of militia. Propaganda pamphlets were freely distributed.
For the first time, Mussolini declared in a manifesto which shows
that he had put aside the Marxist ideas of class war, for the moment
at least. His new hero was not Marx but Mazzini, who dreamt of
a patriotic war to secure Italy's 'natural frontiers' of language and
race.[6]

Italian politics was going through a crisis. The prime minister,
Facta, stepped down. In early 1922, Mussolini saw that the parliamentary system was crumbling and realized that for him and his
party it was the opportune moment to take control. He was getting
ready for his infamous march to Rome with his followers and his
semi-military corps, the Blackshirts (*squadristi*). The march started
from Milan on 27 October 1922. The progress of the Blackshirts was
unhindered; shops were looted on the way, telephone exchanges

were destroyed, government offices were occupied, and any resistance harshly treated; the police watched silently.

King Vittorio Emmanuelle III declared a state of emergency across Italy and ordered the army to impose martial law. Facta had already resigned, and another ex-premier, Salandra, declined to take charge of the country. The king was not keen to offer the post to Giolitti, in whom he had no confidence: Seeing the popularity of Mussolini, the king took an unparliamentarily decision and asked him to form a government, despite cabinet opposition. Mussolini, whose belligerent followers were causing a menace countrywide, became the 27th prime minister of Italy at the age of 39 on 29 October 1922. The frenzied, jubilant followers of the prime minister ransacked the Socialist Party offices everywhere; bookshops selling socialist books and literature were wrecked or burnt down; opposition members were humiliated and tortured. The only consolation was that the Italian stock market stabilized on Mussolini's appointment.

Initially, fascist representation in the lower chamber of the Italian Parliament was insignificant and there was no representation at all in the Senate (the upper chamber). However, Mussolini's skill as an orator, combined with his shrewdness, helped him to earn the confidence of the people. Eventually, he built up maximum number of supporters in the Senate, amongst them the liberal economist Luigi Einaudi and the editor of the much circulated, esteemed liberal paper *Corriere della Sera*, Luigi Albertini. Albertini openly announced in his paper that Mussolini's fascism would save the country from socialism. Some of the senators were even pressurizing him to be a dictator and Mussolini was entrusted with special privileges, such as the power of increasing tax, without the approval of the Senate.

From the very beginning, Mussolini was very cautious in his foreign policy, being convinced that his domestic image would not be improved unless countries outside Italy had full confidence in him. Consequently, he did not take any risks in foreign affairs, but repeatedly told foreign agencies, journalists, and dignitaries that fascism was a special ideology only appropriate for Italy and 'not for export'—something he also expressed to Tagore.

A week after taking up his prime ministerial duties, Mussolini was invited to join the Peace Treaty for Turkey held in Lausanne. This was his first experience of a European programme. It was not clear whether he had any interest in peace in Turkey, but he was interested in giving interviews to foreign journalists. The congress was scheduled to continue for several months, but Mussolini was only present for two days. Within those two days, the other European delegates had heard nothing from Mussolini but 'I agree', while he had given a dozen more detailed interviews to journalists. Coming back home, however, he boastfully told his senate that 'he achieved a brilliant success in persuading the British to accept an increase in Italian colonial territory.'[7]

He had to attend a conference in London within a month. This time the conference's agenda was to consider the allies' war indemnity to Germany. At this conference, Mussolini's role was the same as in Lausanne, but journalists had tired of interviewing him. At the London conference, Mussolini was not only ridiculed but also dejected. But once again, in his own account, 'he was the main political personality in London', casting himself in the role of chief figure in a congress which was 'deciding the future of Europe.'[8]

Mussolini forcefully declared in public that all unlawful activities within his party would be dealt with using the iron hand of his regime. At the same time, he had given standing instructions to his private corps to ruthlessly punish anyone opposing Il Duce ('The Leader'), so that they could not hold their heads high in future. Soon, he upgraded his squad to 'National Militia', giving them legal status.

Meanwhile, Mussolini found that his paper's circulation had fallen rapidly in comparison with that of *Corriere della Sera*, indicating that although people were supporting Mussolini as a leader, they did not always approve of his policies. A section of the people was even beginning to doubt how long Mussolini's regime would last. However, he knew how to handle the situation: He immediately offered the editorship of *Il Popolo d'Italia* to his brother Arnaldo.

The first election since Mussolini came to power took place in the spring of 1924. There were altogether 3,000 applicants for candidates from his party. Outwardly, Mussolini showed his aloofness concerning the candidates, but in private, he scrutinized the suitability of every single one of them for the election. However, to maintain his liberal image, he also selected a few candidates from liberals and conservatives, even including a couple of Catholic clerics. Two past prime ministers, Salandra and Orlando, were also integrated within his team. Although Giolitti did not intend to stand in the election, he was willing to campaign for the party and fight socialism. Two important names in Italian philosophy and poetry, D'Annunzio and Benedetto Croce, also pledged their support.

While the 1924 election campaign was in full swing, the National Militia had been given full authority to disrupt all public meetings of the opposition and, as a result, the whole country was being terrorized. The socialist leader Giovanni Amendola had been barred from organizing any meetings. Another socialist leader, Giacomo Matteotti, was physically tortured. Several socialist candidates were assassinated. Hundreds of people were killed. The foreign journalists who were reporting the news of this barbaric election process had to leave Italy immediately. The police continued to be a silent witness. Outside witnesses concluded from this that 'the fascists are, in their methods, as barbarous as the Bolsheviks: for the moment, at any rate, foreigners cannot regards Italy as a civilized country.'[9] Only the unconcerned prime minister said with a virtuous face that he would not have wished to stain with blood the essentially spiritual movement that he led to victory.[10]

The election was over amidst killing, terrorizing, vote-rigging, and all kinds of unlawful irregularity, and, as expected, the results showed that the Fascist Party won with 65 per cent of votes cast. The office of *Corriere della Sera* was ransacked due to the neutral stance of the paper, thus helping the opposition to gain more seats. Matteotti openly challenged the fairness of the election, preparing a dossier of evidence detailing the illegal aspects of the election and sending copies to Belgium and England. For this offence, he was assassinated on 10 June 1924, and another opposition leader, Amendola, was publicly murdered a month later.

The assassinations of Matteotti and Amendola severely tarnished Mussolini's international image. However, nothing could stop his progress and anarchy reached a critical state: The once anti-imperialist Mussolini was now engaged in the expansion of his territory into the Mediterranean.

The rest of the history of Italy and its involvement in the Second World War is well documented. On 24 July 1943, soon after the start of the allied invasion of Italy, Mussolini was defeated in the vote at the Grand Council of Fascism and was arrested the following day.

On 12 September 1943, Mussolini was rescued from prison by the German Special Forces, and in late April 1945, with total defeat looming, he attempted to escape to the north, only to be swiftly captured by Italian partisans near Lake Como. It was there where he was executed. His body was then taken to Milan, where it was hung upside down at a gas station for public viewing along with his seven followers, including his mistress Clara Petacci—an irony of fate indeed!

Weeks after the assassination of Matteotti and Amendola, Tagore came to Italy for the first time and 18 months later for the second time. The history of the rise of Mussolini is contextually important in understanding and analysing much of the debate and implications of Rabindranath Tagore's second visit to Italy featured in the following pages.

Notes and References

1. Denis Mack Smith, *Mussolini* (Granada: London, 1983), p. 8.
2. Ibid., p. 9.
3. Ibid.
4. Ibid., p. 13.
5. Tom Kington, 'Recruited by MI5: The Name's Mussolini, Benito Mussolini', *The Guardian*, London, 14 October 2009, pp. 1–2.
6. Mack Smith, *Mussolini*, p. 32.
7. Ibid., p. 70.
8. Ibid., p. 71.
9. Ibid., p. 86.
10. Ibid., p. 87.

3

Italian Tour, 1926

Born on 14 February 1871 in Naples, Carlo Formichi developed an interest in India and Indian literature while he was a student and went on to study Sanskrit under Professor Michele Kerbakar at the University of Naples. He was awarded the Sienna scholarship to study Vedic and Buddhist scriptures under Professor Hermann Oldenburg. This was followed by a study of Indian philosophy, the Vedas and the Upanishads under the famous Indologist Paul Deussen in Germany. He also studied smriti and logic with Professor Buhler in Vienna. In 1899, he completed his doctoral thesis based on *Brahmaponisad* and Ethics. He taught in many Italian universities and finally joined the University of Rome as the head of the Department of Sanskrit in 1913 and later on became vice president of the Reale Accademia d'Italia. (The Royal Academy of Italy was an organization of Italian academicians, intellectuals, and cultural figures created on 7 January 1926 by the fascist government of Italy.) Amongst the many books authored by him, the translation of Asvaghosa's *Budhhacharita*, Kalidas's *Raghuvansam*, *Apologia del Buddhismo* (An Apology for Buddhism), and a revised edition of *Kamandaka* were his principal works.

While in Milan, Tagore invited Formichi to join Visva-Bharati as a visiting professor. In the meantime, the ailing poet returned home cutting short his tour. Formichi busied himself in organizing his forthcoming visit to Santiniketan. His immediate priority was to explore his contacts for raising the necessary funds to support the running of the proposed Italian library at Tagore's University. He also had to organize the appointment of an Italian professor for at least a year at Italian expense. These two proposals were taken at the local committee meeting in Milan.

On 20 August 1925, Formichi received a cable from Visva-Bharati confirming his formal appointment. The cable read, 'On behalf of Visva-Bharati I invite you as visiting professor for the period from November to March on the same terms as previous professors. Council's official letter following soon—Rabindranath Tagore, Chancellor, Visva-Bharati.'[1] A reminder from Kalidas Nag soon followed. He wrote: '[…] Please try to bring with you authoritative books on Italian art and aesthetics. […] They would prove extremely useful to us, for we have a good school of modern Indian painting at Santiniketan. […] Except for a few volumes sent by Dr. Tucci, we do not have any Italian books. France, Germany, England and America have already sent a number of books.'[2]

Nag's letter caused Formichi more agony than joy at receiving the appointment. He did not want to reach Santiniketan empty-handed since all his predecessors had gifted the university with treasures of books. By that time, Formichi was convinced that it was impossible to get any financial help from the Italian government on the pretext of a cultural exchange programme. All his earlier efforts to persuade the Department of Education had failed. However, the department suggested that he approach the Ministry of External Affairs since it involved cultural propaganda and they should be able to help. Although the ministry showed an initial interest in Formichi's appeal, the unpleasant subject of Tagore's anti-fascist statement during his earlier visit eventually came up during the course of discussion. The ministry made it clear that they would have to think twice before sponsoring any funds to an institution founded and directed by a person whose controversial statement had sparked off a political debate only a few months ago. 'I can assure you,' Formichi argued, 'Tagore did not come to Italy for political ends. The Fascists' indignation is founded on a misunderstanding, and this is proved by the most correct way he talked about Fascism in an interview released in Bombay and published by local newspapers soon after his arrival.'[3] Not assured, the ministry advised him to refer the matter directly to His Excellency Mussolini for his judgement and ultimate decision. Desperate, Formichi wrote a long letter to Mussolini explaining the situation and seeking his favour.

This was probably his first direct communication with Mussolini. It read:

Your Excellency
The Visva-Bharati University, near Calcutta, is asking the University of Rome to send a representative of Italian indology to that centre of Indian native culture, the most highly reputed in the entire country. In past years other European scholars of Indian studies, such as Sylvain Levi from Paris, Maurice Winternitz from Prague and Sten Kono from Christiania, have been invited there to hold Sanskrit classes. The honour being thus bestowed on Italian science has immediately prompted the authorities to grant me leave. Now, therefore, I am seeking Your Excellency's help in order that I may not present myself empty-handed to those people who are offering their distinguished hospitality to an *Italian* scholar to pay homage to *Italian* science.

The European professors who were there before me brought with them, on behalf of their respective governments, book donations for the Visva-Bharati library. I would like to do the same, particularly since I know they would highly appreciate any publication dealing with our art. To this end I am enclosing a list of books, along with the remark that to this day the Visva-Bharati library almost completely lacks Italian works of any kind. It would be better still if a learned Italian could go to India with me too, in order to present an introductory course on Italian culture there.

The Indian university will defray all the necessary expenses for my travel and stay in India from November to April. Italy, on her part, should take charge of the travel and board and lodging expenses for the other teacher.

A wonderful representative of Italy's new School of India Studies is Dr. Giuseppe Tucci, a deputy-librarian at the Lower House of Parliament, and Professor-in-charge of *Religions and Philosophies of India and the Far East* at Rome University. He has a vast knowledge of oriental languages, as well as a versatile mind, with all the prerequisites needed to uphold the prestige of Italian science.

The President of Visva-Bharati University is the world-renowned poet Rabindranath Tagore, who was here in Italy in January last, and was and still is unaware that he was dubbed an anti-Fascist. I was continuously by Tagore's side from his arrival in Genoa right to his departure at Venice, and I can unhesitatingly testify that the Poet has never had anything to do with any kind of political propaganda. He would be extremely sorry and hurt to learn that he was even suspected of having interfered in a host country's politics. Tagore is a poet and wants to be a poet. If only his health had allowed him to prolong his travel to Rome, as he many times told me, he would have visited Your Excellency with the aim of further strengthening cultural relations between India and Italy.

Besides, my witness is now superfluous on account of the Bombay correspondence which has been so widely spread. It reported that in an interview on the conditions now prevailing in Italy and Fascism, the Poet had expressed only words of approval.

I am glad to see that the misunderstanding has now been cleared, for I know that the great poet intends to come again often to feel the salubrious breezes of our country, as soon as his health will permit. To make him once more the target of wrong suspicions would mean to do injustice to truth and to disavow our traditional hospitality, thereby offending a man of the purest spirit who has fallen in love with Italy and sincerely wishes her a triumphant ascent.

I would be rightly delighted to bring Your Excellency's gift to the poet. However, should this not be possible on account of scarcity of time, since my departure from Brindisi is scheduled for 4th November, I might simply announce that generous offer, which would be later presented through our Royal Consul.

With deep regards I remain, Your Excellency,

Yours very truly,

Carlo Formichi[4]

How eager Mussolini was to establish cultural relations with India at that particular time is anybody's guess. He was extremely preoccupied with his country's serious internal problems. Most of the upper- and middle-class intellectuals were not ready to accept fascism as government policy. Mussolini used his National Militia to silence dissent by instigating widespread brutality against the opposition: Properties were confiscated, the opposition press was banned, and members of the opposition were physically assaulted. Mussolini's international image was considerably tarnished after the murders of Amendola and Matteotti. He had to find a way of diverting the international attention away from this embarrassing situation. Mussolini promptly assumed the part of cultural exhibitionist and seized the opportunity to prove that Italy too had an important international cultural role. He decided to promote a cultural relationship with India using Tagore as a bridge. So, he granted Formichi's plea with unusual generosity. He wrote:

Rome, 21st October 1925

Distinguished Professor,
In expressing my deep satisfaction for the invitation from Visva-Bharati University, which honours not only an Italian scientist but also Italian science and the University of Rome, I am glad to entrust to you the task of taking the books mentioned in the enclosed list as a gift to the University, the main centre of Indian culture. I hope this offer will help in strengthening more and more the cultural relations between India, the classical land and cradle of the world's civilisation, and Italy.
I remain, distinguished Professor,
Yours
Mussolini[5]

Surprisingly enough, while Formichi was organizing his trip to India, Tagore was preparing for another trip to Europe in the summer of 1925. In a letter dated 4 March 1925, he wrote to Elmhirst, 'I have decided to start on the 15th of August, reaching Italy at the beginning of September.'[6] This time he was eager to meet Rolland in Switzerland after his Italian tour, and the meeting was confirmed repeatedly in letters and telegrams. In the end, however, Tagore again failed to keep the appointment. Rolland was very disappointed and wrote in his journal in August 1925:

Tagore has made us disappointed. During last three months he has assured us several times that he would come to Villeneuve in August. Even in the middle of July it was emphatically mentioned in his son's letter that he would start from Bombay on 1st August. However in his next letter we were informed that the journey was postponed due to some unavoidable situation. And yesterday (17th August) the letter we received from Kalidas Nag, made us concerned. He wrote that some attacks on him had come from some quarters of Europe and made him very hurt so he had not decided whether he would come to Europe. Finally we received a telegram today in which he completely abandoned his tour on the grounds of his health. Meanwhile the arrangements for his reception are all complete. […] where the entire youth of the country would have been delighted to welcome him; […] everything now became useless. It is nearly impossible to organise something relying on these Indians! […] Rabindranath himself will never realise the amount of work destroyed by abandoning his trip.[7]

A harsh comment indeed! However, this time Tagore's physician in Calcutta forbade him to take his European trip as the condition of his heart was causing further problems.

Formici joined Visva-Bharati on 21 November 1925 with an agreement to stay for four months. His travelling expenses and honorarium were all paid by Visva-Bharati. He wrote a witty account in his memoirs about his first day's impression and how he was received in the mango grove at Santiniketan.

From Bolpur to Santiniketan it takes 45 minutes on foot, or 15 minutes by car. I was tired and covered with dust, and yet I was inexorably led to a mango orchard. I discerned the Poet in the distance. On his right all the student girls were standing in a line, while on his left were the student boys. Tagore embraced me and hung a flower garland around my neck. He then invited me to stand before him at a distance, near a stool on which incense smoke issued from a metal goblet. The marble-coated stool was only 10cm high; it worked as an altar. Apparently, Indians can hardly keep from using the ground as a table or a chair, and even when they just have to resort to tables and chairs, they do so by making them as dwarfish as possible. They almost cannot resolve to lift themselves from the ground, and at most they get up only a few centimetres, so that they can always touch the soil with their hands. Beds and sofas are equally low, and sometimes it is better to sit on the ground with crossed legs, as their custom, than undergo the torture of sitting on their dwarf stools with one's knees hitting high on one's chin […].[8]

Tagore welcomed Formichi in a solemn ceremony following the usual ritual of receiving a distinguished first-time visitor at Santiniketan. Tagore's address was followed by a speech in Sanskrit given by Acharya Bidhushekhar Shastri. In reply, Formichi spoke with his usual courtesy and friendliness:

[...] When I received Tagore's invitation to come here [to Santiniketan], I informed my government about my departure and urged them to give your library a selection of Italian classics and art essays. The Prime Minister himself saw to it, so that I brought with me a magnificent collection of volumes and, along with it, the expression of his deep satisfaction on the commencement of cultural exchanges between India and Italy. I am, therefore, proud to offer this association of learned men a gift from Benito Mussolini, and to represent not only the intimate and friendly sentiments of my people, but also the benign consent of the great man who holds the reins of my fatherland's fate [...].[9]

Tagore had expected that Formichi would bring some books and resources from Italy for Visva-Bharati's library. The possibility of appointing a visiting lecturer to Visva-Bharati, sponsored by the Italian government, was also on the cards. Tagore was quite sure about these two possibilities, otherwise he would not have mentioned them to the correspondent of *Prabasi* (a Bengali journal of distinction), who reported, 'The people of Italy not only paid tribute to the poet, they will also make a gift of the best of Italian books to the Visva-Bharati library. They also plan to send an Italian professor at their own expense to teach the Italian language and Italian literature at Visva-Bharati.'[10]

Amongst the gifts brought by Formichi were *Storia Arte Italia* by Venturi, *Biblioteca d'Arte Illustrata*, *Pinacoteca Vaticana*, *Biblioteca del Risorgimento* (all 50 volumes), and the complete works of Dante, Tasso, and other classical authors, including Pascoli and Carducci. The sheer volume of the gifts and their value (other than in terms of money) was undoubtedly priceless. On top of that, there was the promise of the service of Giuseppe Tucci as a visiting professor for a year at the expense of the Italian government—a generous gift indeed![11]

Tucci joined Visva-Bharati University in December. He was an Indologist who specialized in Buddhist scriptures and was conversant in several European languages as well as in Sanskrit, Pali, Prakrit, Chinese, and Tibetan. At Visva-Bharati, he was appointed to teach Italian and Chinese for one year.

Tagore was overwhelmed!

Acknowledging the gifts and Tucci's appointment, a deeply impressed and moved Rabindranath expressed his personal gratitude to Mussolini in a telegram dated 2 December 1925:

> In the name of the Visva-Bharati allow me to convey to you our gratitude for sending us, through Professor Formichi, your cordial appreciation of Indian civilisation, and deputing Professor Tucci of the University of Rome to acquaint our scholars with Italian history and culture, also for working with us in various departments of oriental studies and for the generous gift of books in your name. These acts display a spirit of magnanimity worthy of the traditions of your great country. I assure you that such an expression of sympathy from you as a representative of the Italian people will open up a channel of communication for cultural exchanges between our countries thereby possibly developing into an event of great historical significance.[12]

Consequently, the poet expressed his wish to meet Mussolini in person to show his gratitude. Subsequent to his incomplete tour during the previous year, followed by the abortive attempt to visit Italy in the summer of 1925, he had made up his mind to embark on another trip. Formichi and Tucci had not pursued Tagore on this matter.

Formichi now started preparations for Tagore's second Italian tour and Mussolini was informed about the visit. Mussolini was somehow convinced that Tagore's visit would confer a seal of legitimacy on his regime and part of this ploy was to invite him as a guest of the government. Some Tagore researchers believe that by influencing Tagore in visiting Italy, Formichi acted as an active collaborator in this plan. But how much Formichi collaborated in this process or whether he was aware of the ploy at the time remains a question. There is no evidence to support collaboration, and Formichi's memoir counters the accusation. However, the invitation was seemingly unconventional as no official letter was issued from the Italian government prior to the visit. Even the Italian consulate in Calcutta was not aware of the invitation. The September 1926 issue of *The Modern Review* reported:

In May 1926, the authorities of the Visva-Bharati arranged for the Poet's visit to Italy to fulfil his promises to the Italian cities. The secretaries of the Visva-Bharati, Professor Prasanta Chandra Mahalanobis and Sj. Rathindranath Tagore found the Italian Government very willing to provide them with the greatest facilities in connection with Tagore's tour in Italy. The captain of the Italian Steam-boat Naples [*sic*] showed the greatest courtesy to the Visva-Bharati Party as would-be guests of the Italian Government. When the Party reached Naples, His Excellency Benito Mussolini formally invited the poet to stay in Rome as the guest of the Italian Government and this invitation was accepted.[13]

On the basis of this report, Mukhopadhyay, one of Tagore's biographers, probably inferred that the poet was unaware of the fact that he was visiting Italy as a state guest even as he boarded the ship. Nonetheless, Formichi's memoir reveals a different account. According to the Italian professor, he informed the Ministry of Foreign Affairs about the poet's intention to visit Italy again and on 20 January 1926. Through the Royal Consul, the ministry confirmed that the Duce had approved the idea of giving hospitality to Tagore and his entourage in Rome. The poet wrote to Elmhirst on 24 February, 'I wonder if it will be possible for you to meet me in Italy where I expect to have a strenuous time. I wish I could throw off my shoulders all the responsibilities of a *distinguished visitor* and have the freedom of a quiet corner away from the glare of *public honour* [emphases added].'[14] Even the memoir of Nirmal Kumari Mahalanobis supports the fact that the poet knew he would be the guest of the Italian government. Tagore had justified his acceptance of the invitation by stating, 'My acceptance of the invitation does not mean that I accept all their ideas. I will not remain silent about things that I disapprove of. I'll impress on them my idea of "world humanity". One should however appreciate the progress they have achieved.'[15] In a casual conversation noted on 8 December in Formichi's memoir, Tagore had mentioned, 'If I ever go to Italy again, I want to present myself as a poet, just and only a poet. [...] Politics, fatally leads to controversy.'[16] This remark is interesting. Perhaps the poet apprehended some ideological clashes he might face based on his experience during the last Italian tour.

Formichi's tenure in Visva-Bharati was only for four months. Within that short period, the students and teachers were impressed by his scholarship and his in-depth knowledge of Buddhist scriptures. He lectured extensively on the 'Dynamic Development of the Indian Religion from Rig Veda to Buddhism' (which was later published in *The Modern Review*). Many Bengali intellectual ashramites later recollected the erudition of this Italian professor in their memoirs (such as Kalidas Nag, Sayed Muztaba Ali, and Pramatha Nath Bishi) with great admiration. Formichi also visited Dacca, accompanied by the poet, where the Italian professor spoke about Dwijendranath Tagore (who had just passed away) to an assembly of students at the university.

At the end of his tenure, Formichi left Santiniketan for Beneras (4 March 1926). At that time, Tagore was in Calcutta, and so the students and teachers of Visva-Bharati arranged Formichi's farewell in Tagore's absence. The students staged a Sanskrit play, *Mudrarakshaka*. Before leaving Santiniketan, Formichi wrote to Tagore in Calcutta:

Gurudev!
Santiniketan

2nd March, 1926

I am so very sorry to hear that you do not feel well. They in Dacca are responsible for your present indisposition; they took as much as they could of the best of your energies.[17] Now you need rest, because you have to prepare yourself for the long journey to Italy. I hope you know that the Lloyd has arranged for you to leave in April. We shall discuss matters together when we meet in Calcutta.

I am leaving Santiniketan for Beneras the day after tomorrow. On coming back from Dacca I thought it was better to go straight to Santiniketan, deliver all the lectures I had to deliver, and then visit Beneras. My work here is over, for I have lectured twice a day lately, and I could thus go through the whole of the programme.

Tucci is accompanying me to Beneras. We shall both be in Calcutta on Sunday. A telegram will let Mr. Morris know the hour of our arrival, and Mr. Morris will tell us whether we shall have to go to a hotel or enjoy your hospitality. Let us not run the risk of becoming a burden.

I hear I have to lecture in Calcutta on the 8th, the 9th and the 10th. I hope Kalidas knows that on the 10th I must leave for Bombay at 7.34 pm and that my lecture has to take place at an hour that allows me to leave Calcutta the same day in the evening. They are here showing me such sincere regret at my departure that I feel very sad to part with so many dear friends. May I find you on Sunday in perfect health.

With best wishes,

Yours sincerely and devoutly

Carlo Formichi.[18]

In Calcutta, Formichi was given another farewell at the Bichitra Bhavan of the Tagore residence in Jorasanko. The poet himself presided over this meeting in the presence of many members of Visva-Bharati. In his farewell address, Tagore said:

[…] You were a worthy bearer of this message from your own land; but being a true lover of India, you must also act as a messenger on our behalf in carrying our assurance to Italy that this friendly beckoning of hers has given a permanent direction to our mind in its communication with her. And all this is in accord with the ideal of Visva-Bharati which, as you know, is to realise the freedom of the pathway through the vast realm of man, widening our consciousness of the unity of spirit in the different human races. Your genial presence among us, the valuable service you have rendered to our *asrama*, the precious token of sympathy you brought to us from your country and the masterly exposition you gave us of the gradual course of the spiritual illumination running through the period of Vedic India, has greatly strengthened our cause, creating a strong link with Italy in our bond of human solidarity.[19]

In reply, Formichi said:

[…] No, this my departure is not an end: it is a beginning; it is not a sunset: it is a sunrise; it is not a farewell in the sense of our Italian *addio*, but rather a welcome to the starting of a most active and intimate collaboration for the achievement of our common ideals.

I am going to Rome in order to prepare for Rabindranath Tagore a reception that has to assume the greatest cultural importance. This great man of yours, that nations vie with each other in glorifying, must find in Italy his second fatherland. Among nations Italy must be for Rabindranath his last love. It is commonly said that the first love is always the sweetest. It is an error: the sweetest love is the last one. The visit *Gurudev* intends paying to Rome and to other Italian cities is, therefore, full of hopeful possibilities [...].[20]

On 14 March, Formichi boarded the ship from Bombay for Italy. Before leaving Bombay, he wrote to Tagore:

Gurudev

14th March, 1926

In forty-four hours I shall leave India and the dream I have seen, full of beauty and bounty, will be at the end. You are the central figure of the magnificent vision, and I am lingering in looking at you with my eyes dropping tears of deep and sweet, oh, so sweet, thankfulness.

When I become aware and return to reality I know I shall feel stronger and richer owing to the lofty goal of collaboration with you. The beloved India of my young and mature years was only in books or in palm-leaves, but now she is living before my eyes, she is personified in you and you who are an incomparable singer of the blessings of life, can easily imagine what that means, that, namely, a cherished dead thing should become living and loving.

Take care of your health, take as much rest as possible. I am not at all anxious about your feeling unwell, because I know that it is only a matter of fatigue. And, then, too many souls love you and watch over you to allow you to be seriously ill. Old age, moreover, is still far from you and what you suffer from is rather the illness young people are exposed to, namely, exhaustion, dependent on having spent one's own energies with too much generosity. My love to Rathi and Tucci. To you, Gurudev, all my heart, all my soul, and let all that is fire in the world give light to your glorious path.

Yours Sincerely

Carlo Formichi[21]

This emotional and intimate letter was Formichi's last communication with Tagore from the Indian shore.

Tagore sent a letter to Mussolini through Formichi. A draft of that letter dated 10 March still remains in the Mussolini File.

Your Excellency

10th March, 1926

On the eve of the departure of Professor Carlo Formichi, may I be allowed to send you through him our message of deep and cordial appreciation of what Italy has contributed to the growth of Visva-Bharati. Professor Formichi came with a rich gift of a library of Italian classics and of books on art, the value of which will be gratefully inscribed in the memory of successive generations of our students. Professor Formichi's own stay at Santiniketan has been fruitful not only in the formation of lasting bonds of co-operation between him and the scholars who worked with him in his subject, but also in the creation of intimate links of friendship with others who he happened to come into contact with.

We are very thankful, too, that Professor Giuseppe Tucci did at last come to Santiniketan and introduce our students to the study of the Italian language and literature. Professor Tucci's brilliant versatility and talent has made him an invaluable colleague to those of our scholars who pursue studies in Buddhism through Tibetan and Chinese texts. Visva-Bharati scholars recognise with feelings of gratitude the help he has rendered them and earnestly hope that his services may be accessible to them for a number of years to come. I am confident that if the duration of Professor Giuseppe Tucci's stay here were to be of a sufficiently long period of years we shall be able to consolidate the work which has begun, to the mutual benefit of historic cultural relations between Italy and India.

Yours sincerely

Signed/Rabindranath Tagore[22]

On 6 April 1926, a cable reached Santiniketan from the Italian consulate in Calcutta. This cable was in reply to Tagore's letter to Mussolini: 'I thank you for your kind message conveyed to me by Professor Formichi and express to you my satisfaction for the re-blooming of the cultural relations between Italy and India. The agreeable proposal regarding Professor Tucci meets with my full favour, and the study of the possibilities of its realisation will be the subject of my particular interest—Mussolini.'[23] Reference to Tucci in that telegram was perhaps concerning Tagore's request for an extension of another year's service of the Italian professor at Visva-Bharati. Surprisingly, there is no mention of any official invitation in the telegram.

Meanwhile, the time for Tagore's second voyage to Italy was approaching fast. He started from Santiniketan for Bombay on 12 May 1926 and boarded the liner *Aqulica* for Italy on 15 May. Members of the entourage included his son Rathindranath, daughter-in-law Pratima, the three-year-old adopted granddaughter Nandini (Pupe), the prince of Tripura Brajendrakishore Deb Barman, the secretary of Sriniketan Premchand Lal, and Gourgopal Ghosh, a teacher from Santiniketan. Of the latter three people accompanying the poet, the prince of Tripura defrayed his fare for his passage. Fares of the other two were partly funded from the university's coffer. They were not strictly the official guests of the Italian government, though the government provided for their hospitality throughout the tour. The reception of Tagore's party was remarkable on board since this time he was travelling as a guest of the Italian government, of which the captain of the ship was aware.

The Bengalee, an English daily in Calcutta, reported the news under the heading 'Bon Voyage':

After completing his sixty-fifth birthday at Santiniketan, Rabindranath starts to-day for Italy to fulfil his pledge of a second visit to that land from which he had to hurry away on the advice of doctors to save himself from repeated attacks of influenza. But during his short stay at Milan, the poet had a foretaste of the magnificent reception that was awaiting him all over Italy. Distorted accounts were subsequently published in a Calcutta daily which went so far as to attribute motives to the poet for his sudden departure from that land. Protests come from Italians themselves and the letter of Mussolini himself left no doubt about the dis-ingenuousness of the mean insinuations of the Indian daily supported by the meaner suggestions of Dr. Sudhindra Bose of Iowa. Since then, without apologizing for its discourtesy to the poet, it has tried to make up for its lapse by increased attention to the poet's activities. Let us hope that it will join with us in wishing a most hearty bon voyage to the poet on his second visit to the land of the Fascisti, and let us hope that it will send a special reporter to watch the attitude of the Italian people towards the poet without depending upon an

American lecturer who again purposely depended upon misapplied clippings from the rabid Fascisti press of Italy.[24]

According to the Italian consulate in Calcutta, they were not aware of the fact that Tagore was visiting Italy as the guest of the government. They were surprised to find similar news published in *The Statesman* that stated: 'Dr. Rabindranath Tagore leaves for Italy today on an invitation from the Italian Government. Dr. Tagore, who was now at Bolpur, will entrain at Burdwan arriving in Bombay on Friday. He is expected to sail from Bombay on the day following.'[25] The news annoyed the Italian consulate enough to prompt them to write to Tagore's secretary Mr. Morris: 'You know it well enough that the news about the government invitation is not a fact. I'm sure you are equally surprised. We have no idea who sent this report to the press. The fact needs to be made public [...].'[26] The subsequent reaction of the consulate is not known as the file does not contain any further communication in this regard.

Tagore's secretary Prasanta Mahalanobis and his wife Nirmal Kumari were initially included in his retinue, but due to some unknown reason, there was a last-minute cancellation of their bookings and they had to be left behind. However, Tagore's pressing request prompted the Mahalanobis family to find two berths on another liner that sailed from Colombo, reaching Rome three days after Tagore.

The news of Tagore's Italian visit as a guest of Mussolini was politically nuanced. All over the world, the press carried the news in almost identical wordings.

The Standard, an English daily in Buenos Aires, reported on 20 May 1926: 'Rabindranath Tagore is due to arrive soon to thank Signor Mussolini personally for his efforts to increase cultural relations between Italy and India. The Premier has decided that Tagore shall be the guest of the government during his stay in Rome.'[27]

The Manchester Guardian reported on 21 May 1926: 'Signor Mussolini has directed that Dr. Rabindranath Tagore shall be the guest of the Italian government during his stay in Rome, where he is expected shortly for the purpose of thanking Signor Mussolini

Tagore at the Grand Hotel in Rome, June 1926
Source: Rabindra Bhavan.

personally for his efforts towards increasing the cultural relations
between Italy and India.'[28]

On 30 May 1926, Tagore and his party reached Naples. As
he was a state guest, some government dignitaries received him
at the quayside. Besides Formichi and the officials, other friends
of Tagore—Andrée Karpéles and her husband Del Hogman from
France, and Leonard Elmhirst from England—came to meet him.
Although Elmhirst was not his secretary during this trip, Tagore was

very glad to see his good friend, but Formichi was less pleased. The previous year's uncomfortable association with Elmhirst was still fresh in his mind. Though Tagore insisted that Elmhirst join him on the tour, jestingly remarking that only an Englishman could serve as the proper corrective to Mussolini, Elmhirst declined.[29] In the afternoon, Tagore and his party reached Rome by a special train. They were received at the Grand Hotel, where a large suite was reserved for the poet and his entourage.

Rome

On the morning of 31 May, Tagore was driven around the city by car with some Italian friends. In the afternoon, reporters from three leading newspapers came to interview the poet in his hotel. In the evening, he was accompanied by Formichi to Palazzo Chigi, the official residence of the prime minister, to meet Mussolini for the first time.

They met in a long, rectangular hall where the prime minister sat at the far end. On the arrival of the guest, Mussolini stood up from his chair and came forward to welcome him—the meeting of a great humanist with an autocratic despot! Formichi was present, but most of the conversation was in English. Mussolini could understand Tagore's words in English, whereas Mussolini's Italian was being translated for the poet. Mussolini began by saying, 'I am an Italian admirer of yours who has read all of your books translated into the Italian language.' Tagore was visibly impressed by this statement, though Mussolini's biographer believed that his literary and cultural awareness was not as much as he claimed.[30] Tagore thanked Mussolini for his generosity and for sending Tucci to Santiniketan. He expressed praise for Rome and mentioned that he had already seen this ancient city from the top of Gianocola. Mussolini insisted that the poet should extend his stay in Rome for at least two weeks and postpone his visit to Florence, which was supposed to be in the following week. During the course of the conversation, Tagore mentioned that he had not decided on the subject of his lectures. Mussolini enthusiastically interjected, 'Talk about art, talk about art!' Here again Mussolini's biographer stated, 'He liked to stress the great importance of art and he himself, inevitably, was claimed to be a seminal influence upon contemporary artists but [...] privately he resented that Italy had been held back from political greatness by the illusory and corrupting pursuit of aesthetic values.'[31]

The meeting was cordial and continued for almost an hour. Finally, Mussolini said, 'Please don't hesitate to let me know your likings, I shall gladly arrange for everything you wish.' The meeting concluded with a hearty exchange.

On their way back to the hotel, Formichi wanted to know the poet's impression of Mussolini. Tagore said, 'Without any doubt he is a great personality. There is such a massive vigour in that head, that it reminds one of Michelangelo's chisel. Moreover, there is a simplicity in the man which makes it hard to believe that he is really the cruel tyrant many indulge in depicting.'[32] Mussolini's biographer wrote, 'No doubt his personal magnetism worked best with those who saw him rarely; nevertheless he could always impress a visitor when he tried, and all the fascist leaders remembered how they had at times fallen under a real spell, especially in the early days [...].'[33] Tagore was no exception.

On 1 June 1926, Tagore's arrival in Rome was reported in most of the dailies published from Rome. *Il Resto del Carlino* reported:

Arrival of Tagore in Rome

Yesterday the Indian poet Rabindranath Tagore arrived in Rome on the 3.10 train. The famous Italian orientalist, Professor Formichi, who has recently returned from India, went to Naples to welcome him on behalf of Italy and the *Duce*. The steamer, carrying him from Bombay to Italy, was docked in Naples. Also there to welcome him was a representative of Mussolini, Comm. Gino Cecchi, who was the newly appointed plenipotentiary minister in Afghanistan and the ex-General Consul of Bombay. The Indian poet got off the train in Rome wearing his typical oriental costume. He wore a rich and wonderful outfit: a tunic with golden embroidery, a long satin robe and a white turban which gave his lean and dark face a majestic appearance. Tagore has a flourishing look and this gave the impression that he is still vigorously active and strong in spite of his old age. His glance was always moving, sometimes flashing, sometimes veiled with a shadow of undeniable sadness. He was moving with elastic and precise steps, maintaining a special harmony with his loose draping of embroidered tunic and the white satin robe.

All procedures related to the poet's arrival in Rome and whom he was going to meet were of his own choice. Only a few people outside the railway station were able to see for a moment this fleeting vision of the East.

Next to the majestic figure, as a contrast, was the thin, supple and agile figure of his young son. This young man with scarab-coloured eyes and copper coloured skin would escort his father throughout his tour in Italy. Seven people constituted Tagore's retinue. Among them were the most prominent Prince B.K. Deb Barman in his beautiful Indian Army officer's uniform and Gongopal Ghosh [sic]. An English man, Mr. Huherst [sic], his secretary, was also in the group. As soon as they came out of the station, the Indian guests got into the waiting car and were driven down to the Grand Hotel where some distinguished people arrived yesterday. Among these people were S.E. Monoilescu, Under Secretary of the Rumanian Treasury, and Lady Elizabeth Carnavon, who was the first victim of Tutankamen's tomb.

The Italian Government put Tagore and his retinue in a luxurious apartment in the Grand Hotel. As soon as they arrived there the poet had his dinner and went to rest, whereas Prince Deb Barman appeared in the big hall of the Hotel in his dazzling uniform, attracting the attention of the people around the tables. Tagore's plan for the coming days in Rome has not yet been organised. It is not known how many days the poet will stay in our city. It is certain that very soon he will be received by Hon. Mussolini who has inspired Tagore to visit Italy. During an interview Professor Formichi mentioned that Tagore's visit is for expressing his thanks [to Mussolini]. However this tour will help India to know more about life and culture in modern Italy.[34]

Similar reports were also published on 1 June in papers such as *Il Regime Fascista* (p3c3), *Gazzetta del Popolo* (p8c2), *La Tribuna* (p3c6), and others.

The three reporters who together came to interview Tagore in his hotel on the afternoon of 31 May published their accounts on 2 June in their respective newspapers. Of these three interviews, *Il Giornale d'Italia*'s account was wordy and elaborate. The same interview in a condensed form appeared in *Gazzetta del Popolo*. Two of the interviews are cited here. The following interview appeared in *Il Giornale d'Italia*.

A Great Guest of Mussolini
Tagore Speaks to *Giornale d'Italia*
Visit to Rome: An Indian Evocation: The Last Work;
Dress of a Mendicant

When we arrived in the hall, Professor Formichi kindly led the way and presented us [to the poet]. He was sitting in an armchair near an open window, behind him the scene of the Diocleziane Thermal baths.

Rabindranath Tagore stood to receive us with his luminous, serene, guileless smile.

I remember one of his lyrics in Gitanjali, 'Light palpitates and dances in the heart of my life.'

His austere figure, surrounded by an aura of gentleness, appeared in front of us. His beautiful head with white hair and beard on top of his white tunic. His face and features are marked with the characteristic colour of Indians. The magnetic large, black eyes convey the liveliness and the sweetness of his look. His mouth with healthy and shining teeth, preserves his youthful purity.

The Poet, in front of whom the engrossed listeners like us were stretched out, speaks in a soft, musical voice, which often sounds like a subdued song.

He receives our visit with a pleasing simplicity, the way he receives his unknown and universal brothers.

Rabindranath Tagore loves all creatures because he loves God who is the father of everyone and all things. However, his God is not a distant, segregated God in a boundless sky, but a God who is present in Nature and in the manifestation of life:

Thou art the sky and thou art the nest as well. O thou beautiful, there in the nest it is thy love that encloses the soul with colours and sounds and odours[.] (Gitanjali 67)

The poet spoke yesterday in his pantheistic language with a touch of song and colour in it. He told us about his impressions of Rome after his first visit to its ancient monuments:

Rome has a young spirit in a body that is a thousand years old.

He also spoke about Milan, which he visited last year, and seemed to him modern and full of warmth.

The Italian horizons are wonderful; the Indian horizons are wonderful too but at an unattainable distance. The horizon and the sky gradually and slowly approach the earth and meet in a playful joy.

Tagore, at our request, mentioned his literary and philosophical works. He is pleased with his works because he sings for the people and not for the critics.

With his tall figure, his head gently inclined and his eyes cast down to gather his inner thoughts, Tagore talked to us for an hour which passed quickly before our curiosities and eagerness. We learned a lot about the soul from the poet's voice flowing into that quiet, hospitable room.

As the time was passing Professor Formichi reminded us about the Poet's other engagements. Then we took leave of this singular man who brought in his person a rare distinction and understanding of love and creation with the highest sense of life and beauty.

The farewell greetings were full of memories with mystical notes.

We saluted by lifting our arms in the Roman way and he folded his hands in a sign of prayer.

We made the gesture expressing the conscience of the power of a historic race; he, like a priest, passionately folded himself, embracing the universe.

Sun's Man

We introduce ourselves to Tagore like a *trimurti*. However, in the pretentious hall of the Grand Hotel, amidst Viennese and English furniture, the noble figure of the poet seemed out of place. He wore a long white silk garment, like the gown of a 'pandit', with flowing beard and neatly combed hair. Surrounding his venerable head there were brilliantly lit Roman scenes appearing from the windows, such as the thermal baths of Dioclezianetion, Isiaco's obelisk and the Esedra fountain.

—Friends of mine told me I carry with me the sun of my country— Rabindranath said with a smile.

I was observing him very closely, he is one of the best models of the Indian race and as people know, the most beautiful among the whole human race.

Last 6th May he became 66 years old. There is not much baldness, and he preserves his youth both in mind and in body. He has an upright stature, an agile and slim physique; symmetrical and proportionate limbs; aquiline nose, swarthy copper complexion, aristocratic hands, tapered fingers adorned with rings; dark searching eyes, calm insinuating voice. While he was speaking his eyelids came down to concentrate on finding the exact eloquent words. He speaks in English which he knows very well; speaks clearly, elegantly and sententiously. He is imaginative like Shelley. In his writing he uses a style that is musical but difficult.

He took us back to an ancient time when the poet and the priest were the same person. Yet in his deep religious speeches we seem to catch a fine vein of irony and scepticism. However, in India this is not new. 'Goodness,' from Hymn 10 of *Rigveda*—'being itself the fruit of creation, doesn't know when this universe originated.['] Then who knows? Who knows how the created world comes out of the uncreated world? Then a thousand years later, Indian wisdom says, 'think you about the origin of things because neither goodness nor the supreme Being knows this.' The spirit of tolerance and the sense of the relativity of things which we find in Tagore's words are ancient words.

His philosophical and religious arts are similar in vein to the Franciscan character. Aren't the most delicate lyrics of songs 60, 61, and 62 of the Gitanjali on children similar to the canticle of creation? The way the St. Assisi was raised in his father's house full of music in search of the harmony of the world. He [Tagore] is also satisfied to discover the soul of the same Indian civilisation and surrenders spontaneously to her voice.

Italian Impressions

—I shall stay in Rome for a week and maybe I shall have occasion to talk to the public.

Tagore speaks in a lively way about Rome, and how it appeared to him yesterday while driving around in a car with some of his friends and Mrs. Pavese, who speaks English and is able to write down the words of the poet faithfully.

—Milan, where I was last year, is a modern city. Rome is modern too: but here the ancient and the modern both continue to exist with each other. I am sorry to come to your country so late and not when I was as young as Shelley, Keats and Goethe. Now I am old.

At this time we asked him about his health, mentioning his malady which affected him last year.

—I feel well now but as my heart is weak, my doctor said I shouldn't feel tired. To me the forced rest is painful. I like to work and give my heart to my people.

—But you have given your heart a lot through your books. The Poet's face becomes illuminated. He was happy to know that in Italy he is well known by all classes of readers. He asked Professor Formichi and Dr. Assagioli, sitting next to him, for information about the most read of his books amongst us. In Italy there is a large number of 'Tagorean' translators, namely Alfia Valli, Verdinois, Clelia Zannoni-Chauvet, Arundel and so on.

—I am happy to learn that all sections of people have read my books. I want to light the [mind] of the people and not the men of letters.

He told us in simple words about a Maltese soldier who went to see him in London and told him, 'I am not a well-educated man but I have read a book of yours. My commander kept it under his pillow, and he lent it to me. The book was good for me at that time and I have come here to thank you.' I want to give the people light—insisted the poet.

—What work are you doing now?—we asked.

None at present. The last one was 'Worship of a Dancing Girl' [Natir Puja], performed by the girls of my Indian school on my birthday on 6th May whereby I wanted to show the dance as a form of religious cult. After that I left.

—What kind of work do you prefer most?

—I don't know, it all depends on my mood. I prefer one kind of work in a particular mood and another kind of work in another mood. You know writers are heartless with their work. When they finish a piece of work they don't look at it anymore.

Meanwhile, the sky over Esedra Square was overcast. One of us recited a verse from Leopardi which was translated for the Poet.

D'amore digiuna
Siede l'anima di quello a cui nel petto
Non si rallegra il cor quando a tenzone
Scendono I venti e quando nimbi alduna
L'olimpo e fiede le montagne il rombo Della procella …

[That man must be unloving and unloved
Who is not happy in his deep heart's core
When high Olympus gathers up the clouds,
When all the winds from far and wide are moved
To war, and thunder strikes the mountain-sides and shatters them][35]

—I love thunderstorms too. You should see our thunderstorms over our boundless plains. They come down suddenly in early summer, the horizon grows black, dust whirls through the air, and rain comes down furiously; then our children go out in the storm and race with the wind. Our plains are boundless.

The Reflection of the East

—Does it remind you of the Roman Campagna?

—No, our Bengal plains are limitless, desolate, enormous, immense sky and plains scarcely relieved by vegetation.

The lively Poet recalls:

—There, spring arrives slowly, oozing between the sky and the earth. It grows rosy with the *palasa*. Our sky seems monotonous to some people, but to him who observes it every day it has continually new and surprising beauty.

After a pause Tagore turned his bright look around, lowered his eyelids and leaned his head forward. That gesture allowed us to observe his tunic and his lightly coloured, simple robe. From his neck was hanging a black ribbon; tied at one end were his glasses.

—Is your dress that of a Pundit? We asked him.

—No, it is of a mendicant. My own personal fashion.

Time passed; it was nearly the time to visit Mussolini. We asked him if he found analogies between the Indian and Roman civilisations.

—Analogies and differences are same as between different human beings. Are we not physiologically alike but physiognomically different?

—Do you believe in the continuity and persistence of supremacy [of races] in the world?

—Before the great emigration which led to the formation of the Indo-European world, there were many other similar movements in the world. We find relics of such movements in many countries, for example in South America. When a people attains an excessive height of energy, it becomes like a river overflowing its own banks. Emigration is not always a sign of pauperism, but may also originate from the fact that nations which enjoy an exuberance of life must find outlets for their civilisations [to spread]. Do the primitive people of Africa feel this necessity? No, but the races rich in life and vigour do.

—You Italians know very well how the phenomenon of migration took place. I feel that these ancient Indians, when they first felt the exuberance of life, crossed the Pamirs and crossed the deserts and brought their civilisation into the Gangetic peninsula of India. So, the Indians carried civilization out of their cradle and spread it all over the world. Because of the perpetual Indo-European supremacy the movement of expansion is still going on.

The time is pressing. Tagore's son came to remind us that his presence is needed at the Palazzo Chigi.

One more question:

An Autograph

—What is the maxim you would choose as an aid to the best conduct of life?

—It is not easy to say. The words which help me to explain my ideas may not have the same meaning to other people. So they might misunderstand me.

—But the people have understood your books so they will also understand the maxim.

—It is not really a maxim. These are the ancient words which help me shape my life. But those are not the things you expect.

Tagore hesitated to reveal his secret.

—Those are not as you are expecting, but they help me in my life. Those are modest words inherited from ancient times.

So we insisted he wrote those Sanskrit words on a piece of paper, with an explanation by Professor Formichi.

Truth, complete knowledge, infinitely supreme soul, who reveals itself in immortal shapes of joy, peace and happiness are all in One.

Rabindranath Tagore (or Tagor, which is how we Italians transcribe it) signed with a paint brush like fountain pen in Indian calligraphy. So satisfied were we, the Trimurti, that we left holding the autograph very carefully so as not to spoil it.

Tagore's Life

The Indian Poet Rabindranath Tagore became popular in Europe soon after he was awarded the Nobel Prize. Before that he was known mainly to Sanskrit scholars.

In Italy Tagore's name became popular after his first visit to our country in 1925. The visit was interrupted in Milan and this gave rise to some misunderstanding.

Now he has returned to find out about the young country and civilisation of a thousand years. Tagore has been received with enthusiasm. He arouses an interest in the Italian soul by his unusual charm and through the philosophical values of his vast literary works.

A learned Indian told us about the great poet.

Tagore was born to a family of artists. Gaganendranath and Abanindranath Tagore are famous painters and Dwijendranath, Rabindranath's brother, is a philosopher. His father, the Maha Rishi, was also a contemplative soul who sat for a whole day enraptured in front of the splendour of nature.

Rabindranath has grown up in an environment of literature and music. When he was nineteen and still unknown, he wrote his first romantic work.

When he was young he was a passionate and contemplative lover of nature and his poems written at that time were hymns to creation and the creator.

Afterwards he wrote dramas which are still performed in Calcutta.

From the age of 25 to 35, affected by enormous tragedies, he wrote the most beautiful lyrics of love based on some of the themes which exist in Sanskrit text. Then his art became deeply religious and philosophical.

The following years reflected his aspirations and passions for humanity. His lyrics are full of soft rhythms as in Gitanjali, the votive collections, and in Stray Birds, and are full of untranslatable shades and original meters which reveal a world of dreams and wishes.

Tagore's work presents a special interest, as it brings forth, in European terms and values, the Indian soul; that is why he is considered the greatest among the old living poets. So in India this age is called Rabindranath's age.

Tagore also excels in music. His songs are sung in the west of India and Burmah, wherever Bengali is spoken.

He is considered a 'saint' too, one who doesn't disdain to live. His word is born from the same life, as his compatriot says 'we give him our love.'

A visual and significant sense of beauty always vibrates in Tagore's thought; moral and intellectual beauties remain hidden in the physical aspect of everyday objects.

He is a contemplative man who is stirred and moved by nature such as birds singing, the murmuring of water, the fragrance of flowers.

Every morning, the Poet wakes up before dawn, sits below the trees of his garden and remains absorbed for hours.

From this meditation bursts forth the powerful hymns.

What divine drink wouldst thou have, my god,
from this overflowing cup of my life? (*Gitanjali* 65)

Tagore is a Pantheist, following an ideal pantheism which Saint Francis extolled in an immense laud to the good and beautiful things of the creator. Similar to Saint Francis, to Tagore also: life is a joy and death is the crowning glory.

This is the poet who India admires and loves and worships, who is filled with sweetness and spirituality, where the voices of sense and soul are admirably fused in a serene peace.[36]

Facsimile of Tagore's interview in *Il Giornale d'Italia*, 2 June 1926
Source: National Library of Rome.

La Tribuna on 2 June published the following report:

'Italy—Clothed in Quenchless Light'
Our Interview with Rabindranath Tagore

Is he celebrating an Eastern solemn ritual sitting in front of a snow white altar and making offerings?

The poet's robe, like his beard and long hair, are snow white; his gesture is slow, aesthetically sacerdotal.

Will you have a cup of tea with us?

The invitation to take a cup of tea actually implies that Rabindranath Tagore is going to attend his 'five o'clock' tea session in one of the most modern private suites of the Grand Hotel. His voice seems to us not like the murmuring prayer of a thousand faithful Indians but the fine voice of the fountain of Esedra.

During the whole interview the atmosphere is such that one cannot get rid of the impression of a dream.

The poet himself unintentionally encourages us in this illusion.

My visit to Rome appears like a dream. I can hardly believe that I am really in the country which I have learnt to love through the poems of Shelley, Byron, Browning and Goethe. I wish to admire and often remain ecstatic observing the marvellous reproductions of your art and literature which are kindly sent to us by the Italian Prime Minister for my boarding-school library.

The poet spoke with enthusiasm about the collection of books, albums and photographs sent through Professor Formichi to his college at Santiniketan by the generosity of the Duce.

He spoke above all with gratitude on behalf of himself and his numerous students who study Italian art, literature and language. He also mentioned that the Italian course which our Professor Tucci runs and which is taken up by many pupils who will one day come to Italy—'the land of hope and glory'—to complete their studies.

The Prince of Tripura, regent of East Bengal, who has accompanied the poet in Italy, is also an enthusiast about our country. [He said] when he returns to India he will spread throughout his country the spirit of Italy.

Rabindranath Tagore is also accompanied by his son Rathi and his wife, and a little adopted daughter. In his entourage are also his secretaries Mr. Ghose and Mr. Elmhirst [*sic*], who has been for a long time the poet's secretary.

Their small mission will be, when they return, to speak nicely about the sentiments that were expressed yesterday:

We owe much to Professor Formichi for initiating this cultural rapprochement between Italy and India. While we cannot yet foretell what results may come from this more intimate communication between India and Italy, I feel sure that it will help both countries to fulfil their historic function in the world.

The great poet of Asia then made a rapid comparison between India and Italy: India is a peninsula, the civilisation of which spread throughout Central and southern Asia, and which has remained up till now a centre of faith and culture; Italy also is a peninsula which had a similar mission in the West, and has retained up to the present time a living spiritual heritage[.]

I believe these two people [Tagore and Mussolini] are destined for an intimate understanding with each other.

—You can help us in our progress, and will also find something [for Italy] helpful in the depth of the Indian soul.

The same view was expressed by the poet to the Duce yesterday evening during their cordial conversation at the Chigi Palace … [The line of this paragraph is illegible in the original source.]

His Excellency Mussolini seems modelled body and soul by the chisel of Michelangelo.

The poet told us something about this extraordinary man—that he was convinced 'his every action shows intelligence and force.'

I see a great future for your country, a future as great as her past, after she rises glorious and beneficent, to herself and also to others, from the terrible scourge that shook the whole world.

Asked by us from *Tribuna* to say something about Italy, he gave the following lines, which we reproduce from his own autograph: 'Let me dream that from the fire bath the immortal soul of Italy will come out clothed in quenchless light.'

From page to page, from mouth to mouth, the words of the poet will reach the extreme boundaries of Asia.

We expect the wish he expresses and firmly believes will be realised.

Tagore to Mussolini

Yesterday at 7 pm the head of the government received the great Indian poet Rabindranath Tagore and his companion, the Sanskrit Professor Formichi. The conversation was long and difficult as it was in English. The

"*L'Italia, ammantata di luce inestinguibile,*"

Let me dream that from the fire bath the immortal soul of Italy will come out clothed in deathless light.

May 31ˢᵗ 1926

Rabindranath Tagore

Tagore da Mussolini

Un libro di Roberto Farinacci

Concorso d'Arte e Musica

Libri ricevuti

poet, who had already seen Rome from the top of Gianocolo, expressed his enthusiasm and admiration for this eternal city.

He will stay in Rome for a fortnight.

The Governor will receive him at Campidoglio and a pompous welcome will await him at the historic Hall of Wisdom at the University.[37]

The poet's remark, 'Let me dream that from the fire bath the immortal soul of Italy will come out clothed in quenchless light', in his own handwriting with his signature was highlighted in a box in the paper. The aforementioned news was replicated in a slightly shortened version in *Il Regime Fascista* (p3c5) on the same day.

Il Popolo di Roma published the following article on 2 June 1926 with a signed photograph of Tagore.

Tagore and Italy

Rabindranath Tagore, now the guest of His Excellency Mussolini, has always given proof of his love for Italy and his appreciation of the ardent desire of the Italian people to fathom the depths of Indian culture and Indian spirit.

In gratitude to the Italian Government for the gift of a library of Italian classics and books on Italian art that Professor Formichi took with him to Tagore's University, Visva-Bharati, Tagore wrote a letter to the Italian Prime Minister expressing the hope that there will be lasting relations of cooperation between Italian students and the learned men of India. After Professor Tucci, a member of the Italian mission, had conducted a course of lectures on the Italian language and Italian literature at Santiniketan, the poet expressed through his interpreter a vibrant message of thanks which ended as follows: 'I am sure that if Tucci's sojourn in India is prolonged for a number of years we shall be able to consolidate the work he has begun with admirable energy, the results of which are a promise of great mutual benefit to the history of cultural relations between Italy and India.'

But his love for Italy has had other manifestations in messages and letters of a more intimate nature; his intuitive soul of a poet and Seer has penetrated the soul of today's Italy, the Fascist Italy. This love and understanding were expressed to the full in the message to Professor Formichi prior to his return to Italy that, both here and in India, assumes a significance for the whole Italian people: 'In your temperament there is something that is not only the fruit of a long training of scientific study but something native to the gentle soil of your mother country. It is that generosity that has the magic power of opening the door of the inner shrine of an alien race.' Praising highly the profound culture of Professor Formichi he speaks to him as an old friend, 'Your arrival in our hermitage accompanied by the gift of an Italian library from your country is a gift of surprising magnificence. It had already awakened the desire in our students to honour it by truly acquiring the possession of its contents and thus getting into direct touch with the great sources of inspiration which, during a period of rebirth in the history of Europe, brought forth such varied and fertile, artistic and intellectual productions to the Western Continent. This library was a generous invitation from your country to our people to participate in her festival in her hospitable home, open to all ages and to all humanity. You are a worthy bearer of this message from your country but, as you are a true friend of India, you must also take back a message from us to Italy: our assurance that her symbolic invitation has conferred on our hearts a permanent desire for communication with her. All of Professor Formichi's work is forging a gallant link between the two countries.'

The letter which Professor Formichi brought with him and showed to the Prime Minister concludes with these affectionate words for himself and Italy: 'Before departing let me say that my relationship with you is not only based on the cause to which I aspire for my institution. It is a fervidly personal link and intimately associated with my love for Italy and the exuberant welcome she has given me. If on account of my increasingly infirm health I should be obliged never to ask her hospitality again her breath will remain always in the many memories of our mutual life and in the permanent impression you leave in our hermitage of treasures of thoughts and dreams, and in the greatness of heart of her people.'[38]

Meanwhile, Tagore's visit to Italy and his various remarks about Mussolini were highlighted in newspapers outside Italy. *The New York Herald* published the following news on 2 June.

Tagore Lauds Duce in Visit to Rome
Hindu Philosopher Urges Exchange of Students between India and European Countries

Rome, Tuesday—'Let me dream that from her bath of fire will emerge the immortal soul of Italy, with an aura of quenchless light,' said Rabindranath Tagore, who, with his wife [*sic*], his son and daughter-in-law, their adopted daughter, and an entourage which includes Prince Tipura of Bengal [*sic*], is visiting Rome as the guest of Premier Mussolini.

'Mussolini is a great hero, whose every word and action is a proof of his force and intelligence. Body and soul, he might have been formed by the chisel of Michelangelo,' added Rabindranath.

'If the West can learn the art of contemplation and gain a mastery of thought by studying the East, it can on the other hand teach the East action,' said the Indian philosopher, 'and an exchange of students between India and the various European countries will be an important instrument for bringing this about.'[39]

Though most of the reports in the Italian press were friendly towards Tagore, there was some criticism too. A slightly sarcastic comment appeared in *La Voce Ripublicana* on 4 June 1926:

Tagore said: 'The Indian and European mentality are complementary to each other. Obstacles to freedom are of two kinds, material and spiritual. Europe has overcome material difficulties through science. India seeks to overcome spiritual difficulties with her life of contemplation. These two far-away worlds can collaborate in winning the freedom of the whole world.'

He accentuated Indian discipline in concentrating the spiritual aspect of life. He spoke of an ideal city of the poet where, like in Italy, an attempt is being made to blend the old and the new.

The idea of a 'mixture of diverse elements' is constantly occurring in Tagore's speeches. He wants to unify in one civilisation the characteristics of East and West. [...] But it is not sufficient to speak in English, to stay at the Grand Hotel, to study Western texts, to give interviews, and to have a secretary engaged in writing letters on a machine, to know the spirit of the West. To appreciate our nature it is necessary to come into contact with our world and our life. [...] The civilisation of Europe is essentially dynamic, while the civilisation of India is essentially static and dualistic, and Tagore's idea of a meeting of the two is absolutely utopian.[40]

There was no report in the press on the details of his movements for the next couple of days after his meeting with Mussolini, although in some newspapers the news of his proposed visit to Turin was published in advance on 3 June. During these two days, the poet was either busy sightseeing or resting.

The next engagement of the poet was lunch with Sir Ronald Graham (1870–1949), the British ambassador in Rome, on 4 June. Formichi was not present. In the afternoon, he met Tagore in the hotel. In the course of the conversation, the poet told Formichi, 'As long as Mussolini lives [...] Italy can be said to be safe. Now I know what I shall answer when, after crossing the Italian border, I hear people speak ill of your country.[41] It was an irony that Tagore had to contradict his statement later after leaving Italy.

Il Regime Fascista published another wordy report entitled 'Tagore' written by Franco Cassetti. In it, Cassetti discussed Tagore's idea of the meeting of eastern and western civilizations without losing their identities, within the personae of the ideal 'citizen of the world'.

Tagore

The poet of *Gitanjali* and *The Crescent Moon*; the playwright of *Chitra* and the *King of the Dark Chamber*; the bard of the *Offering Collection* and *The Gardener*; the thinker of *Sadhana, Dharma* and *Samaj*; the Bengali reformer; the educator of India, the great follower of humanity and of the extraordinary Brahamanic teaching, is in Italy.

An exceptional and ancient civilisation briefly becomes part of another magnificent and imposing ancient civilisation by testing it and testing itself in comparison. Rudyard Kipling was the first to draw a clear line of demarcation between the West and the East, which is probably a divide that cannot be filled. These two eternal and immanent colossi have looked at each other over the centuries and become confused, entangled and mixed. Nevertheless, they have never lost their own indelible effigies, carved in porphyry in order to survive and withstand forever.

They represent Meditation and Action; Doing and Thinking; Strength which wins, rises above and triumphs, and Strength which lets the other win, exceed and triumph.

Both sides triumph in this century-old battle. This fight has lasted from time immemorial and originated at the dawn of time in order to move forward and occupy the destiny and story of humankind with a roar. Perhaps this is the intimate centre, the deepest germinal node from which every event originates, every human complication derives, every tumult of races and peoples proceeds with the incessant violence of a stream that relentlessly goes from a known origin to an unknown outlet. The heroic thirst for conquest, which wants to see the earth yoked to men as the panther to Dionysus' chariot, is the mystical heat, the ascetic vehemence that wants to destroy every earthly craving of humankind to drink at the universal spiritual springs of Brahma. Brahma gathers in himself every source, every instinct, every force, every sufferance and every soul, and submerges them again forever.

The West and the East are not two civilisations but two poles. They are two developments, maybe intended by the providence that governs humans, so that the races accomplished a divine plan of wonderful achievements and moving experiences, which make human beings superior and higher beings by indefinitely moving from one side to the other, towards one and the other direction.

As a guest in Italy, Tagore represents the encounter between the enlightened Calcutta and the pagan, Christian, and fascist Rome. Calcutta and Rome become the synthetic tangle of a symbol; a form of approach which Mussolini first understood and comprehended in its intrinsic essence, in its fullest reality—despite some hue and cry against Tagore which has emerged in the last two years in Rome itself.

Who is Tagore, Rabindranath Tagore, the prince Tagore, who lays down religious and political creeds, a priest and a master, a poet and philosopher who was awarded the Nobel Prize for poetry in 1913?

He is a reformer of institutions, a guide for humankind. In 1828, his grandfather founded the *Congregation of God* (Brahmo Samaj) to fight against idolatry in India and spread the monotheistic principle. As well as having run and reformed the *Congregation of God* since 1872, Tagore has founded Santiniketan, *Sanctuary of Peace*, where he is a teacher and an initiator of souls.

When the hatchet of death struck his adored family three times in a year and killed his wife, his young daughter, and his little son, this missionary of good suddenly expanded his love for his dear ones to the wider circle of a family whose members he heard groaning and whose suffering he saw as they were corrupted or hit.

He did not curse when he felt overcome by this wave of adversity. He collected his thoughts in prayer. His prayer is known all over the world as poetry. His poetry poured from his soul as sanctified tunes stream from an immense silver organ. Like a religious priest, he gave us the teachings of God and redeemed human beings with the melody of his poems, which seem full of the imponderable that only souls can handle. He said that above, around and inside human beings there is one truth, one life, one force, in which one being exists and survives. This is Brahma, God. Nothing exists and nothing is conceivable but Him. Everything belongs to God, is in God, and is God: from a blade of grass to a constellation, from the invisible germ in the earth to the galaxies that swathe the sky, to Ursa Major and Ursa Minor that govern it, and the immense thoughts of the creatures that ascend into it.

His poetry encompasses monotheism and pantheism. It is a premonition of Christianity and a legacy to the anchoritic ancient Wisdom.

Tagore said—May human beings be like God. He is the only example whose soul is full of the destiny and reminiscence we should pursue. If God is just, human beings are just. If God is immaterial, human beings win against the material. If God is holy, human beings are ascetics. If the whole of God is love, human beings are without hate. If God is an eternal creative energy that bestows life and joy upon his creatures, human beings are tireless makers of good through deeds in favour of their fellow creatures.

From his hermitage, the monolith of the Indian sphinx came to the surface of the Holy Ganges and was shattered by a sudden vein, an immense crack, an unexpected dividing furrow. What was one became duality, complementary, distancing and reconciliatory at the same time. A contemplative life is complementary to an active life. The ascesis of repentance, solitude and ecstasy integrates in the ascesis of human labour, which prides itself, its neck, muscles and soul, on the enormous effort in establishing good on earth. The admonition of Tagore's gospel is to be active and meditative. One must meditate to work, and work to meditate. This gospel's foundation eternally washes the oceanic flow and tides with incomparable sincerity.

What is the human being if he is not an ensemble of masks placed on top of masks? Man—he adds—you need to be naked at all times, as if you were always in the presence of God. You human being, there is a child at the heart of you. In your living and truthful centre there is a child who ignores the sad wisdom of the world. The margin of this person overlaps with the margins of infinitude. You human being, you are a global person who can set the child free in the same way as the statue breaks free from the block. Lead the child to the light and offer him all of your space. You will be immensely happy. You will make your fellow humans immensely happy.

This is Tagore. This is the axis of his inspired poetry, of his propagated science, of his vibrant philosophy. This axis is raised on the world as a condition to a glorious resurrection.

What is the essence of the other soul, that soul which is Roman, Italian, fascist and occidental?

It is certainly other and different. It is certainly an advance. However, there will always be touching lines and inserting planes between the two ancient civilisations.

The touching lines are the religion that re-emerged from the bare land of ruthless materialism, the religion of action that works towards the good and redemption of the race. Patriotism is conceived as a rewarding gift and a gift to be deserved at every moment of Eternal Justice. The inserting planes are sincerity raised to worship and unalterable duty, a spiritual understanding of life as force, inner joy, and useful sacrifice.

All that does not exclude an antithesis. Diversity remains and contrast survives. Well, then we think this is the reason why the hospitality offered by Mussolini and the gift he presented Tagore (a collection of the principal works of our Latin, Italian and Occidental culture) have a higher meaning as well as the sense of profound admonition.

We must integrate. The peoples who are destined to live and triumph must now integrate. In integration, there is an enrichment of all that is homogeneous to one's nature; a perpetual fulfilment; a daily shape and reshape; daily and tireless moulding with new elements of the malleable matter of race.

To integrate stands for giving, trying one's best and working with faith for the progress of others, so that the spirit always triumphs over the darkness of primitive animal nature and becomes purer and grander.

Franco Casetti[42]

On 5 June, Tagore was exclusively received by the king of Italy, His Majesty Vittorio Emmanuelle III. The king was fluent in English so Formichi was not present. The interview lasted nearly an hour. The following summary of the conversation, as recorded by Tagore's secretary, is quoted from the *Visva-Bharati Quarterly*.

The King received me with great cordiality. I was much touched by his simplicity and his great sincerity. He speaks excellent English. He asked me whether I was being shown the different sights of Rome, and how I liked them. I told him that I was enjoying everything but not in a perfectly natural way. There were always too many people around me. I often wish I could go back to my former obscurity.

The King smiled and said: That will never happen, you will never get an opportunity of enjoying things in your own way.

He had an interest in Indian people and asked me how many different languages there were, whether there were big differences in customs and manners and whether there was intimate intercourse between the different parts of the country. I said, 'There are at least a hundred different languages and there are many obstructions to communication. In addition there are big differences in race and cultural status. This is a great difficulty. It takes a long time for an idea to spread over the whole country. Cultural problems are much simpler in a small country like Japan. Ideas become diffused easily. There are no big differences in the level of culture and civilisation. I was much struck for example by their intense love of beauty. The interesting thing was that it was not confined to any particular section of the people. It was equally marked in every social stratum.'

The King told me that at one time cultural intercourse between Italy and India had been active and deplored that there were no adequate facilities for this at the present time. I told him that things were getting better in this regard. There were arrangements for the teaching of Sanskrit in several Italian Universities. I also told him that we hoped to achieve a closer connection between Italian and Indian scholars through our institution, the Visva-Bharati. The King was very pleased to hear this, and told me that though he knew very little about the East he had a great interest in it, and hoped our efforts would be successful.

Before leaving I said, 'It is a great honour to have had this audience with your Majesty.' He appeared distressed and stopped me, saying, 'Please do not say that, please do not speak of honour. It has been a great pleasure for me to have met you.'[43]

King Vittorio Emmanuelle (1869–1947) was born in Naples. He was the constitutional head of Italy for a period of 46 years (1900–46). According to Mussolini's biographer, the king was a timid enigmatic person who in principle wanted to take political decisions constitutionally, but failed to do so on several occasions. Temperamentally, he was drawn to anyone who would take firm decisions and control domestic unrest. That was the reason why he, initially, fell back on Mussolini, but later on, felt some guilt for appointing him as prime minister.

After his meeting with the king, the poet also met the ex-premier and the most senior senator, Luigi Luzzatti (1841–1927). The ex-premier invited Tagore to visit his institution Orti di Pace (The Garden of Peace).

Tagore in front of Orti di Pace, June 1926.
Source: Rabindra Bhavan.

On the afternoon of 7 June, the poet was given a civic reception at the Roman Capitol. This was his first public appearance.
The reception was organized by the governor of Rome, Senator
Cremonesi, and the reports of this reception were published in
several dailies. *La Tribuna* published the following report with
a photograph of Tagore with his friends and Formichi with the
Capitoline Hill (Campidoglio) in the background:

Rabindranath Tagore's Reception at Campidoglio

Yesterday at 5 pm Governor Cremonesi received the great Indian poet
Rabindranath Tagore together with his family and followers at Campidoglio.
The Governor was also accompanied by Vice-Governors Darbesio and
Veselli and his wife; the Rectors Duke Caffarelli and Duchess; Dukes
Foschi, Giglioli, Mariotti, Pirera, Secreti; and the chief officer Laurenti.
    The Governor saluted the poet, and in conveying the greetings of the
city, he expressed his gratitude for the honour done to the city by his visit

to the Campidoglio. He added that in Rome his name was surrounded by great admiration and deep love.

Rabindranath Tagore also saluted the Governor and courteously expressed his profound love for Italy and its glorious capital Rome, whose beauty he deeply admired.

Senator Cremonesi then showed the illustrious visitor the magnificent vista of the Roman Forum from a lodge and offered him hospitality in the Sala Rosa (Red Room).

Before leaving Rabindranath again thanked the Governor for the exquisite reception, saying that it would always remain one of the most memorable days of his life.

A Lecture Given by Tagore

At the invitation of the President of the Union of Intellectuals of Italy, Luigi Luzzatti, the Indian poet and thinker Rabindranath Tagore will deliver a lecture on Wednesday at 5 pm at the Quirino Theatre on the subject of 'The Meaning of Art'.

All authorities and world intellectuals of Rome are invited to this lecture which will be briefly introduced by Professor Carlo Formichi, the Sanskrit professor of the University and also the fellow founder of the Union.

Tickets will be provided by the librarian, Dr. Antonio Rovini, from the Office of the Deputy.[44]

Another engaging article about Tagore, written by the ex-professor of history and senator Alessandro Chiappelli, appeared in *Il Giornale d'Italia* on 8 June. The professor contradicted Tagore's idea of the East–West fellowship. He maintained that the *dhyanyoga* and *karmayoga* of the East had no relevance in the West. His article expressed a clear nationalistic stance.

Tagore, the East and the New Italy

A whole swarm of our mystics and contemplatives moves around Rabindranath Tagore, the excellent British–Indian poet who is presently in Rome.

Tagore visited Honourable Mussolini, the *Duce*. What an incredible contrast they are. If one needs to symbolise contemplative life and active life, nothing would be better than opposing these two great figures, as they represent the existing contrast between the Indian and the Roman civilisations. Tagore himself highlighted this antithesis while talking to a reporter from *Il Giornale d'Italia*. Tagore pointed out that each of the two civilisations has its own physiognomy and character. We are, he said, physiologically similar but physiognomically different, are we not? Well, this is exactly what spoils the naturalistic pantheism at the core of the Indian understanding of life. [...] The more nature rises to the realm of the spirit, the more it perceives the individuality of shapes. Thus the individual, who becomes a person in the human world and the civil State, is the product of constant effort. This is a product of crucial and immortal value and, therefore, it excludes extinction and annihilation in Nirvana or in the cosmic Brahma. Thus, every occidental civilisation has its living and individual character. Quiet peace is not preached in the West as it is in India, but activity and life. This difference keeps India under English supremacy despite Mahatma Gandhi's preaching. He is the other great personality of present-day India.

We respectfully welcome and honour this great British–Indian Poet as Italy and, for her, the Honourable Mussolini do. However, we do not spread the word of resignation and renunciation in a country that wants to play a major role in the world and has a duty to take determined and powerful action. It needs strong characters, vigorous and tough wills. It does not require anything of mystics or the contemplative submissions of dreamers. We do not belong to a pantheist civilisation but to that of the Christian creation, with a God who carries his children and his people's children on his wings like an eagle, in accordance with the powerful biblical image. Our God is not a nest for conformity with Rabindranath Tagore's image, nor a living God who is the creator of human beings who are themselves autonomous creators of the values of will and life. We shall not spoil the heart of the Christian idea of the West that all peoples are free and active. Saint Francis loves all beings too but he loves them because they are children of a creating God. They work and love for God. They are not vain and transitory aspects of an undetermined universal essence in which they blend like waves in the boundless ocean. Our country does not have the endless plains of Bengal but it has the variety of its mountains, which at times are rugged and at other times descend onto the plains, of its winding and open lakes, of its various and exciting seas. Our art is not uniform and symbolic like Oriental art but it is classical. It is unwavering and romantic, varied and free in inspiration and form. Its variety includes the Etruscan Apollonian of Veio and the Jupiter of Otricoli, the dramatic pulpits by Pisano and Gilberti's golden doors in Saint Joseph's, the Medicean tombs and Michelangelo's Moses, the paintings in the Christian catacombs and the glorious achievements of Raphael and Michelangelo Buonarroti in the Vatican, the *hypogea* of the Etruscan tombs, Giotto's tower, and Saint Peter's dome.

Such is the fruitfulness, the active and diverse freedom of Occidental and Christian civilisation. Such is the reviving genius especially of the ancient and new Italy that rises again, bold and pugnacious in the heart of decadent Europe, which moves back and forth between the allures of the old East and young America. The East represents an ancient contemplative, idle wisdom and the apathy of unchangeable casts and mystic doctrines. America fascinates with a tumultuous busy life and a dominant longing for business. Italy and Rome still have a role to play by giving the old Orient, decadent Europe, and the transoceanic femme fatale called America a new ideal in words and inspiration.[45]

Tagore visiting the Roman ruins, June 1926
Source: Rabindra Bhavan.

Between 3 and 6 June, some members of a ladies circle in Rome came to meet the poet in his hotel. Besides the following report, there is no other source confirming this meeting. However, a member of that circle, Marga Sartorio Savilla, wrote about the meeting in an article published in *Il Messaggero*, where she expressed her profound admiration for Tagore, symbolizing him as a prophet with a mystical aura. She was overwhelmed by the sight of the poet as she found the wisdom of the East before her.

Tagore

I did not expect to see him. For me he was as far away as his mysterious India, which my soul longed to visit, but always returned without being able to reach it.

I did not think I could look into his eyes or touch his garments with my timorous hands. This mythical figure, towering over the sky above our wandering dreams, seemed so unreachable that I would never believe seeing him with us as a man amongst men. It was true that since our adolescence we received the light, love and serenity oozing out from his heart—yet our thirst was unquenchable. It was also true that he was with us since then; but how could we reach him? His purity, concealed by simplicity, we tried to grab in our hands like a toy; the way a child from his play *The Post Office* would try and reach out for. His purity was like a gift from a kind soul. However, would a child ever truly own it? Perhaps he believed he owned it. That was the truth, the illusion; could he hold this gift of purity in the empty cupped palm of his small hands?

In my opinion, he was the King of a 'dark chamber' [through] which sunlight rarely entered. From this deep and mysterious darkness, an outline of a soul would appear brighter in the true light of reality. And in that light, the blurred outline of this great figure, stood alongside the forms of our unsatisfied desires.

The other women around me, however, wanted to see him in the flesh, breaking the spell of this fascinating mystery.

Suddenly, his presence was announced here in the hermitage. The news reached the women waiting—causing some uneasiness—for some it seemed like it would never happen, like a ray of light breaking through a horizon of unstable clouds. The announcement came like the blossoming of a miraculous flower in their outstretched hands. Immediately these women felt less anxious as sense of calm prevailed. They knew their wish was finally being granted. Each one of them waiting to receive the announcement; 'He waits for you. Go.'

'I will meet Tagore. I will be with him in a few minutes'; I repeated those words to myself. The meaning of those words sounded completely new and though I was addressing myself, I was still not sure.

In that lavish setting of the wide hall some people sat with dull faces dressed in colourless clothes. I wanted to remove this melancholic atmosphere. I wished I had worn a tunic that held the earth's colour, the earth we all walked in. I wished to scatter some of that earth on my head.

I sat in a corner where there was barely any light; I wanted to remain anonymous so no one would notice my pilgrimage. At the time some kind of emptiness prevailed in my mind.

At last! As I stepped onto the carpet, all in white, and nimbly moved towards my great expectation, a 'colourless' assistant came before me and asked coldly; 'Are you the lady in white?' I looked around in despair. Could it even have been possible that I was the only person dressed in white in the world at that moment? I could not deny it —'It is me' I said. Then I received a precious note: 'You must tell Tagore how many Italian women read and admire his enlightened works'.

I entered the huge and lavish living room full with many useless objects, but, it seemed empty to me. For there, in the middle of the room, stood a tall, straight and still figure; it was Him.

Did his hands reach out gently towards me? Or did mine violate a century-long custom to clutch his hands and join them together in such a solemn gesture? Did I rest my face in them?

Eventually I spoke about social struggles, politics and human bonds, and pronounced his name. At one stage I felt I could deflect that ray of sunlight. Nowadays we Italians live by action more than we did in previous years—by virtue of our great 'Italianness'. I understand that our way of living is different from those living a long distance away from us, as far as the furthest stars even. Nevertheless during the course of our journey we recognise those who come to us directly from the country of poetry. Although our national life demands our time, we still spare a few minutes to an hour in a day, isolating ourselves within a small tower (alas! a very small tower indeed, but high enough), and we celebrate our spiritual feast. Today we felt that the Poet, with purity, has come from faraway to preside over our festivities.

He spoke—did he immerse in depths of thoughts?—it seemed to me he was exploring an unknown mystery of an 'enclosed garden'. His hands were very beautiful and slim; moving gently as he spoke. They seemed to twist and unwind delicate garlands of flowers. The room was full of flowers.

Although my eyes stared at him constantly, an intense perfume encased me. At first I thought it was coming from the open windows but it was not. It was also not the fragrance of the flowers in fact, I had not experienced that aroma before and it bothered me, as one is always bothered by the unknown.

He spoke and his voice was like music; so sweet and penetrating that no instrument could ever reproduce it from its strings. It was a feminine voice projecting willpower and firm reasoning; sweet but not honeyed in an expression of uncertainty. He spoke in English that sounded like harmony. It felt like a prayer, a faraway chant, but in equal measure a commanding voice, like that of an older brother towards a younger sibling.

I think the language he spoke stood above all other languages. Maybe this is because it brought all our souls together in harmony.

He said, 'My Italian friends, I promised to learn your language. I am very sorry I failed to keep my promise. Besides, I am too old to learn it.'

During the course of time, his long hair and beard had become tinged in a silver colour but it did not leave any trace on his perfect face, or on his smooth forehead, or inside his eyes, or in his hands. I could not see a single wrinkle. His face looked darkened as a contrast with his silver flowing hair, the colour of his skin seemed brightly exposed to constant light. Occasionally he raised his glance and looked towards me, and then immediately lowered it as he had found the answer he was looking for. His eyes were black and bright like two fireballs in a dark night. His gaze was sharp, detached from trifling thoughts veiled by a superhuman gentleness; that appeared to be sent from God's kindness. He wore a wide robe and a tunic. The colour of the robe resembled the night sky shaded by lunar sand and the tunic was sand-coloured, but its gold shade did not shine. I thought the garment showed his regality.

He said, 'People often stare at my clothes and I feel they do not see the person inside the garment. However, in your Italy I can feel the soul of the country. I feel Italians are people who understand me, with whom it is easy to live and communicate my ideas and goodwill.' He said many other things which are simple and like undiscovered treasures lying deep under clear water awaiting disclosure. However, for our conversation, he needed to hear my voice too. So, I opened our dialogue with the words of one of our poets so that he could hear more than just a human voice—a voice expressing harmony.

Che giunto sopra la cima udrai, e giovine, in chiare parole, risponderti non un poet; ma l'adulto cuore tuod'uomo. [Once on the peak, I wish you will not hear the answer of a poet, young boy, but the clear words of your grown-up heart.]

There was a moment of silence. The invisible trail of perfumed air was slowly disappearing. He said, 'I have not understood the words but everything a human voice could express goes beyond those words'.

I stood up because I could not stay any longer. He stood next to me and joined his hands. I passionately kissed them, first one then the other, as if we kissed our holy image. He let me kiss him; looked at me and smiled. His smile was very similar to the smile of a two-year-old child: it radiated serenity.

Tagore moved a step backwards and bowed his head with his joined hands. I know now this is a habitual greeting in his country. Sisters, in that moment I sincerely thought he gazed upon us to give us his blessing. He also blessed our children and our country through us.

Standing on the threshold, I wanted a final look at everything around the room—to frame it in my memory, but I could only see Him. I saw Him alone within this banal, wide and sumptuous hotel room. All useless objects disappeared and his figure seemed to walk between a display of flowers: one with golden bloom and the other with white lilies. I was then able to identify the perfume that enwrapped me. It was a scent of a Son of the Sun and of purity.

I had to wait a few minutes in the hall where my preoccupied mind caught the voices of Indian princes and princesses who arrived with Tagore. There were also some musicians who were adjusting their instruments for a forthcoming jazz recital. I ran away into the Roman night, led by a brighter light than the one that brought me there. I kept the whole picture in my heart so that my inner eyes could see it forever; otherwise it would be lost as an illusion?

Marga Sartorio Savilla[46]

Savilla's gripping account reminds us of a similar emotional experience of another woman, Victoria Ocampo. In her memoir, *The Balcony*, she recorded her first meeting with Tagore at the Plaza Hotel in Buenos Aires, where the poet fell ill on his way to Peru. She wrote:

[…] we went to Tagore's suite and his secretary left us alone in the sitting room. I was worrying about the outcome of this interview and felt so shy that I even considered flight, when the object of my restlessness put a stop to this waiting by his appearance on the scene. Silent, far away, mild but unapproachable (or so he seemed to me), his way of carrying his head […]

would have expressed sovereign disdain, an inhibiting haughtiness if it had not been corrected by extreme gentleness. On his light-brown face there was not a single wrinkle in spite of his 64 years […]. A smooth brow, as if no worry had ever marked this even skin and left its trace on it. Abundant white hair, wavy and falling on to a firm and well-rounded neck. The lower part of the face was hidden by the beard. This gave more prominence to the upper part: an aquiline nose; the structure of brow and cheekbones, strong and delicate, had a rare beauty, well caught in certain of his photographs. The eyes, black, with often lowered, perfect lids, still retained their youth and fire […]. Tall, rather slim. His hands, extremely fine and expressive, moved with a slow grace and seemed to talk a language of their own […]. I felt frozen by the sudden and real presence of this distant man with whom my dreams had made me so familiar and who had been so close to my heart when all I had known of him were his poems.[47]

On the morning of 9 June, the poet visited Luigi Luzzatti's colony school Orti di Pace. This school belonged to children who were orphaned in the War and was similar to two other colony schools: Paterna Domus in Citta di Castello and Ospedione di San Francesco sited in Collestrada. Not only did the school have a similar name to Tagore's institution, but also, like Sriniketan (Tagore's other school of rural regeneration), it trained pupils in a life of self-dependence and good health.

The pupils welcomed the poet at the gate. He was shown around the school's orchards and scattered some olive seeds, at the request of the school authorities, to commemorate his visit. This was followed by a recital of Roman classical and modern songs by the students, which impressed Tagore. At the end, a student offered him a floral wreath which he accepted, and then he blessed the students in the way he blessed his own pupils in Santiniketan.

The Unione Intellectale Italiana organized a gathering of intellectuals including the city's artists, literary figures, and philosophers on the evening of 9 June at the Quirino Theatre. Many government officials, including the prime minister, were present. The prime minister, who was 280 miles away from Rome the day before, drove back to Rome himself non-stop to attend this particular meeting.[48] The theatre was full in spite of the expensive tickets, and in that star-studded, distinguished assembly, Tagore gave the first lecture of his tour, 'The Meaning of Art'. The lecture, originally an essay written in English, was first published in *Visva-Bharati Quarterly* in 1921. Tagore had probably written this lecture to deliver during his tour of Europe in 1921. This long and elaborate lecture has now been made available in a major compilation of Tagore's works—*The English Writings of Rabindranath Tagore* edited by Sisir Kumar Das[49] and, therefore, not included here. In 1969, this essay was separately published by the Lalit Kala Akademi of India in the form of a bulletin with an introduction by Mulk Raj Anand. In this thoroughly philosophical discourse, Rabindranath Tagore revealed his fundamental ideas about art and aesthetics.

We cannot be sure whether the entire essay was delivered as a lecture at the Quirino Theatre. The newspaper reports mentioned certain points that were not included in the published version. Although the audience that evening comprised the distinguished intellectuals of Rome, this complex subject might not have been easily comprehensible due to the language barrier. Formichi's paraphrasing in Italian was probably not adequate for a complete understanding of the complex nuances of Tagore's lecture. The press reports accentuated this possibility.

On 10 June, reports of the lecture at the Quirino Theatre appeared in most of the dailies, but the reports were very brief and the actual lecture was hardly reviewed. The following brief review appeared in the 11 June issue of *Il Giornale d'Italia*, which also included the report of Tagore's visit to Orti di Pace.

Tagore in Rome
A Conference at Quirino

Yesterday evening at the elegant hall of Quirino the Indian poet Rabindranath Tagore delivered to the waiting crowd his lecture 'The Meaning of Art' organised by the 'Unione Intelletuale Italiana' (Italian Intellectuals' Union).

All intellectual people of our city were present at Quirino yesterday evening. The Head of the Government, the Honorable Mussolini himself wanted to be present. Accompanying him was the Under-Secretary of Foreign Affairs the Honorable Grandi, and among the audience we saw the Honorable Salandra, the Prefect Count D'Ancora and numerous personalities from the political, artistic and cultural world.

Rabindranath Tagore was introduced to the audience by Professor Formichi, the learned Professor of Sanskrit from our own University who has just returned from a trip to India. Formichi soberly summed up the success of the work of the great Indian poet and philosopher, mentioning that Rabindranath Tagore who is now the guest of the Duce, expressed his love for Italy in his recent statement about Italy: 'that from her bath of fire will emerge the immortal soul of Italy, with an aura of quenchless light.'

At this point there was an enthusiastic applause which obliged the president [Prime Minister] to lean out of the box with a request not to interrupt the speaker.

Professor Formichi expressed Tagore's regret that he was not able to address the conference in Italian but he [Formichi] announced that as soon as the poet returned to India he would learn our language so that he would be able to read the magnificent collection of classics which Benito Mussolini gave him.

At the end Professor Formichi summed up the content of the poet's lecture for an easy understanding by the audience.

Amidst an air of peace and serenity, Rabindranath Tagore started his lecture in his melodious voice and conquered the hearts of the audience immediately.

According to his theory, to understand the true meaning of art it is wrong to assume that art is the equivalent of beauty. Art is rhythm and harmony and it symbolises the inexhaustible magnificence of the creative spirit.

Many tragedies of our daily life cannot be called beautiful but if the descriptions of those, as the poet expresses, move us deeply, then those are manifestations of art. If I tell a child, who knows of tigers through his school book, the story of a tiger who is displeased to see his magnificent black-striped fur and so asks a man to brush off his stripes—then, according to Tagore, he creates in the child's imagination an artistic vision of this tiger. So the child finally visualises a tiger from the story she listened to and the images of what she has seen will eventually fade away.

For Tagore, art is a vision.

Science—he says—is impersonal, whereas art is only personal through the way physiology becomes physiognomy and philological literature.

In this century, characterised by an unbridled run for power and wealth, the poet and the artist, who are poor, have their only infinite true wealth which is the creative power.

There was endless applause at the end of the lecture. Tagore was visibly moved and thanked the audience with his hands folded in front of him.

This evening at 7 pm in the hall of via Greoriana 5, Professor Mahalanobis, the Secretary of Tagore's University will give some information about the University in English. Admission free.

A Call at 'Orti di Pace'

Senetor Luzzetti, honorary co-operator of Colonies of the youth workers, invited Tagore for a tour around the pleasant 'Orti di Pace' (Garden of Peace) at Gianicolo. The poet, who has founded a school in India where he tries to lead the youngsters back to the simple and healthy pastoral life, was interested in this type of school and accepted the invitation. Yesterday Rabindranath Tagore accompanied by Professor Formichi, who was acting as interpreter, and the President of the Colonies of Young Workers Professor Dr. Levi Morenos and Miss Margherita Parazzoli, came to the 'Garden of Peace'.

He was received by Countess Anna Piccolomini of Triana and Countess Contini, one of the promoters of 'Orti di Pace', lady Lucia Penremoli Luzatti, Comm. Rosmini, the councillor of the Colonies, the Gr. Officer Dante Merchori and others. Also present were various personnel and teaching staff of the institute.

The orphans were assembled close to the big fountain decorated with lictorian bundles. Tagore greeted them sweetly. Then he proceeded with the students towards the Colony farm. He was listening with great interest to Professor Levi Morenos, who described the horticulture, fruit-growing and gardening done by the pupils. Then there was a touching and symbolic ceremony when Tagore scattered some olive seeds into a demonstration field for growing olives. After the ceremony the pupils sang some ancient Roman religious melodies and hymns, directed by their music teacher Sabatini. The poet was pleased to listen to the choral singing, which he believes is one of the major tools in educating children.

On behalf of the rest of the children one of the orphans offered Tagore some publications about the 'Garden of Peace' with some flowers collected from the school garden. Tagore, who liked the gift, addressed the children with affection saying that he blessed them with the same sentiment as he blessed his students in India, and he wished them a very happy and prosperous future.[50]

On the afternoon of 10 June, Tagore attended the annual choral concert at the Coliseum (or, Colosseum). The reception was organized by the governor of Rome, Senator Cremonesi. This was an unprecedented experience for the poet. According to Mahalanobis:

The huge Coliseum was a seething mass of human faces. The overtopping galleries, which in the Imperial age seated from sixty to eighty thousand spectators, are now mostly in ruins and yet offered standing room to several thousands of persons. The central arena was filled with visitors. The choir, which consisted of more than one thousand children, was grouped on a huge wooden gallery erected on one side of the arena. As we entered the whole audience, numbering perhaps twenty or thirty thousand, rose from their seats and gave such a welcome to the Poet as we shall never forget. The singing was marvellous, more than a thousand voices singing in harmony making us realise how thoroughly even art in Europe has been brought under their genius for organisation. At parting the audience rose and saluted again in Roman style. In its tremendous dimensions, as also in its perfect harmony, this farewell salute was scarcely less wonderful than the choral music. The poet was visibly touched, and raising his arms blessed the children with all his heart.[51]

In the evening, the poet was welcomed at the University of Rome. The Great Hall (Aula Magna) of the university was nearly overspilling with its audience. A few hundred students were also present. A thunderous applause followed the poet's entrance into the hall. The rector, Professor Del Vecchio, in his welcome address said:

This is a happy and solemn occasion for the University of Rome which has today the honour of welcoming one of the purest, loftiest and most representative spirits of the modern world. It gives me pleasure to thank you, Sir, for having accepted our cordial invitation, and I thank you also for the fraternal reception you have accorded in your wonderful land of India to our esteemed colleague in this University, Professor Formichi.

You are no stranger to Rome, for Rome is the seat of the Universal spirit. Your poetry is full of human feeling, which is at the same time a great humanistic philosophy, and has met with a profound echo in our hearts. You have affirmed in sublime and mystical words this eternal truth: that above the greed of riches, the thirsting after pleasure and power, there is the Kingdom of Spirit, of goodness and of love. You have recalled men, too often intent on fighting and destroying themselves for particular interests, to this health-giving principle, which comforts and illuminates the path of life: you have exhorted them to accomplish the mystical union of the individual with the universal soul. Your doctrine, however, does not end in a vain asceticism; it is also a poetry and philosophy of action, which is fostered by wisdom, justice, concord and love. This is, if I understand it rightly, your Supreme Ideal, and it is also ours. This ideal, according to the classical forms of our civilisation, is expressed in the symbol of the University of Rome, which I am happy to offer you, Sir, as a memorial of this day. I beg you to accept it as a sign of our reverent sympathy and profound admiration.[52]

Tagore at the University of Rome, June 1926
Source: Rabindra Bhavan.

At the end, the chancellor handed over the address of honour with the embossed university seal to the poet which is still preserved in the Italy File of Rabindra Bhavan, Santiniketan. Welcoming the poet, Formichi said:

King of Poets! It is with great honour and a still greater joy for me to convey to you the greetings and the homage of the Faculty to which I belong. Do please hear in my voice, the voice of all my colleagues and of the students of Philosophy, Philology and Literature, who are best qualified to appreciate your wonderful feats in the different provinces of thoughtful research and artistic creation. When last February we were together in Dacca and I could see with my own eyes the boundless enthusiasm with which the clever and energetic Indian students of East Bengal gave vent to their feelings of love and worship for their great and glorious *Kavi* [poet] and their revered *Guru* [master], I was dreaming all the time that you might one day find myself also among the students of my own university, for I foresaw that our Roman youth would not be inferior to their Indian brothers in showing their unbounded admiration for you. I remember to have said to the Dacca students: If *Gurudev* comes to Italy you will find rivals, formidable rivals, among the students of the University of Rome.

The dream has become a reality today, and today I cannot help realising the truth proclaimed by our great poet Carducci: 'Life is beautiful and the future is holy.' You don't know Italian, nor do these youths understand Bengali; the means for the interchange of feelings is lacking, and yet you have to grant that these Roman youths are as much filled with love and admiration for you as the Dacca students.

The reason is that personality reveals itself by a medium which transcends language and makes it superfluous. You can be mute, never utter one single word, and yet you will reveal yourself wholly. But you are not mute, you have already spoken to the students over and over again. They all have read some of your poems translated into Italian. They know, of course, only fragments of your gigantic creation, and these fragments themselves have reached them under a shape which is not the original and genuine one, for every translation is always a misrepresentation. We say in Italian: *traduttore traditore*—a translator is always a traitor. But a Latin adage says that from a single nail one is capable of inferring the whole structure of a lion. Don't think, therefore, these students clap their hands unconsciously and without a proper understanding of who you really are. They all see the lion from the nail, they all feel the touch of your lofty personality.

King of Poets! Our intense wish is that your journey to Italy should be a thing of beauty, a joy forever; but the air you breathe on this soil, the water you drink from our wells, the food our fields and our trees offer you, and above all the warmth of our loving hearts should give strength to your body and allow you to dispose of the feeling of fatigue you complain of. We don't consider you as old, you are not old. We all know your age, you are only 66, and the lightning in your eyes proclaims the heydey of life and inspiration.

What you want is only rest. And I know it is not easy for you to get it. We are ourselves wishing to see you, speak with you, hear you talk in private and in public, prevent you from taking rest.

These are days of great strain for you, but you, O eagle, know where your nest is; and when you go back home, and climb into your nest, there the echo of our applause, which is a strain on you today, will be soothing and, we hope, a source of inspiration.[53]

Following Formichi's emotional address, Dr Vera Sarta, a Sanskrit scholar presenting a bouquet of white roses to the poet, said on behalf of the students:

In a language which is not mine I feel more than ever incapable of giving expression to the emotion which overwhelms us in this hour, when we meet you, after waiting so long, since you gave your promise last year to come to us, waiting for you with thirsty souls. Let these flowers convey to you the greetings of the students of Rome:

> *Vadantu tani pushpani asmakam sneham manam cha:*
> *Pushpani etani tu mlanam gamishyanti, na tu asmat sneham manan cha:*
>
> [Let these flowers tell you of our love and reverence;
> these flowers will fade, but never our love and reverence.][54]

Finally, Tagore addressed the students:

My Friends, it is a great regret that I speak in a language which is neither yours nor mine. I have seen your beautiful country and I loved it. Nature herself in her youthful spring has welcomed me. But today it is not Nature but the voice of youthful Italy which spoke to me and touched my heart with the music of Italy. I had a splendid introduction to this evening in the singing of the children at the Coliseum, and that music is still vibrating in my heart.

My friends, I bring you greetings of love from the youthful minds of India. I hope you will accept me as a fit messenger; though old in years, yet being a poet, I am young in heart, and as such claim to represent the youth of India. Students everywhere belong to a country of their own, which has no distinction of nationality or race, a land of human hope, a land of young minds seeking life and light; and in this land guidance and leadership belong to the poet. Therefore I find myself at home among you just as I find myself at home among the students of my own country. For you also belong to that land where one can hear the music of life, that music which is the true language of man. I wish I could bring to you this music, instead of these futile words.

But perhaps I have given utterance to my thoughts in the music of my poetry, and I am glad to know that that music has reached you. It is a great joy for a poet to realise that his words do not belong to his own language only, but somehow by breaking through the barrier of languages, they reach your soul and find expression in your love and admiration.

My young friends, the great sensitivity of your mind seems to me like that of the flowers listening to the spring breeze which comes across the sea and whispers to them of the coming of spring, and speaks of the song which summer sings to them. You have opened your hearts to my greetings of love, and I am thankful that it is given to me to realise this. I feel that I have won my place in this country; that you acknowledge me not only as a poet of India, but as a poet of young hearts, so that I belong to you as well as to my own country.

What a great privilege it is for me to serve as a medium for the union between the peoples of India and Italy. It has existed in the past, but must be made new and alive. My friends, this is my mission—I have been dreaming of this day, when it will be possible to bring to your door and to your heart all the treasures of my country; and let you know that she has something to offer to you, some truth which is of eternal value.

Today I am your guest, and after a few more days I shall take my departure. But I know I shall still live here, when I am no longer here—I shall live in my love for you in your hearts. I shall come over and over again, like flowers which fade but come again.

My journey of life has come to its end, and it gives me great satisfaction that I could come to Europe in this my last visit and leave imprinted on your youthful hearts my hope for and my faith in the future humanity. We, the different peoples of the world, have our different interests, and there we can never come together. But above our own self-interest, there is a region of common aspirations and common achievements, which is the true meeting place for all humanity.

You see how ancient races, though no longer existing, still speak through their ruins and in their contributions which are immortal for humanity. You remember the great period of your own history—the period of the Renaissance—when a new light shone from Italy on the whole of the western world. The flame of that light is still inextinguishable and is still inspiring art and literature in Europe. Those who realise that this is the true light of humanity—they can never grow old, they can never die.

Do you not believe that there is hope for humanity? Let my presence, as a messenger from the East, be not in vain. That you have been able to receive me in this way, and that I have been able to appreciate you, this is not without significance—it is not a passing event in your college life—here the East and the West have actually met. We realise in our meeting today the spiritual unity of man, and I aspire that this moment will not be a small thing that found expression in the voice of a thousand children in your ancient Coliseum, but it is the true music of the meeting of the East and West. I hope you will remember me not as a casual visitor, but a messenger from the ancient East, and as the poet of youthful humanity. I shall be fortunate if I can help to establish a guest house in the heart of young Rome for pilgrims of truth and love who will come in future.[55]

Formichi was translating the poet's lecture section by section. The lecture was frequently interrupted by applause. At one stage, the poet had to put on the university headband (Goliardic cap) at the request of the students, and at the end of the lecture, the main entrance of the hall was so crowded that the poet had to take his leave through the rear exit way.

Il Messaggero published a detailed report of this reception in its 11 June issue:

Reception of Tagore at the University

The announced solemn reception for the poet Rabindranath Tagore took place in the main hall of the Royal University yesterday afternoon. There was an immense audience including the Minister of Education, S. Fedele, the Chancellor Professor Giorgio Del Vecchio, the Professors Millosevich, De Francisci, Rostagno, Vivante, Brandileone, Vittorio Rossi, Almagià, Gabetti, Vacca, Dionisi, Bonfante, Benini, Manfroni, Mallino, Mercati, Pirotta, Bonanni, Pettazzoni, Curis, Matronola, and many others. General Varini, who is commanding officer of the Tenth Zone of the Army, commander Scazza, who is the revenue officer, Count Salimei, who is director of education, commander Fraschelli, who is general director for secondary education, together with commander Martini, and many other senior officials from the Ministry of Education, were also present. Many of the women and students were wearing their university hats.

The poet arrived at 17.45 and was welcomed by thunderous applause. He was accompanied by Professor Formichi, the Maharaja of East Bengal, his son, his daughter-in-law, and other Indian people, who wore their picturesque Indian costume.

Firstly, Chancellor Del Vecchio spoke in Italian and in English. Amidst much applause, he said:

> 'This is a happy and solemn day for we welcome one of the most represen-
> tative minds of today's world. I would like to thank Rabindranath Tagore
> for accepting our invitation. I would also like to thank you for the fond
> welcome given to a dear colleague of this university, Professor Formichi, in
> your wonderful India.
>
> You are not a foreigner in Rome because Rome is the seat of the universal
> spirit and does not regard any human as alien. Your human poetry, which
> is also human philosophy, has found a deep echo in our hearts. You have
> claimed this eternal truth with mystical and sublime words: the realm of
> the spirit, kindness and love is above material life, and above the human
> craving for richness and pleasures. Human beings are too often busy at
> fighting and tearing each other to pieces because of private interests, but
> you remind them of a healthy principle that comforts and enlightens. You
> urge upon them a mystic union of the individual with the universal soul.
> Your teaching is not vain asceticism: it is also poetry and a philosophy of
> action. If I understand correctly, your supreme ideal, which is also ours, is
> represented by deeds, actions nourished with wisdom, justice, harmony,
> and love.
>
> In the classical shape of our civilisation, this ideal is represented in the
> emblem of the University of Rome, which I am pleased to offer you,
> Rabindranath Tagore, as a memento of today. I hope you will accept it as a
> symbol of our friendship and our deep admiration.'

The chancellor gave Tagore a silver copy of the new seal of the University with a brief inscription carved on the reverse in honour of the poet.

Professor Formichi then gave a speech in English and, amidst the applauses, touched upon the poet's highest genius, which the Italian readers know of because they appreciate his works in translation.

In English Dr. Vera Certa also welcomed Tagore on behalf of the students of Rome and presented him with splendid bouquets of red and white roses.

Finally, Rabindranath Tagore stood up and delivered a noble speech translated sentence by sentence into Italian by Professor Formichi.

He mentioned the unforgettable show he saw at the Coliseum, as a worthy preparation for the reception organized by the University. He thanked the Italian youth for the warm welcome, and gave them greetings from the young hearts of India. He greeted the Italian land by claiming he was happy he did not feel a stranger here but, on the contrary, he was understood. The poet's word—he said—is the zephyr and you, the young, are the flower in the wind. My day is ending, and I am happy to have lived long enough to bring my voice to the West for the good of humanity. He ended amidst enthusiastic applause by exalting the Italian ancient civilisation, the greatness of Rome, and the influence of the Italian Renaissance on Asian culture, and by celebrating the future of Italy.

Some students offered a University hat to the poet who placed it on his head amidst thunderous applause.

The ceremony ended with tea served in the Rector's hall. Then the poet left the University accompanied by the chancellor and other dignitaries. The crowd, gathered around his car, hailed him warmly.[56]

The same news appeared in *Il Popolo di Roma* (p5c4, 11 June).

On the morning of 12 June Tagore received a group of a hundred students at the hotel who came to collect his autograph on their school cards. After signing the cards the poet said to one of the students who spoke with him in English, 'You made me work hard for half an hour, but I shall keep the memory of this labour with good spirit. Without this small suffering I couldn't have the pleasure of being with you. These cards will remind you of today during your studies.[57]

The afternoon of 12th June was spent in visiting the Roman forts and other places of historical interest. The poet and his party were taken to a health resort on a hilltop near Grottaferrata. The poet was overjoyed looking at the beautiful view; he appreciated the aims and objectives of this new institution, and he and his party wrote words of inspiration in the visitors' book. Following this, the party went to nearby Frascati.[58]

During Tagore's stay in Rome, an arts organization, Ars Italica, produced one of his plays *Chitra*. The director of the play, after prior consultation with the poet, designed the scenery and costumes. On the evening of 12 June, *Chitra* was staged at the Argentine Theatre. At the beginning of the play, Professor Pusnini, on behalf of Ars Italica, invited the special guests to watch the performance. Annibale Ninchi and Elisenda Annovazzi, two leading actors of the time, took part, and, at the end, the poet appeared on the stage. *Chitra* was followed by another play *Edipo Re. Il Popolo di Roma* published a notice of the performance on 11 June and the following review on 13 June:

Tagore's *Chitra* at Argentina

The story of this drama—rather, of this dramatic poem—is very simple. It goes back, if our memory serves, to a well known and ancient Indian legend. There was a hermit warrior Arjuna who had made a vow of chastity for twelve years. There was also the daughter of a king, 'Chitra', who had fallen in love with the famous hero. The king's daughter was the first child and therefore the heir to the throne. Although she belonged to noble stock, by the grace of the Numi (according to the legend) she turned into a rough and brave warrior. She was trained by her august father in the art of running government and war. As a result her pretty feminine charm disappeared. So there was scant possibility of Chitra luring the renowned hermit into her trap. The two benign Numens—Madana, the god of love, and Vasanta, the god of eternal youth, both necessary according to need— were touched by the despair and prayers of the young girl, and so made her a gift for one year of a seductive beauty. This perishable mask succeeds in winning the heart or, more precisely, the senses of Arjun. However, after the first throes of love Chitra became displeased with her deception, thinking that she had played a trick on her hero. She realised that her body and charm were false but not her worthy spirit. She earnestly requested the Numens to take back their gift, as it was not worthy of securing her happiness. She was warned, however, that this would inflict on her beloved a cruel disappointment followed by a cruel forsaking. She stopped the pretence before the year finished. But her destiny was different to that which she feared. Some of her countrymen were screaming in terror as invaders came to devastate the country and they came seeking Chitra, the Princess, to save them from misfortune. This incident made Arjun's soul suddenly anxious to know who the heroic woman wearing male costume was, being both mother and father to her people, possessing the power of arms and tenderness of heart. Now the enchantment was over; Chitra, quivering and freeing herself from her distressing torment, offered herself to the hero. He, this time, gazed fondly at her, and found how real she was and her true soul. He also found her humble and passionate in her devotion.

This plot is pallidly summed up; we must say that in an opera like this the story only serves to render the poet's thought. If we faithfully interpret the drama it represents the glorification of woman as envisaged by Tagore. This is the woman whose charm is not bound by seduction of the flesh but rises into everlasting merits like virtue and sentiment. This is a drama of thought, absolutely poor in action and not at all theatrical, which disdains the technique of the form we commonly understand. This play only renders truth across the few scenes between the main actors.

The audience—a large number—listened to the play and gave a warm ovation for the poet, who assisted the performance.[59]

A short report of the performance was also published in *Il Messaggero* (p5c4).

Tagore's visit to Rome was coming to an end. On his last day, the poet had two very significant meetings: the first one was the farewell meeting with Mussolini, and the other—more dramatic—was with the Italian philosopher Benedetto Croce.

Benedetto Croce (1866–1952)
Source: Biografías y Vidas, http://www.biografiasyvidas.com/
reproducir.htm.

Prior to his departure from Rome on 13 June, the poet, with his usual escort, Formichi, went to bid farewell to Mussolini at the Chigi Palace. According to Formichi, the second meeting with Mussolini was longer and heartier. The transcription of the meeting with Mussolini, prepared by Mahalanobis, was first published in the *Visva-Bharati Quarterly*, although there is apparently no report of the meeting in the Italian press. The following exchange is cited from Mahalanobis's transcription:

TAGORE: Before leaving Rome I wish to thank you and the Italian peo-
            ple for your great hospitality. I have been deeply touched by

the warmth of their feeling, and I shall carry its memory away with me.

I am grateful to you for opening cultural communications between Italy and India; for the chair of Italian which you have established in Santiniketan; for your magnificent gift of books, photographs and albums. I hope this may be followed up by giving an opportunity to Indian scholars and students to come to Italy.

I have felt gratified to hear that the students of Rome are trying to form an association for helping Indian students who may come to Italy. We shall also try to do the same. We must encourage an interchange of scholars between our two countries. This has a great historic significance.

I hope you will help me in my mission, in bringing about a meeting of East and West. The basis of a new civilisation will be laid in such meeting. You in Europe are objective, while we in the East are introspective; the synthesis of these two elements is required for the civilisation of the future.

MUSSOLINI: I admit it. The East has got her spiritual wealth. We require it. Science is not sufficient; without spiritual life we shall not be complete.

TAGORE: Science has power, but it cannot create. It can accumulate vast heaps of materials, multiply an unending succession of things, but that is not creation.

MUSSOLINI: It is true; in reality multiplication is nothing. Look at our multiplicity of electric lamps; they are the same in every room; they have no variety.

TAGORE: This is typical of science. Only life has variety. I believe the present moment offers a great opportunity for a true union of East and West. It will have great significance in history, and I hope we shall succeed in our efforts.

(Mussolini nodded his head. He wanted to know whether the Poet had seen the ancient monuments in Rome.)

TAGORE: Yes, I have seen everything, and I have enjoyed seeing your ancient ruins. But I have also seen youthful Italy and I have great hopes for its future.

In Europe I see a big wilderness of machines and factories: there is power, there is intellect, there are stupendous organisations, but I do not see any vision behind it. Material wealth and power cannot make a country immortal. She must contribute something which is great and which is for everybody, and which does not glorify her own self. Your Excellency! Italy possesses a great personality, and therefore she as a nation is most suited to promote a rapprochement between both the Asian and the European civilisations, and to allow the dream I have cherished and pursued throughout my life to finally come true.

(After a while the poet remarked) Your Excellency, you are the most slandered man in the world.

MUSSOLINI: I know but what can I do? I have to carry out my duties.[60]

The conversation then turned to the possibility of starting a scholarship scheme with the aim of prompting an exchange of students between India and Italy. Mussolini's spiritual aspiration was a revelation! Equally amusing was his comparison of the multiplication of materials with electric lamps. Also, Mussolini's response on the subject of the East–West fellowship during the discussion was minimal.

Tagore visiting Hendrick Anderson's studio, June 1926
Source: Rabindra Bhavan.

This was only a part of the long conversation between Mussolini and the poet. They also discussed other aspects, which we learn from Romain Rolland's journal. The date of Rolland's journal was 24 June 1926 when Mahalanobis and the poet both were in Villeneuve, so presumably Rolland's account was based on his personal conversation with Mahalanobis. Rolland wrote:

During his second interview with Mussolini Tagore brought up the subject of Italian politics. They discussed freedom and autocracy. Mussolini said, 'Often there comes a historic moment when dictatorial administration becomes inevitable for maintaining peace and order, and when freedom has to be kept at bay. But that phase would be temporary.' Although Tagore agreed with Mussolini he emphasised that two things can never be compromised—cruelty and lies. The *Duce* nodded his head.

At the end of the meeting Tagore expressed his intention to meet Benedetto Croce. 'One more big favour is that Your Excellency,' he said, 'shows me the briefest way to meet the great philosopher Benedetto Croce; I would feel ashamed if I left Italy without getting to know the highest thinker in the land whose works are closest to the speculations of Indian philosophers. The latter would never forgive me for going to Italy without meeting Croce.'

With this proposal, Formichi instantly shouted 'Impossible! ... impossible!' Mussolini more calmly said, 'In fact he is not in Rome'. 'Yes', Tagore replied, 'but he is in Italy. And I am ready to go and meet him, wherever he is'. Mussolini again repeated, 'What a pity! No one knows where he is.' But Tagore insisted that nobody in India would understand it if he were to leave Italy without seeing the man who is regarded as the highest embodiment of Italian thinking. In the end Mussolini entrusted Formichi with the task of tracing Croce.[61]

There is another version of this meeting found in Mahalanobis's transcript, which matches the description in Formichi's memoir, and this version seems to be a more plausible account of the dialogue between Tagore and Mussolini. According to Mahalanobis's version, when Tagore enquired about Croce, Formichi instantly cried out—'this is not possible, this is not possible.' Mussolini shut him up, gesturing imperiously, 'Sure,' he said, 'we shall send him a telegram.'[62]

Rolland's description was slightly embellished with a touch of ridicule as if Tagore knew Croce was anti-fascist and wished to provoke the Duce. However, up to that point Tagore had no idea or interest of Croce's political standing. According to Prayer, it was often a favourite pastime in European anti-fascist circles of that period 'to depict Mussolini and his faithful yes-men in grotesque colours', and Rolland's description had been spiced up a little.[63] At the end of the meeting, Tagore asked Mussolini to give him a signed photograph and he immediately obliged. Finally, before they left the Chigi Palace, Mussolini drew the poet's attention to his proposed project of 'The International City'. Tagore was fascinated.

'The International City' was the original idea of the American architect Hendrick Christian Anderson. He had planned an international centre in Rome where the entire legacy of knowledge and culture from all nations of all times was to be preserved. He called this a 'Laboratory of Civilisation'. A team of about 40 architects designed an elaborate plan to build a series of townships such as the Temple of Arts, Conservatory of Music, International Institute of Letters and Science, and Palace of Scientific Research. This township was planned to be built in Austria beside the Tiber, a site where Roman civilization had been initiated a thousand years ago. This township would be more spectacular and unique than St. Peters or even the Coliseum. It would include the world's tallest marble column, 36 metres high, weighing 770 tonnes, on the top of which there would be a bust in the semblance of Mussolini. Tagore was told about this plan because Mussolini had approved this project. Tagore was so impressed by this plan that the same afternoon he went to Anderson's studio to see the blueprint of the project, accompanied by Rathindranath and Signor and Signora Rapicavoli.

This project never materialized. After using 100 tonnes of metal, there was no money left and the project was abandoned.

The meeting between Benedetto Croce and Tagore was rather dramatic. Benedetto Croce was one of the foremost Italian philosophers and historians of his time. He had influenced Italian aesthetics in the early years of the twentieth century. Croce was initially a proponent of fascism, but after 1925, he was disillusioned and had dissociated himself. Mussolini wanted to install him as the education minister in his cabinet. Later, he had selected him as the chief of the Italian Academy, but Croce had turned down both offers.

Mrs Moody, who was the poet's American hostess and friend, had insisted that the poet meet Croce before leaving Italy. The poet wished the same, but was not sure how to go about it. Formichi did not offer any help in this respect and was trying to avoid the issue. Later, Mrs Moody introduced Tagore to Carmelo Rapicavoli, an officer of the Italian Army, who worked in the external affairs department. Although Rapicavoli had little respect for fascism, he had worked in the government out of personal compulsion. When he was approached, he made it quite clear that the meeting was only possible with Mussolini's approval. Finally, when the Duce's permission was accorded, Tagore wished to bypass Formichi for this particular meeting. Rapicavoli flew to Naples and secretly accompanied Croce all the way to the poet's hotel early in the morning after a nightlong train journey while Formichi was still in bed. The poet met Croce secretly behind closed doors in the presence of Rapicavoli and was with him for about an hour. When the meeting was over, Rapicavoli smuggled Croce back to Naples even before breakfast! Formichi expressed his disapproval when he came to know of it at the breakfast table.

Three records of the dialogue between Tagore and Croce are now available. Mahalanobis was present at that meeting and took a note of their conversation. This note was originally published in the Visva-Bharati Bulletin and is quoted below. The second transcription of the conversation now available was noted by Rapicavoli who was present as an interpreter (indicated within square brackets) during the meeting. The third one is by Formichi and is largely based on Mahalanobis's and Rapicavoli's accounts.

TAGORE: I am sorry to have troubled you to come to Rome, but I could not leave Italy without seeing you. I would have been ashamed to have returned to India without meeting you. I did not know you were in Naples, otherwise I would certainly have seen you there.

CROCE: The pleasure is all mine, in having been able to come to see you. You do not know how much I admire your poetry. Not only for its thoughts, but for its sober form—as we Italians call it—its classical form. This is quite different from our ideas of oriental poetry which we usually think of as steeped in fancies.

TAGORE: And I am an admirer of your philosophy and your literary criticism. Your 'Poetry and non-Poetry', which I read in English translation, appeared to me as a very concise and yet full treatment of the subject.

CROCE: My idea of divinity is similar to yours: God is not a being amongst beings, but the Being of Beings.

TAGORE: That is exactly my idea.

CROCE: Not to divide the world into two water-tight compartments: material and spiritual, but to see the working of the spirit in the totality of the two—the idea has found expression in your thoughts in a perfect form.

TAGORE: I believe your Italian mind is synthetic; you see things in their integral aspect.

CROCE: Italian genius is something mid-way between the French and the comprehensive character, which is sometimes apt to become confused, of the German. The Italian mentality seeks to reach profundity, but at the same time demands clarity.

TAGORE: This is a great asset. If this is so, then your country is a fit place for a synthesis of Western Science and Eastern Philosophy. We look at Italy as a country where something new in the field of culture is developing, and we want to grasp it and take it back with us.

CROCE: That is true. During the twenty years before the war, there was a new cultural movement in Italy. The confusion caused by the world war has, to a certain extent, arrested this development. But I think this temporary suspension, rather than damaging it, may have beneficial results. The scattered seeds will bury themselves in the ground and will render good fruit in the future.

TAGORE: Western civilisation, for which we had at one time a great reverence, is showing a tendency to give great reverence to the things that are of the outside world. This is a unilateral development and is causing the loss of a good deal of prestige which it had in the East. The development of elements which have reference to the inner life is also necessary.

CROCE: Yes, it is true, but the external things must not be rejected. They cannot be isolated, they must be permitted by idealism. The most difficult thing is to unite the Oriental and Occidental attitudes of mind: to look upon ideas as facts and upon facts as ideas.

TAGORE: In the Visva-Bharati in India we are trying to form a centre where the greatest minds of this age can come and meet. I would be happy if you would come once and join us.

CROCE: I sincerely hope it will be possible some day. In the meantime let me take the liberty of sending you my works, but at present I do not wish to trouble you any longer.[64]

* * *

[CROCE: Some time ago an Indian Professor, Mr. Das Gupta,[65] the author of a history of Indian philosophy, came to meet me at my residence. It was a real feast for my girls to see him in his Indian costume. He gave a public lecture on the relationship between my theories and Indian philosophical ideas.

TAGORE: I know Dr. Das Gupta. He was very happy to have spoken in Italy at a conference presided over by you. If your girls had seen me in this costume, it would have been once again a feast for them.

Croce: It would be an event they would remember all their lives. Three years ago I received a long letter from another Indian.[66] He mentioned his idea of creating a common language for all India, also with the aim of promoting the making of national unity. He wanted to come to Naples and seek my advice, as he had gone through my works on the philosophy of language.

TAGORE: India is a continent, not a nation like Italy. In India there are various languages which differ in origin, words, grammar and sentence-building. Italy, instead, was able to give herself a unified language through Dante, by raising one of her dialects, Tuscan, to the dignity of a common national language.

CROCE: Therefore, the idea of India's unification amounts to the institution of an artificial language.

TAGORE: Exactly so.

CROCE: Could you tell me something about the University you have
            established, which I find so interesting?

TAGORE: I can do more. I shall send you all that has been written about
            it. There is, however, only one thing you will not find in those
            writings, namely the atmosphere of the University itself.

                                    * * *

TAGORE: Now, is your philosophy the expression of the Italian mental-
            ity, or a particular aspect of your solitary spirit?

CROCE: My philosophy is strictly connected to the traditions estab-
            lished above all in Southern Italy, and originated by Vico and
            Bruno. In some respect, these traditions cannot be separated
            from German philosophy.

TAGORE: Today I have got my share of spiritual food. Could this be
            so every day! Everything cannot be absorbed at once. I shall
            send you my works in exchange, and read yours in English.
            Those I already possess in Italian will be included in the
            Italian section of my University's Library.][67]

It is interesting to note that the subject of Italian politics did
not come up at any stage in their conversation. The news of the
meeting between Croce and Tagore or their dialogue was not published in any Italian paper. The poet later wrote to Duke Scotti
about the interview:

With some difficulty I secured a glimpse of your great philosopher Croce,
for my delight is in meeting the heroes of the free mind. When we come to
Europe it is to have the inspiration of the liberty of thought and of creative
spirit and not to be bewildered by the spirit of the athletic vigour of your
efficiency, which you have newly borrowed from America, the continent
which seems to believe that growing fat is to be growing great and is therefore suspicious of idealism and the free expression of truth.[68]

Before leaving Rome, the poet said in an interview with an
American journalist:

I am not really competent to judge what the Italians think and wish. I
hope they will realise that the mere pursuit of material wealth will

never make them great. They will be a great world power only when they give the world permanent gifts of the spirit. Otherwise national prosperity and political power die with them. These are consumed in the process of enjoyment: but products of the spirit are for all time and for all countries.[69]

Florence

On 14 June, Tagore and his team left Rome for Florence by train. Gourgopal Ghosh and Premchand Lal were not part of the entourage on this occasion. Ghosh had joined the International Institute of Agriculture for a training course on cooperative agricultural production—a training that he could apply in Sriniketan. Lal left Rome for another destination. The poet and his retinue reached Florence railway station at 11 pm. Mayor Senator Garbasso, the rector of the university, Dr Burci, another renowned Indologist and Sanskrit scholar Pavolini, and some other distinguished people were at the station to welcome the poet. As a guest of the Municipal Board of the city, they were lodged at the Grand Hotel. On 16 June, *La Tribuna* published a short report on Tagore's visit.

Tagore and Florence

Florence, 15th—Yesterday at 11 o'clock at night the Indian poet Tagore arrived in our city. He was received at the station by the Mayor Senator Garbasso, Prefect Regard, Rector of the University Professor Burci, Professor Pavolini and others. Then the Mayor and Prefect escorted him to the Grand Hotel by car where he had been lodged. During the week the famous Indian poet will give a lecture in the Grand Hall of the University.[70]

On 15 June, the poet and his team were taken on a tour to Fiesole, a nearby village. Many important citizens including Cardelli, the mayor, were present to welcome him. 'Now I realise why Fiesole has always attracted the poets,'[71] Tagore remarked, seeing the landscape of the countryside.

In the meantime, on 16 June, *Gazzetta del Popolo* published a final programme for the remaining days in Italy.

Tagore's Lecture

The programme for the forthcoming visit by Tagore was finalised yesterday evening at the meeting held at 'Pro Cultura Femminile' (Association For Women's Culture) where artistic and literary celebrities and representatives of the local press would participate. The Honorary Director of Pro Cultura Femminile Association Dr. Lisetta Motta Ciaccio, the President Dr. Lea Mei, and most of the members of the Association Council were present. Also present were Professor Bertoni, who represented the Rector of the University, the Honourable Professor Cian, Professors Pastore, Pivano, Vidari, Vezzani, Domenico Lanza, and Commodore Laudi, who represented the Education Deputy Officer, Professor Collino and many other distinguished people.

Dr. Mei confirmed that Rabindranath Tagore would arrive in Turin on Thursday or Friday. On his first day he will visit the city and its picturesque surroundings. On Saturday, after a visit to the Casa del Sole, there will be a reception arranged by Pro Cultura Femminile at its premises at 3 Mercantini Street. On Sunday, the Indian poet will deliver a lecture on 'City and the Village' in the hall of the Conservatory at 5.00 pm. Professor Formichi will precede the lecture with a detailed presentation. This will be followed by a musical concert, the programme for which has not yet been finalised.

The interest in Tagore's arrival and the anticipation of his lecture, which will be a hymn to simple life and the countryside, is growing keener and keener. The Pro Cultura Femminile Association is receiving many booking requests but, as everyone should know, the number of seats is very limited.[72]

The next day, the poet was received by the Leonardo da Vinci Society. The hall was filled with the distinguished members of the Society. Welcoming the guest, the president of the society, Marchese Corsini, said:

You do not come to us as a stranger, for your great fame has preceded you and we know you through your writings. We offer our greetings in this old city of Florence in the name of our Society. This name—Leonardo da Vinci—stands for whatever is great in art and creative impulse in Italy and therefore in the whole world, and in association with this name we greet you. We welcome you as a Master, what you call in your language Gurudeva, of our Society. You represent the unity of life in the midst of a diversity of activities, and we feel proud at having you in our midst today.

In reply Tagore said:

I wish I had not been preceded by my fame. I could then come closer to you, like the English poets, Browning, Shelley, Keats and Byron. I ought to have come when I was younger and was less known, without my burden of fame. Until my 50th year I lived in comparative obscurity. I had my solitude on the banks of the rivers of Bengal, on the wide stretches of the Ganges, in the nooks and crannies of our quiet villages. I had no desire for fame. I find it a burden, yet it gives me the opportunity of meeting you and making friends with you. I feel honoured by your greetings. I feel glad, for through me you have also honoured my motherland.[73]

On 16 June, Tagore was presented with an elegantly bound volume of Dante's *Divina Commedia* (Divine Comedy) in a special ceremony held at the Grand Hotel organized by the Fascist Association of Florence. *La Stampa* reported a brief news of the ceremony in its 17 June issue (p9c2).

Tagore addressed a full auditorium in the Great Hall of the Royal University on 17 June. Artists and intellectuals of the town were present. More than 100 students of the different university departments along with the representatives of the American and British communities in Florence were also there. The cadets of the Milittzia Volantaria lined up on the steps to form a guard of honour, and a little before 5 pm, the poet entered the auditorium and was received by the rector of the university, Dr Burci. The audience welcomed Tagore with thunderous applause: the poet accepted the honour with folded hands and took his seat on the stage. Dr Burci and professors Gatti, Pavolini, and Pelezzari shared the stage with the poet. Throughout the programme, two students in army uniform stood on the two sides of the stage as standard-bearers.

Burci introduced Tagore to the audience as the best friend of Italy and so, he said, Florence is welcoming the poet as the friend of Italy. Pavolini said:

In Europe we know very little of his works, we know him only as a writer, and even that only through a few books. Yet this little is sufficient to make us admire him and love him. Today he comes in a new role, as a man of action, who has introduced great reforms in Bengal, one of which, perhaps the most important one, being in the sphere of education. He comes to us today as a great educationalist, and we shall all hear with interest and respect what he has to tell us about education.[74]

Tagore made an address in English about his Santiniketan school, which was translated into Italian for the audience by Pavolini. Again, this lecture 'My School' is incorporated in Das's compilation of Tagore's works—*The English Writings of Rabindranath Tagore*—and, therefore, excluded here.

Il Nuovo Giornale, a Florentine paper, published the following report on 18 June. Surprisingly, we find in this piece the actual review of the poet's speech minimized into a single sentence, while the rest of the report is devoted to the addresses of the distinguished fascist personalities sharing the platform with Tagore—a representative feature of fascist journalism.

The great event of the artistic world, the long-expected lecture of the Indian poet Rabindranath Tagore, came off yesterday in the Great Hall of the University. From 4 o'clock the Great Hall overflowed with the elite, among whom figured the greatest names in science, art, literature, and the aristocracy—both Florentine and foreign. A large number of students from all the faculties, and a large number of representatives of the English and American communities in Florence were also present.

Along the staircase of the University and the Great Hall the student soldiers of the University's Militzia Volontaria (Volunteer Corps) were drawn up as a Guard of Honour under the orders of Commander Professor De Vecchi, the Centurion Ricardi and the Decano Pavolini.

A few minutes after five, greeted by a warm ovation, the poet Rabindranath Tagore reached the University with the other members of his party dressed in their own characteristic Indian costume. The poet was received by the Rettore Magnificio (Vice-Chancellor) Professor Burci, the authorities of the University and the academic body. When they entered the hall the poet was received with the liveliest applause which lasted several minutes. Rabindranath Tagore acknowledged the imposing demonstration with a salute of his hands (*namaskara* in the Indian style) and took his seat on the platform together with the Rettore Magnificio and Professors Gatti, Pavolini and Pellizzari.

On the platform and around the hall the soldiers of the university students corps stood on guard; two standard bearers stood on the platform holding two large standards.

The Rettore Magnificio Professor Dr. Burci welcomed the poet on behalf of the University in a short speech in Italian. He said that they all knew that the poet was a great friend of Italy, and he was proud to welcome the poet to Florence as a friend of Italy.

Professor Pavolini, the University's Professor of Sanskrit, then spoke in Italian, and told the audience about the wide sphere of the poet's activities. 'In Europe we know very little of his works, we know him only as a writer, and even that only through a few books. Yet this little is sufficient to make us admire him and love him. Today he comes in a new role, as a man of action, who has introduced great reforms in Bengal, one of which, perhaps the most important one, being in the sphere of education. He comes to us today as a great educationalist, and we shall all hear with interest and respect what he has to tell us about education.

Professor Pavolini then gave a short summary in Italian of the poet's lecture, saying that 'he would now change the gold of the poet's words into the flimsy paper of poor resumé.'

The audience heard the lecture with great attention and hailed him with warm cheers at the end of the lecture.[75]

In Florence, Tagore went to visit the famous galleries such as Palazzo Vecchio, the Uffizi, and Palazzo Pitti, where he witnessed the richness of Florentine art. The entourage spent three nights in Florence. On the eve of their departure from Florence, Pavolini offered the poet a Sanskrit quatrain composed by himself in honour of his farewell:

Pushpapuramiti khyatam
Shrutva vakyakamritam guroh
Eshyatyabhinabham Sangam
Phalapuranatahparam.

[The city of flowers as it is known before, will henceforth be known as City of Fruits having heard the words of *amrita* from the Guru.][76]

While in Florence, the poet had given an interview to a reporter, Aldo Sorani. In which Italian paper the interview was published is not known. In Britain, *The Observer* published the English version of the interview on 27 June 1926. Excerpts from the interview are quoted below:

A Message for Europe.
Talk with Rabindranath Tagore.
The Malady of Unrest.
East and West.
(By Aldo Sorani)

Rabindranath Tagore has paid his second visit to Italy, this time in response to Mussolini's personal invitation, and Mussolini welcomed him in Rome with all the honours. The poet was much feted not only in Rome, but also at Florence and at Turin, where great crowds came to hear his public lectures on 'The meaning of Art' and on his 'School', lectures he will repeat in London. In the meantime he proposes to make a sojourn in Switzerland and Austria, and also to consult some specialists about the heart trouble which impairs his health at present.

In Florence I was privileged to have quite a long talk with the poet. We met in the sunny sitting-room of his hotel that dominates the Lung' Arno, and the poet talked with me in a low and sweet but rather tired voice; sunk in a deep armchair, caressing in his hands an English translation of the last novel by Selma Lagerlof.

'Italy appears to me ever more beautiful', he said, 'and Florence fairest among Italian cities. But I would have preferred to come to Italy not laden with years and fame, but in a neophyte's pilgrimage, even as Shelley and Keats came. Youth would have appreciated better still the message Italian poetry conveys. Yet, neither celebrity nor old age are of my making or fault!'

The Burden of Fame

Tagore returned to the burden of his world celebrity. 'I am not made to run about the world and to be pointed out to the crowd, especially the European crowd. My life and its message are interior; all true life is interior. The multitude gather to behold the poet, to hear the poet, yet, having seen and heard him, it does not know him, for the poet remains concealed, and the louder the clamour and the larger the multitude, the more deeply will the poet withdraw himself within the shelter of his soul and rest unknowable. But how can I now rid myself of the burden of renown?'

I asked him, pointing in the novel by Selma Lagerlof, if he read many European tutors, and he replied that he read many of the English, like all the pupils of his School, who devour English books with ardour. Nordic literature makes the strongest appeal to him, and especially the Russian; above all, Dostoievski, Tolstoi, Turgheniev, and also Gorki.

The Inner Discord

Almost inevitably our conversation touched upon the relations between East and West, the two civilisations.

'I always think', said Tagore, 'that the two civilisations can and should remain distinct, and, at the same time, complete and harmonise each other. In Asia we are already too much apart and divided into countries, races, and cults of diverse origin. You in Europe, despite many divisions and many struggles, have succeeded, after long efforts, in attaining to a unity of culture, and this unity has an element of the miraculous, especially in the field of the organisation and co-ordination of scientific knowledge, and hence has a supreme importance.'

'But does it not seem to you that the world war has interrupted and menaced even this cultural unity?'

'Maybe, but not for ever. You are today more crude, more wilful, more exacting, and, even after the war, more aggressive and at variance. Yet the greater danger for you would lie in the acquired habit of belief in discord as an ineluctable and fatal law of life, and, above all, in believing necessary and beautiful the interior discord, that is to say, the warring of man's soul with itself. There are people today who hold that true life lies precisely in the continual contradiction with themselves, this intimate fight of ideas, sentiments, passions. It is a dangerous error. The ideal life consists not in a state of perpetual contradiction with ourselves and with others, for life should achieve harmony within us; it should radiate peace and union.'

Riches and Freedom

'It is true, however, that the catastrophe of the war suffices to explain this restlessness within and without, which nevertheless cannot endure for ever. The day will come when it will be borne in upon you that the desire for exterior benefits and their accumulations is useless and dangerous, and you will feel the need of a true peace and to put order in your houses and in your souls.

'You will then recognise that much you held as goods is not so in reality, but are the rubbish of centuries, and then you will set yourselves to sweep away the dross that today hampers and oppresses you. Then, indeed, you will possess, both within and without, a new land of promise whereon to build, wherein to sow the seed of coming harvests, and you will reach a higher plane of civilisation and neighbourly life with others and with yourselves.'

'Do you share the belief of some others that assistance for this necessary word of clearance and rebuilding could profitably come to us from America?'

'No: America is too far away, too much a prey also to the same ills that agitate Europe, too preoccupied with this world's goods, and too rich. One could quote to her the words of Christ: "It is easier for a camel to pass through the eye of a needle than for a rich man to enter the kingdom of Heaven". For America to prove of aid and inspiration to Europe, it would behove her also to have gone through the deep waters of calamity. Moreover, America is not free. We in India are, it is true, under a foreign domination, but we are freer men by far than Americans—spiritually freer.'[77]

Turin

Turin was the poet's last stop before leaving Italy.

On 18 June, Tagore and his party arrived in Turin by train. Earlier, Duke Scotti had met him for a brief moment at the Milan station. The duke appeared rather nervous during his conversation with the poet and secretly told him, 'There's hardly time for a detailed conversation. Please don't be impressed by what you have seen as an outsider. The condition of Italy is really bad [...] no one is free here!'[78] Tagore often heard his companions discussing the dismal political condition of Italy. But this was the first time he heard something from a direct, dependable, and discrete source.

Unlike most other cities and towns of Italy, Turin was primarily an industrial town. It housed the famous industrial complexes such as Olivetti and Fiat. The communist party and the socialist parties of Turin were very active. The poet's party reached Turin around midnight when the members of Società Pro Coltura Femminile received them. They were checked in at the Hotel Europa. The news of the poet's arrival and a provisional itinerary were published in *La Stampa* on 17 June (p6c3), and *Gazzetta del Popolo* on 17 (p6c3) and 18 June (p7c3).

To encourage the cultural activities of working women, Signor Motta had established Società Pro Coltura Femminile in 1911. In its tenth year, in 1921, the society planned to open a school in Calabria. Within a few months, the school was opened under the leadership of its president, Dr Lea Mey. In 1926, its new building was completed on the main avenue of the town, Via Mercantini. On 19 June, Tagore was invited to inaugurate the building: As usual, the most important people of the society, including artists, litterateurs, and industrialists were present at that meeting. After the poet and Formichi took their seats on the stage, the president of the society, Dr Mey, welcomed the poet, presenting him with a leather-bound album containing her illuminating address in English (reproduced here) which was read by Amelia Alan Civita after Tagore had finished his speech. Tagore said:

My hostess—in India we have a special ceremony, *varana*, performed by the ladies of the household in receiving or bidding farewell to a welcome guest. According to Indian ideas a farewell is not complete until the ceremony has been performed. On the eve of my departure from this beautiful country I feel that your reception today is a kind of *varana* performed by the daughters of Italy. This has great significance for me, I realise that I have been taken into the heart of the country, for that is what women truly represent. You have accepted me as your own poet, and you have shown your willingness to share the friendship of a poet with the women of his own country. This is a cause of rejoicing to me, for it proves the right of a poet to own all the countries of the world. I take my leave from Turin and I take away with me the remembrance of all the beautiful towns I have visited; I have imprinted in the heart of the women of Italy my great love for their country.[79]

Amelia Alan Civita then read the content of the welcome address transcribed in the album, a summary of which is given here.

Sir—It is with a sense of real exultation that we welcome you here among us at the new seat of our Society. We consider your visit not only as a great honour done to us, but as an encouragement, as a good omen for the success of our work […].

There is a great affinity between your aim and ours, that is why our welcome is so warm and sincere, why your books are so popular and so much appreciated, and your heroines so familiar to us.

The Society is not a literary academy for lady scholars; its chief ambition is to encourage women in their love of a simple mode of life, to prepare them for the sweet yet hard tasks that await them, to make them sensitive to currents of world-thought, and to help them to [be] judge of life in accordance with a high and serene standard of values […].

You have done that on a much larger scale. Still wide and small paths lead to the same goal.

But you have a peculiar and greater claim to our gratitude. It is your delicate understanding of women's heart, your way of entering into its deep mysteries, your appreciation of her humble virtues and the discovery in them of an inexhaustible source of poetry. This is why we tenderly love your Chitra and Beotrae [Binodini?], sweet Mashi and passionate Bimala, and the sensitiveness of their souls finds a deep echo in our own […].

May you continue to lead us with your knowledge and wisdom to those regions where only love and purity reign; may the applause of the Italian people follow you in that wonderful country of yours, which has for us all the charms of a dream.[80]

The poet was so touched by the reception that he stood again to say a few words.

I am deeply touched by what you have said about my love for the Eternal Woman and the Eternal Child. It comes as a surprise to me how truly you have grasped my own feelings. In our country it is said that God manifests himself in Woman, that His creative activity finds true expression in the nature and form of the eternal woman. If I have gained success in singing the praises of this aspect of God which is the eternal feminine, I have ample recompensation in the praises which I have received to-day from you.[81]

After the felicitation, the poet was handed over the album. The felicitation was followed by Adelina Mazzoni's songs, with piano accompaniment by Michelle Losogna.

On 20 June, Tagore, accompanied by Signore Agosti Dina of the Società Pro Coltura Femminile, paid a visit to the Casa del Sole (House of the Sun), a school for orphans.

In the afternoon, Tagore gave a lecture on 'City and the Village' at the Liceo Musicale. The lecture is omitted here as it is included in Das's compilation. Tagore first delivered this lecture while travelling in China (22 May 1924).

Duke and Duchess Galeratti Scotti were present at the lecture in Turin. Later, they went to the Hotel Europa to meet the poet. They met after a gap of 17 months. In that apparently guarded environment, the earlier warmth was missing, although later Scotti wrote to Salvemini:

We did not contact him while he was in Rome surrounded by a world that abides by Mussolini. We intended to express our disapproval by our silence. At Turin, he wanted to see us. We attended the lecture and spent an hour with him at the Europa Hotel which was as sublime and interesting as usual. He did not hide that during this second trip to Italy he was surrounded by an atmosphere and people which was so different that he felt very uncomfortable. He felt he could not establish a spiritual connection; of course I did not hide our feelings from Tagore, but it did not seem correct to express our detachment and severe criticism of this great old man, who appeared to us as if he was humiliated by the unsuccessful visit to fascist Italy.[82]

During this meeting, Italian politics was not touched upon as Scotti had indicated to Tagore to avoid the matter.

The extract of Tagore's lecture at the Liceo Musicale was reported in *La Stampa* on 21 June 1926:

Tagore in Turin
Lecture and Concert at the Lyceum

Yesterday, on the occasion of the announced lecture of Rabindranath Tagore, the beautiful auditorium of the Musical Lyceum was crowded with an elegant audience. Among others, there were the highest authorities and the most representative personalities in Turin: the prefect Cav. di Gran Croce D'Aamo, the City Chief Officer Gen. Etna, the Senator Professor Loria, Professor Bertoni, Professor Vidare, Professor Pastore, Professor Faggi, Hon. Olivetti, lawyer Bandanzellu and the working unit of the Society 'Pro Cultura Femminile' that arranged the gathering. Furthermore many scholars, journalists, poets, artists and ladies attended the lecture.

The thoughtful and solemn Indian poet was greeted at his entrance in the auditorium with long applause. He was followed by his son and daughter-in-law, the Maharaja of Tippura [sic]—Holder of East Bengal—his secretary Professor Mahalanobis and his wife and Professor Formichi of the University of Rome. When Tagore took his place, the audience was told by the Italian scholar that first of all, the poet wished to present his friendly salutation to the noble citizenship of Turin.

'Last year,' said Professor Formichi, 'Tagore was most regretfully forced to decline the invitation to be the guest of Turin but he distinctly recalls the display of warm admiration he received by some "Pro Cultura Femminile" associates who brought him fervid greetings from Turin. Now, for the second time, the poet considers himself as your guest and is delighted to be a friend as well. Neither the bright grandeur of Rome nor the incommensurable artistic beauty of Florence could decrease the feelings of love, gratitude and admiration he feels for Turin.'

Professor Formichi gave an outline of the poet's lecture, City and the Village, in order to make it easier for the audience. There was another burst of applause for Rabindranath Tagore when he was about to commence his lecture. After addressing a warm greeting to the auditorium and to the city of Turin, the poet started to read his lecture in English.

In our modern society—he said—the standard of living is much more than adequate for the simple necessities of existence. When luxurious temptations are widespread, a society could face the great danger of dissipation. Property is a deep-rooted concept in human nature, therefore it is vain to make any effort to eradicate it. Material possession is not only money and furniture, or for a mere acquiring of power but has to be intended as an object display of our taste and imagination, and the proof of our creativity and self-denial. Property is therefore an expression of our personality. When life-style is basic, wealth is not exclusive. On the other hand, if excessive mania for luxury is in the ascendency then property becomes egoistic, generating envy, fomenting class-hates and developing anti-social tendencies.

Tagore carried on his speech pointing out that being unable to face one's neighbours' opulence is nowadays felt shameful. As a matter of fact, society itself—that is supposed to be collaborative—became fertile soil for hard competition. This universal greed is the real origin of the mischief, cruelty and lies that infest policy, trade and the whole atmosphere of modern life. The most evident proof of such a situation is the impressive wealth of our cities despite the physical and moral weakness of our villages. Villages are just like women: in their conservation is the future of mankind.

As women, the role of a village is to provide people with food, bliss and even to make noticeable the poetry of life. To the contrary, when immoderate greed and ambition impose on villages a continuous and weakening effect, the city has no longer to be considered a consort but the village a slave. Modern civilisation needs big cities in the same way the human body has vital organs such as brain, heart and stomach. These organs will never overcome physical harmony, but they will cooperate in promoting and preserving the whole organism whilst maintaining their own features. In this sense, our modern cities seem to be many tumours with congested blood that suck out the vital lymph of the villages.

As a conclusion to his fascinating speech, the poet supposed that the Moon was inhabited long before the Earth (who knows?) and Life was prosperous and happy till the moment when a new human race with a solid intelligence was born there. Those men, fully dedicated to luxury and intolerant of any moral law, cut down all the trees, drew water from the springs and made the surface of the planet a desert in order to satisfy their own desire. In the end, they killed each other for supremacy over the planet. According to Tagore, something like that is now happening on the Earth. Our planet is actually producing what its sons do really need, but it cannot satisfy the greed of such vicious people who hardly recognise what real happiness is, 'the only one that is kept within the borders of the dominion above us.'

Long unanimous applause saluted the end of the moral and poetical speech. Then Madame Matilda Lipovetzka, accompanied by violinist Mr. Giaccone and timpanist Mr. Mena, started to sing with her delicate and melodious voice some of Tagore's own compositions namely one 'Qliquore divino, o mio Dio' (*Hey more Devata*)—a passionate song; 'Ti conosco bene dolce straniera' (*Ami chini go chini tomare*)—a melody of joy; and, 'Se nessuno risponda' (*Jodi tor dak shune*)—a popular melody. Furthermore Mr. Giaccone and Mr. Mena continued playing Tagore's 'Intermezzo per archi'. The audience displayed through much spontaneous applause a sincere enthusiasm for those kinds of melody that were brilliantly interpreted both musically and vocally by a splendid Madame Lipovetzka.

Acclaimed and applauded, Rabindranath Tagore warmly thanked the interpreters of his music for a truly outstanding interpretation and then read two lyrics in the Indian language in order for the audience to perceive the verbal melody naturally belonging to the Bengali idiom in which they were conceived.

This morning Rabindranath Tagore visited the 'Gaspare Gozzi' School and in the afternoon he will be solemnly received in the University at four o'clock. Most probably the poet will know of the Duchess d'Aosta, who—as a fervid lover of his poetry—let him know she hopes for a meeting.[83]

Gazzetta del Popolo published an interview with Tagore on 21 June 1926.

Tagore in Liceo Musicale

Rabindranath Tagore: a solemn and austere prophetical figure with long white hair down to the shoulders and a majestic beard. Tall and upright in posture, the poet discloses that his age, almost sixty-six, and the huge amount of his works does not drain his energies. On the contrary, his physical vigour is in contrast to the infinite sweetness of his look and the calm and melodious tone of his voice. His shape of the body is that kind of figure you cannot forget and it seems perfectly fitted to embody the poet's spiritual personality.

Yesterday, when I was kindly received into his beautiful hall at the Hotel Europa, Tagore was dressed from the chin to the feet in a loose hazel tunic with wide monastic sleeves. The same kind of garment that reminds one of the 'crocea stola' that was said to be worn by his great and far-off precursor: Sakya Muni, the Buddha.

It is quite unusual to have a conversation with such a high and solemn personality but Tagore's faint and harmonious voice encouraged me while a kind smile shone as a vivid light on his magnificent and spiritual face. His complexion is lighter than his retinue's and the widespread paleness of his face does resemble a sort of diaphanous alabaster concealing an eternal blaze.

Italian Culture in India

The poet showed himself to be overwhelmed with joy about his travel in Italy. I was told that our country deeply touched his heart with strong impressions and even the welcome was capable of arousing deep emotions. He promised to spread through Asia the culture and history of our country and to testify to the will of renewal that is nowadays moving the Italian people. Tagore is persuaded that Italy, because of its geographical position, is the most suitable country to permit a new approach between East and West. Such a mission rightly belongs to Italy because of its history and its role as a civilising country both in the Middle Ages and in the Renaissance.

Professor Carlo Formichi, learned and genial scholar of the Department of Eastern Studies in the University of Rome, has been recently sent to India by the Government as an ambassador of Italian culture. On his way back, after a long journey with Tagore through many Italian cities, he gave me examples of the poet's thinking and explained that the cultural relationship between India and Italy has already commenced. Under an initiative of the Foreign Office, Italy has sponsored some scholarships for those young Indians who wish to study in our country, and Italian naval companies have promised to offer transportation facilities. Tagore himself asked some Indian maharajas for financial aid in order to support Italian scholars during their cultural missions to India, which is one of the most interesting countries for archaeological studies and research in religion, philosophy, science and, particularly, medicine.

The poet believes that an intense reciprocal knowledge is conducive to an intense reciprocal love. He is persuaded that the more you increase in spirituality, the more you reject and forget every inner conflict. Above us, only brotherhood.

For several years, Tagore has been used to inviting reputed European scholars to attend Sanskrit classes. The most worthy Professors Formichi and Tucci were recently asked to represent Italy in the country that was the cradle of Western cultures. Moreover, Mussolini himself gave an entire library of Italian books to Professor Formichi, who shipped it to India to spread our culture and, most of all, to initiate a course in the Italian Language and Literature at the University of Calcutta.

'With these boxes of books—Prof. Formichi told us, displaying satisfaction—Italy began to be known in Asia. Indeed, our nation made a very good impression because no other countries in the world can boast such men as Dante, Galileo and Leonardo, among others.'

Visiting the King and Mussolini

To express his gratitude toward our Government, Tagore came back to Italy where Mussolini expressed his willingness to have him as a guest.

The Indian poet was received by Mussolini and the figure of the Italian Prime Minister deeply touched Tagore. As an Indian, he believes that the world runs because of men, not machinery. From age to age, it is necessary that extraordinary men come to push and stimulate people and countries. Therefore the progressive leap being applied by the Italian people seems to Tagore a certain guarantee for a glorious future.

King Vittorio Emanuele [*sic*] gave an audience to Tagore and stayed with him for nearly an hour. Tagore showed himself enthusiastic about the Italian King's education and knowledge about Asia. Furthermore, the King was said to be fluent in English and to speak with a perfect accent and elegance. The poet noticed that his own peculiar appearance and old-fashioned face were attracting the King and so he took off his dark spectacles in order to reveal his face. He reminded us of that moment in which the King smiled because of that kind and jocund gesture.

According to the Indian philosopher, one of the most interesting places in Rome is the Appian Way. He noticed a close relationship between Latin and the Indian world: as a matter of fact, in India the dead are not set apart, on the contrary they keep on staying among the living. He was moved by the students' parade that took place at the Colosseum. Tagore loves children and when he is amidst them he feels younger, despite his weakness.

The Italian city that most of all overwhelmed Tagore with joy was Florence. Having carefully studied English poets like Shelley, Byron and Browning, he declared now to be able to understand why those artists extolled Florence to such an extent. In its atmosphere, the city was said by the poet to be intimately aristocratic, certainly because of its artistry displayed in temples and museums. Coming out of the Louvre in Paris, the passers-by are projected into a modern city that resembles any other one. On the contrary, Florence is different: its own shape and the distinct surroundings do not oppose the poetry generated by the place.[84]

There is some ambiguity in the poet's visit to the Gaspare Gozzi school. According to the report in *La Stampa*, he visited the school on the morning of the 21st, but actually he failed to visit the school due to a mild indisposition. However, the party went to see the Fiat automobile factory and a chocolate factory in the afternoon. In the late afternoon, a reception was arranged for Tagore by the university's Academic Council. The report of the reception was published in *Gazzetta del Popolo* on 22 June 1926.

Tagore at University
The Poet Leaves Today for Switzerland

Yesterday afternoon Rabindranath Tagore, accepting an invitation by University Council, went to a party in his honour at University of Turin.

The ceremony was not open to the public and took place at the University's Council Hall in the Department of Humanities. To welcome the poet were Professor Bertoni representing the chancellor, the professors of several faculties: Senetor Brondi, Honourable Cian, Pastore, Olivero, Paletta, Chisow, Vidari, Peano, Faggi, Tedeschi, Giglio-Tos, Rinaudo, Romano; the librarian Professor Torri, the local director of education Comm. Renda, the director of the University Secretariate Comm. Gorrini. There were also present the representative members of the University Fascist group.

Accompanied by Professor Formichi when Rabindranath Tagore entered the hall, the waiting crowd of students applauded. With the poet were his son, the Maharaja of Bengal, his secretary and his wife, who wore Indian dress. Tagore, who was wearing a blue tunic and no hat, greeted the audience by folding his hands in a gesture of prayer.

Professor Bertoni, on behalf of the Chancellor, teachers and the students welcomed the poet in English, saying that the poet brought the message of poetry and love to this seat of learning. He also mentioned that his books, which revealed the Oriental soul to the West, are highly admired in Italy.

Tagore, in his gentle and mellifluous voice, then spoke to the students, and was translated into our language by Professor Formichi. 'I am very much ashamed,' the poet said, 'that my debility in health prevents me from expressing the sentiments and gratitude to you in the way I would like to express them.'

'I must confess,' the poet said in smiling, 'I am always afraid of a University because I have never attended one, as I was almost a dissolute.'

Tagore's frank confession of his aversion to school was received by the youth with ardent approbation, especially because at the time they were preparing for their exams.

'More than ever,' the famous poet said, 'I am grateful when Universities greet me. If I could get the time and opportunities to come into contact with the professors and students I would do so because that is the time when I feel in touch with their souls. I am always a student like you, young like you, and may be younger than some of you. Students are not belonging to any particular country and a poet is like a bird which transmigrates from land to land when the poet and the students meet to understand each other.[']

Addressing the students the poet concluded, 'I am feeling at home when I see your faces and hearts are radiant with youthfulness.'

At the end of his cordial speech a great tribute was paid to the poet. He stopped to have conversations with some of the professors. Tagore told Professor Olivero, professor of English literature at our University, that he was glad to see that his works have also diffused into our country which he loves. To the question of how he translated his works from Bengali to English while keeping the harmony, he said that it came spontaneously to him at a time when the doctor had forbidden him to perform any intellectual work. During that period of rest he thought again of translating into English those works that his heart had expressed in his native language.

After his visit to the University, Rabindranath Tagore went to the Cisterna Palace to be received by the Duchess d'Aosta at her request.

Yesterday morning (Monday) the poet was supposed to visit the children of the Gasper Gozzi primary school to listen to the concert conducted by the genius conductor P. Vanet. But the sudden indisposition of the poet caused great disappointment to the children who did not have the pleasure of meeting him.

In the afternoon when he felt better he again went to the University to meet the principal, Bertoni, the professors of several faculties, and a group of students who received him with an enthusiastic ovation. The students enjoyed the witty conversation of Rabindranath Tagore.

Local factories also joined in honouring the great Indian poet and his group: 'Fiat' and 'Unica' offered visits to their large factories. These were appreciated considerably by the Prince of Tripura, the poet's son and his wife, and by Professor Mahalanobis and his wife.

Today at midday the poet is leaving for Switzerland where he will rest for a short time. Then he will go to Vienna to consult a famous physician about his health.[85]

After his farewell to the university, the poet went to visit the Duke and Duchess d'Aosta at the Sisterna Palace. A brief report of this visit was published in the 22 June issue of *Il Regime Fascista* (p6c6).

On 22 June, Tagore and his party left for Switzerland. Formichi escorted the party up to the Swiss border, Domodossola. Before leaving Italy, Tagore sent the following message to Mussolini through Formichi: 'I take leave with hearty thanks to Your Excellency, and to the Italian people represented by Your Excellency, for your generous hospitality and kind sentiments towards me—Rabindranath Tagore.'[86]

With that note, Rabindranath Tagore left Italy, never to set foot there again!

Notes and References

1. Carlo Formichi, 'On Tagore', tr. Mario Prayer, *Rabindra-Viksha*, vol. 39 (2001), p. 46.

2. Ibid.

3. Ibid., p. 48.

4. Ibid. The date of the letter is not mentioned.

5. Ibid., p. 50.

6. Krishna Dutta and Andrew Robinson (eds), 'The Tagore–Elmhirst Correspondence', *Purabi: A Miscellany in Memory of Rabindranath Tagore, 1941–1991*, Letter no. 28 (London: The Tagore Centre UK, 1991), p. 89.

7. Prasanta Kumar Paul (tr.), *Rabijibani*, vol. 9 (Kolkata: Ananda Publishers, 2003), p. 244.

8. Mario Prayer, '*Carlo Formichi: India e Indiani*', *Rabindra-Viksha*, vol. 40 (2001), p. 18; translated from Carlo Formichi, *India e Indiani* (Milan: Edizioni Alpes, 1929).

9. Ibid., p. 19.

10. Somendranath Bose (ed.), *Samayikpatre Rabindra Prasanga—Prabasi 1308–1348* (Kolkata: Tagore Research Institute, 1976), p. 85.

11. Kalidas Nag, 'The Visvabharati and Prof. Carlo Formichi', *The Modern Review* (December 1925), pp. 710–12.

12. Prabhat Kumar Mukhopadhyay, *Rabindra Jibani o Rabindra Sahitya Prabeshak*, vol. 3 (Calcutta: Visva-Bharati, 1952), p. 277.

13. See section titled 'Notes' in N.G., 'Rabindranath Tagore Visits Italy', *The Modern Review* (September 1926), p. 338.

14. Dutta and Robinson, 'The Tagore–Elmhirst Correspondence', Letter no. 45, p. 97.

15. Nirmal Kumari Mahalanobis, *Kobir sange Europey* (Kolkata: Mitra and Ghosh, 1969), p. 8.

16. Prayer, 'Carlo Formichi', p. 22.

17. The University of Dacca invited the poet and the two Italian professors on a lecturing assignment. Along with Formichi and Tucci, Tagore reached Dacca on 7 February 1926. Formichi spoke about Dwijendranath (who had died earlier) in an assembly. The poet became overexhausted due to continuous lectures and travelling in Dacca for one month.

18. Formichi File.

19. 'Farewell Address to Prof. Carlo Formichi', Visva-Bharati Bulletin, *Visva-Bharati Quarterly* (April 1926), pp. 91–3.

20. 'Prof. Formichi's Parting Address', Visva-Bharati Bulletin, *Visva-Bharati Quarterly* (April 1926), pp. 93–5.

21. Formichi File.

22. Mussolini File.

23. Ibid.

24. Newspaper clippings, 1926 folder, Rabindra Bhavan.

25. Ibid.

26. Italy File.

27. Newspaper clippings, 1926 folder.

28. Kalyan Kundu, Sakti Bhattacharya, and Kalyan Sircar, *Imagining Tagore: Rabindranath and the British Press, 1912–1941* (Kolkata: Sahitya Samsad, 2000), p. 410.

29. Rathindranath Tagore, *On the Edges of Time* (Calcutta: Visva-Bharati, 1981), p. 136.

30. See Denis Mack Smith, *Mussolini* (London: Granada, 1983), p. 152:

> There is little confirmation that he knew more of Shakespeare and Molière than he could have learnt from the encyclopaedia or indeed from the mere titles of their plays; nor can we accept the assertion that Defoe was one of his favourite writers, or that he was a devotee of Whitman, Longfellow, Emerson, William James and Mark Twain. These were just names to drop, not authors to be read.

31. Ibid., p. 155.

32. Prayer, 'Carlo Formichi', vol. 40, p. 25.

33. Mack Smith, *Mussolini*, pp. 127–8.

34. *Il Resto del Carlino*, 1 June 1926, p2c4.

35. This is the fourth stanza of Leopardi's poem '*Nelle Nozze della sorella Paolina*' (For the Marriage of His Sister Paolina). The English translation is taken from J.G. Nichols, *The Canti* (Manchester: Carcanet, 1954), p. 23.

36. *Il Giornale d'Italia*, 2 June 1926, p5c1–3.

37. *La Tribuna*, 2 June 1926, p3c3/4.

38. *Il Popolo di Roma*, 2 June 1926, p3c4.

39. Newspaper clippings, 1926 folder.

40. P.C. Mahalanobis, 'Our Founder-President in Italy, 1926', Visva-Bharati Bulletin, *Visva-Bharati Quarterly* (October 1926), p. 283.

41. Prayer, 'Carlo Formichi', vol. 40, p. 26.

42. *Il Regime Fascista*, 4 June 1926, p3c1/2/3.

43. Mahalanobis, 'Our Founder-President in Italy, 1926', p. 290.

44. *La Tribuna*, 8 June 1926, p4c5–6.

45. *Il Giornale d'Italia*, 8 June 1926, p2c4.

46. *Il Messaggero*, 9 June 1926, p3c1/2/3.

47. Victoria Ocampo, 'Tagore on the Banks of the River Plate', *Rabindranath Tagore: A Centenary Volume 1861–1961* (New Delhi: Sahitya Akademi, 1961), pp. 27–47.

48. Krishna Dutta and Andrew Robinson, *Rabindranath Tagore: The Myriad Minded Man* (London: Bloomsbury, 1997), p. 266.

49. Sisir Kumar Das (ed.), *The English Writings of Rabindranath Tagore*, vol. 3 (New Delhi: Sahitya Akademi, 1996), pp. 580–8.

50. *Il Giornale d'Italia*, 11 June 1926, p2c4/5.

51. Mahalanobis, 'Our Founder-President in Italy, 1926', p. 289.

52. Italy File.

53. Mahalanobis, 'Our Founder-President in Italy, 1926', pp. 286–7.

54. Ibid., p. 287.

55. Ibid., pp. 288–9.

56. *Il Messaggero*, 11 June 1926, p7c1.

57. *Il Regime Fasista*, 13 June 1926, p3c5.

58. *Il Popolo di Roma*, 13 June 1926, p3c3.

59. Ibid., p6c2.

60. Mahalanobis, 'Our Founder-President in Italy, 1926', p. 291.

61. Mario Prayer, 'Tagore's Meeting with Benedetto Croce in 1926', *Rabindranath Tagore: A Timeless Mind* (London: The Tagore Centre UK, 2011), p. 266.

62. Ibid., p. 267.

63. Ibid., p. 266.

64. Mahalanobis, 'Our Founder-President in Italy, 1926', pp. 291–2.

65. Surendranath Dasgupta (1887–1952) was a scholar in Sanskrit and philosophy. The subject of his doctoral thesis was 'The Philosophy of Benedetto Croce'.

66. Dr Suniti Kumar Chatterjee (1890–1977) was an Indian linguist, educationist, and littérateur. Chatterji accompanied Tagore during the tour to Malaya, Java, Bali, and Sumatra in 1927. Later, he became the president of Sahitya Akademi, India.

67. Prayer, 'Carlo Formichi', pp. 31–3.

68. Rathindranath Tagore, *On the Edges of Time*, p. 138.

69. Mahalanobis, 'Our Founder-President in Italy, 1926', p. 293.

70. *La Tribuna*, 16 June 1926, p2c5.

71. Mahalanobis, *Kobir sange Europey*.

72. *Gazzetta del Popolo*, 16 June 1926, p6c3.

73. Mahalanobis, 'Our Founder-President in Italy, 1926', p. 294.

74. Ibid., p. 295.

75. *Il Nuovo Giornale*, 18 June 1926; the original paper is missing in the National Library of Rome. The present citation is quoted from Mahalanobis, 'Our Founder-President in Italy, 1926', p. 295.

76. Mahalanobis, 'Our Founder-President in Italy, 1926', p. 291.

77. *The Observer*, 27 June 1926, p11c4.

78. Mahalanobis, *Kobir sange Europey*, p. 44.

79. Mahalanobis, 'Our Founder-President in Italy, 1926', p. 296.

80. Ibid.

81. Ibid., p. 297.

82. Scotti's letter written to Salvemini, cited from G. Salvemini, *'Tagore e Mussolini'*, in *Esperienze e studi socialisti in onore di U.G. Mondelfo* (Florence: La Nuova Italia Editrice, 1957), pp. 191–206.

83. *La Stampa*, 21 June 1926, p4c1/2.

84. *Gazzetta del Popolo*, 21 June 1926, p3c2/3.

85. Ibid., 22 June 1926, p3c1.

86. Prayer, 'Carlo Formichi', vol. 40, p. 34.

4

Post Tour

Villeneuve, Switzerland

The Italian tour was over. The next destination for the poet and his entourage was Villeneuve in Switzerland, where they arrived on 22 June 1926 by a special invitation from Romain Rolland, which, in fact, had been offered the previous year. Rolland wrote to Tagore: 'Under normal circumstances I would have travelled to Rome to meet you. Rome is my most favourite of all European cities. But now the Italian soil is forbidden for me.'[1] Rolland's letter expressed an undertone of disapproval of fascism.

Tagore arrived at Montreux station in Villeneuve late in the evening. Since Rolland was out of town, Marcello Martini received the poet. The party stayed in the Hotel Byron in the suite once occupied by Victor Hugo, which opened onto Lake Lemon surrounded by mountains. Exhausted but contented, the poet was looking forward to several days of peaceful rest at this beautiful spot. Rolland and his sister Madeline lived nearby at the Villa Olga.

From Villeneuve, Tagore wrote to Formichi about his health, his future plans, and, once again, of his successful trip to Italy. Formichi replied on 29 June 1926:

Gurudev

You can easily imagine the kind of joy your dear letter just arrived brings to me. It was just what I was longing for; to hear, namely, that at last you are taking rest and enjoying peace.

You went through very strenuous weeks in Italy, and I sometimes felt ashamed to be obliged to add to your strain. But I did it, I assure you, feeling utterly miserable in the bottom of my heart. But think of the glorious results of your visit, think that you have opened a channel of deep and sincere friendship between India and Italy, the benefits of which for the future of mankind can be easily foreseen.

A Committee has already been appointed to found an Italian Visva-Bharati here and to start a work by which students of the two countries will largely profit. The meeting took place on Saturday last at the University, and the next one will take place at the end of this week. Meanwhile I shall manage to be constantly in touch with the Foreign Office. It is of permanent importance to beat the iron while it is hot, and the iron is hot indeed in the present moment.

You say you are happy in being free from the swarming interviews whose ephemeral wings fill the air with hum, not always of truth. And you are the man that has heard the least of falsehood in the world, if I have to judge from what has happened in Italy twice: all that were brought near you were utterly sincere in their admiration of you.

If you feel so well in Switzerland I hope you will remain at Villeneuve two and why not, three weeks, instead of the only one projected.

Had you any inconvenience on account of the heavy luggage sent from Turin by a wrong train?

As soon as I came back to Rome I found that the exams were going on at University, and I can take no rest yet. But I feel so happy of the splendid success of your visit that I hardly need any rest. The epithets Shakespeare gives to sleep might as well be given to joy: Sore labour's bath, chief nourisher in life's feast. My sisters and my children are proud to be remembered by you. They all send you wishes inspired by the purest loving worship.

Remember me, please to Mrs. Tagore, to Rathi, to the Prince, and to Mr. and Mrs. Mahalanobis and just enough to believe in my boundless love and endless devotion.

Yours forever

Carlo Formichi[2]

That evening, back in town, Rolland, accompanied by Madeline, came straight to see the poet at his hotel. This was his second meeting with Tagore: They had first met in Paris in 1921.

Throughout his Western journey, Tagore met and befriended many internationally acclaimed writers, intellectuals, philosophers, and thinkers such as Albert Einstein, Thomas Mann, Albert Schweitzer, André Gide, and Paul Valéry, but he felt at home with Rolland, in spite of the language barrier, as both of them intimately shared some common ideals of raising the moral consciousness of humanity. Also, both of them were pacifists and champions of civil society. Rolland too had a similar reverence for the poet. In a letter to Kalidas Nag, Rolland once wrote, 'In my mind and spirit I feel more close to Rabindranath than any contemporary European poet and thinker.'[3] However, the meeting was brief on that late evening.

The following day, Tagore and Rolland casually started discussing various issues of Indian politics, with the help of Madeline as interpreter. The failure of the Khilafat Movement, the boycott of British-made goods, the idolatry of Indians, the poet's difference of opinion with Gandhi, Indian, and European music—all came up in their discussion. But Rolland wanted the poet to reflect on his experience in Italy. He was anxious to inform Tagore that the Italian fascist press was utilizing the poet's innocent but positive comments, made during his tour, to establish his support for fascism. The anti-fascist quarters of Europe had already started expressing their disapproval. The British *Daily News* wrote on 11 June 1926:

Rabindranath Tagore, the great Indian poet, is staying in Italy as the guest of Mussolini. He has changed his opinions regarding Fascism and its leader, though he agrees that no good would result from the extension to other countries of methods which have been found suitable in Italy.

'It is for me to study, not to criticise from outside', he said, when I asked him for his opinions. 'I am glad of this opportunity to see for myself the work of one who is assuredly a great man, and a movement that will certainly be remembered in history'.[4]

L'Humanité and other socialist journals published in France were echoing a similar condemnation based on these reports. Letters arriving from France about Tagore were extremely critical of him. Not only in Europe but also in some parts of India, there was a strong voice of disagreement with the poet's visit to Italy. The *Madras Mail* on 17 June 1926 expressed some doubts on Tagore's humanist ideals, with a touch of sarcasm:

[...] Dr. Tagore's praise of Fascism, even though narrowly qualified, uttered after a few days' residence in Italy and apparently before he had met any of the persecuted minority, among whom are to be found some of the most intellectual men Italy possesses, is strangely at variance with the liberalism of his own creed of tolerance and human brotherhood. What does Dr. Tagore really think, we wonder, of Mussolini's militant Imperialism as manifested in Tyrol?[5]

Realizing the international implications of the situation, Rolland wrote to Nag:

Tagore's views against narrow nationalism were expressed in his speech delivered in Japan. Based on that a small discerning group in Europe have been considering Tagore as their guru and revered him as an emblem of justice and freedom of mankind. How disillusioned they were when they found that Tagore became the state guest of Mussolini, the most hated oppressor and murderer of millions including Amandola and Matteotti.[6]

Clearly, Rolland was anxious to convey his concern about these unacceptable circumstances. However, he was not being given the opportunity to discuss it.

Rolland had jotted down the details of his conversation with the poet during his stay at Villeneuve in his journal *Inde*. As mentioned earlier, this journal is an important document that records the mutual anxiety of two intellectuals who shared similar views on the contemporary politics and social and humanitarian problems of India and Europe, as well as the exchange of ideas and personal thoughts. Apart from his direct interactions with the poet, Rolland had collected facts about Tagore for his journal through his detailed conversation with Mahalanobis, often without the poet's knowledge. In *Rabindra-Viksha*, Mahalanobis published his transcriptions of the elaborate Rolland–Tagore conversation about the Italian experience.[7] Both these sources are important in establishing the nuances of these two great minds while analysing the Italian trip.

Finally, Tagore raised the subject of his Italian tour:

TAGORE: I want to tell you about my Italian visit. In India I was full of hesitation whether I should come to Italy at all. In an Italian steamer in which I came I had a long talk with the Captain. He was full of admiration for Mussolini and Fascism. He told me how things in Italy had changed for the better during the last few years. My Italian friends in India has also said the same thing. Just on my arrival in Rome I met the French ambassador. They all said Mussolini had saved Italy from utter ruin. I said, this is not the most important thing. I was however trying to understand their point of view. They all agreed in thinking that during the great war something had happened which made Italian people extremely undisciplined. They all confessed about something in the Italian people which was against order and self-government. They said that those who cannot govern themselves must be governed by some external agency just as we have to put restrictions upon lunatics and fools. If a large majority of people themselves confess that they have lost the capacity for self-government or self-control, it seems reasonable to admit that a different course would become applicable in their case. Then I saw Mussolini. In certain ways he has a striking appearance and I thought that his personality may have had a direct appeal to the Italian people. I tried to reconcile the whole situation in the following way.

            With the tremendous growth of science it was thought that the human factor could be eliminated through machinery. In fact, as machinery was supposed to be absolutely free from mistakes it was thought that society could be saved better by mechanical organisation rather than by human personalities but the great danger is that if something goes wrong with the machine there is an immediate deadlock. Owing to the great war the social and administrative body in Europe broke down and there was a great misery, the people who suffered cried for help and they found that they could not get any help from machines but had to depend on individuals. If at this stage somebody comes forward with a forceful personality and announces that he has saved them, then the people naturally accept him as their saviour; specially when they saw that Mussolini succeeded in clearing away the wreckage of the parliamentary machine and substituted his word as law. The common people in spite of all their weakness are human beings. The personality of Mussolini could not but have a great effect on them, specially at a time when they had lost faith in their old mechanical contrivances.

ROLLAND: The question is whether it would be worthwhile to lose one's reason in order to live.

TAGORE: It all depends on the actual facts. A situation may come about in which a temporary surrender of one's own initiative may be welcomed. I was told that Italy had become a land of lunatics. It was the best that could happen for the people themselves to put the whole country under the control of a masterful personality which alone could bring back order. Once this was achieved, they could hope for higher things to come back in time. I have been told that this is what actually happened. Mussolini has succeeded in bringing back law and order to the people. Now they are prosperous and happy, in fact, far better than they were just after the war. I am told that formerly peaceful citizens could not go out without weapons and ran the risk of being assassinated and looted at any moment. One thing is now changed—the foreigners can now travel with security in every part in Italy and I was assured that all this due to forceful personality of Mussolini.

Then the conversation ended that morning. In the afternoon, during tea at Villa Olga, Tagore picked up the incomplete thread of the morning's conversation.

TAGORE: There are some people in Italy who are not satisfied with
              the fascists. Duke Scotti of Milan told me that his mouth
              is shut. My guide Formichi told me that Duke Scotti was
              an incorrigible anti-Fascist. While I had been talking with
              the Duke from time to time he got extremely nervous so
              that I did not get any opportunity of having a quiet talk
              with him.

ROLLAND: I realise the difficulties of the situation in Italy. England,
              France and Italy were three countries where parliamentary
              education began centuries ago and a sound, reliable civic
              consciousness has steadily grown up and matured. When
              the parliamentarianism is in danger voluntary organisations
              simultaneously spring up to defend it and lend their support.
              This has made political conditions in England extremely suit-
              able. In France, love of liberty is strong among the individuals
              but there is very little organization. They cannot resist effec-
              tively the encroachment of the liberties of the people. They
              submit easily. In Italy it is still worse. There is very little
              initiative among the populace; they submit to the least show
              of organised force. In the case of France I have myself known
              many critical periods. I remember in 1877 Gen. Boulanger
              was almost on the point of becoming the Dictator of France. If
              he had shown a little more initiative he would certainly have
              become Dictator. Most of the people were Republicans, but
              they would have failed to resist him. My own brother was at
              a Teachers Training School where everybody was Republican.
              Many of them wanted to issue a manifesto protesting against
              Boulanger, but out of about 130 only 8 actually signed and
              the rest were afraid; although the Dictator was not actually
              in power, they were afraid of their future.

                  I believe the same thing or still worse is actually happen-
              ing in Italy. In reality only a small group of Fascists [who
              are] very ardent, very sincere, have power. I have lived in
              Italy for a long time and my own impression is that the
              people are extremely undisciplined. The very huge crowd
              which immensely admires Mussolini today would crush him
              tomorrow if he shows the least weakness. I remember them
              shouting *Viva Cresfi* one day and breaking his statue the next.
              I have seen [them] breaking the doors of the French Embassy

one day and threatening the German legation the next day.
Mussolini will remain in power so long as he is absolutely in
form and strong. If he shakes a little the whole country will
rapidly turn against him.

I feel very sorry that a large number of ardent idealists
who are followers of Mazzini were prevented from speaking to you in Italy. A young Italian came to see me. He had
started several philanthropic and educational institutions
before the war and had gathered a group of teachers, but all
this was broken up, as he was opposed to Fascism and would
not agree to the instruction of the Fascist organisation in his
own institution. He saw the minister of education himself
and asked the minister. 'Do you want to lose my soul?' To
that the minister replied, 'It is written in the Gospel that you
must lose your soul to win it.' And he said that he could not
advise any teacher to help him with the work of the institution; for it would be over with him immediately. I have
heard the same story from Dr. Salvemini, the great historian of Mazzini and Italian liberty. He had to leave Italy and
settle in England which also was only possible because he
had some private fortune. Mussolini has issued a decree
under which exiles from Italy lose their rights of citizenship and their properties in Europe are confiscated. I have
also seen Fascist papers writing editorials about the 'sacred'
murder of Salvemini.

A young man about 25 came to see me from Milan. He
was a delegate who spoke as a representative of the people.
He told me 'We have suffered from physical oppression and
our mouths were forcibly shut. I have come to talk to you so
that you may tell Tagore.' The young man went to Germany,
I shall try to put you in touch with him.

I realise fully how the present dominance of the Fascists
has come about: the political crisis after the war was aggra-
vated by the failure of the socialists who proved doubly unfit
for governing the country. I recognise that the seizure of
power by Mussolini was inevitable. It was a logical necessity.
Conditions in Italy at that time were somewhat similar to
those in France at the end of the last century when Bonaparte
came to prominence. A great deal depends upon the man but

even Napoleon had done greater harm to France than good. I believe Italy is in a much worse condition because Mussolini has not got the personality of Napoleon. The people of Italy are more impulsive and Mussolini is playing with fire. He is constantly speaking against foreign governments and is missing on the patriotic ambition of his countrymen. When he speaks to big gatherings and asks, 'To whom does Nice belong, to whom does Savoy belong?' And they all shout together—'To us'. He is rousing them and he is appealing to their hatred of other nations. I have no doubt that he is the greatest menace to the whole of Europe.

Tagore was listening with rapt attention. Now he was in a state of confusion! Despite the sincere, spontaneous, and overwhelming reception of the people of Italy, the unreserved hospitality of the government and Mussolini's munificent grants for Visva-Bharati, Tagore could not ignore the accounts of the inhuman fascist government that he was receiving from dependable sources like Scotti and Rolland. Still irresolute, Rolland's persuasions led the dithering Tagore to express his disapproval against the fascist regime on paper.

Initially, Rolland wanted Tagore to register his protest through an interview in favour of the intellectuals who were persecuted and exiled from Italy. But Tagore refused because, till then, he had not come across any such person. Also, whatever the hidden ploy of the Italian government, apparently there was nothing objectionable in what was showcased to him. In spite of that, the poet agreed to publish a written protest, which, he was told, would be published in a French daily. In the meantime, Rolland arranged to bring the French poet George Duhamel and publisher Ronniger to Villa Olga in order to ensure a proper and wider publicity of the poet's protest in the print media. It was suggested that Duhamel would produce a set of questionnaires on the basis of which the poet would frame his statement. On 30 June, Duhamel's questions were translated and submitted to Tagore in the morning. Confined to his room, he spent the whole day answering questions.

On the evening of 30 June, Tagore invited everyone in his suite to listen to his statement. Here, we turn to the pages of the journal *Inde* for the reactions of his French audience:

30 June, 1926 [...] we finished our supper and Tagore summoned us to listen to his statement. My sister translated for us from the beginning to the end.

And, that was a dreadful scene!

Tagore was convinced that he has touched on all the points made by Duhamel in his statement. In fact Tagore wrote a statement before he got the questionnaire and this one was a slightly modified version of the previous one.

The statement was haphazardly expressed, and neither forceful nor clear. He mentioned that he had received the love and respect from Italian people. He cautiously pointed out that he was the guest of the fascist government and he had seen everything through their eyes. He also mentioned his satisfactory discussions with one of the Italian professors [the name was not mentioned] about the abstract policies of fascism. Of course he also mentioned he did not agree with everything that the professor said. Abruptly he added that he was not in a position to judge the activities of fascism, he hadn't seen anything, heard anything or understood anything to judge the policy otherwise. He wanted to be clean and washed! He concluded his statement by briefly mentioning his interviews with Mussolini. [...] He compared him with Alexander and Napoleon.

We were listening to this with bewilderment, not even daring to look at each other. When he finished, a cold silence befell on us.[8]

Quite clearly, Tagore's statement disappointed his listeners. The poet's protest did not have any impact on Rolland and his French guests. Duhamel was dismayed; angry to the point of outburst. However, Rolland tried to ease the situation by requesting Tagore not to make any public statement before meeting, in particular, the exiled intellectuals from Italy, Salvemini in London, and Salvadori in Zurich. The poet also promised to revise his article, more critically expanding his views on fascism. Rolland told both Salvadori and Salvemini to ensure that they meet the poet at the appointed locations. Duhamel, in frustration, returned to Paris. Tagore's days in Villeneuve were over.

Rolland's telegram to Salvadori informing the day of
Tagore's arrival in Zurich, July 1926
Source: Archivio Salvadori Paleotti, Fermo, Italy.

Zurich

On 4 July 1926, Tagore and his entourage reached Zurich. They
were lodged at the Dolder Grand Hotel. On 5 July, Salvadori's wife,
Signora Giacinta Salvadori, visited the poet with a letter from the
professor, who was indisposed. The letter carried an underlined
note of discontent. He wrote: '[...] It was extremely painful to us all
lovers of Liberty, Justice and Peace, that you should have accepted
the hospitality of a government which is a shame for Italy and a
dishonour to humanity and civilisation.'[9]

Guglielmo Salvadori was professor of philosophy at Florence
University. In 1924, he wrote in an article in *The New Statesman*,
which was published in Britain that 'the great majority of Italian
patriots look with great suspicion at the new state of things, and

are extremely anxious as to what it may bring about, for no good patriot and law-abiding citizen can look with approval at illegality and dictatorship.'[10] Mussolini's followers were furious to see such a bitter truth expressed in the article. The 'Blackshirts' arrested Salvadori, beat up his son, and even threatened to kill them. Finally, they had to seek asylum in Switzerland.

Guglielmo Salvadori with his family. From left: eldest daughter Gladys, Salvadori, youngest daughter Joyce, son Max, and Signora Giacinta Salvadori.
Source: Archivio Salvadori Paleotti, Fermo, Italy.

Mahalanobis had carefully recorded the conversation between Signora Salvadori and Tagore. This dialogue is of immense historical importance since, after this exchange, Tagore's impression of Italy took a completely different turn. The Tagore–Salvadori dialogue was published in the *Visva-Bharati Quarterly* (1926) and also in *Rabindra-Viksha* (2000) with some omissions in the latter (marked within square brackets).

SALVADORI: My husband is so ill, that although he wanted very much to come to see you, he could not do so. He feels very sorry for this, but he sent me to speak with you. We have seen in the paper that after your interview with Mussolini, you have expressed your admiration for him and for the Fascist movement. We are feeling very unhappy about this. We know there is some misunderstanding. We are fighting for the cause of freedom, and it is very sad for us that we are not getting your support.

                  We, who have been exiled from Italy on account of the Fascist regime, have been feeling unhappy ever since we heard that you had come to Italy. You, who are so good, why did you come to Italy, now the land of violence and persecutions? We have been asking this question since you came here as I mentioned in a letter to a Paris paper recently. I sent you a copy of this letter.[11]

TAGORE: Yes, I had received it, but as I do not know Italian I could not understand it. But now that you ask me this question, let me tell you why I came to Italy this time.

                  As you know, I had been invited by your people in Milan last year, and I came into touch with them during the few days I could stay there. I was strongly moved when I found that the people loved me and wanted me to be with them for some time. I however fell ill and had to return to India before fulfilling my engagements in other towns. I promised to come back in the following summer.

                  In India reports of Fascist atrocities reached me from time to time, and I had serious misgivings about coming back to Italy. About this time Prof. Formichi came to Santiniketan, bringing with him from Mussolini a wonderful gift of books and valuable collection of art reproductions for my institution. He also brought an appreciative letter from Mussolini himself. Now this gift struck me as particularly appropriate as helping us in our work of building up an international institution of fellowships which should be a true centre of the meeting of East and West. The services of Prof. Formichi and Dr. Tucci which had been lent to us also helped in our work. In my message to Mussolini I expressed my thanks to him for his gifts—but this was purely in connection with my own work, and had no reference to his political activities.

Prof. Formichi and Dr. Tucci continually pressed [encouraged] me to come to Italy, but my misgivings were not dispelled and at one time I had practically decided to give up my projected tour in Italy. However, I had my promise to fulfil. I also had a strong desire to meet and spend a few days with Rolland, and this seemed the last chance of doing so. So at last I came to Italy and was taken to Rome.

I had no opportunities to study the genesis or the activities of the Fascist movement, and I did not express any opinion about it. In fact, in all my interviews I was careful to explain that I was not competent to say anything about organised Fascism, not having studied it.

About Mussolini himself I must however say that he did interest me as an artist. His personality was striking. As an artist [poet], the human element—even in politics—touches me more deeply than abstract theories. Modern civilisation is too scientific, too impersonal for me. Therefore personality is always interesting to me. Take our own Indian Emperor Aurangzeb—he was a ruthless monarch, yet he is interesting. Interest in his personality does not imply moral approbation of his actions. [The expression of the personal man in his work may or may not be good, may even be terrible, but when it makes itself powerfully evident it is fascinating.] Moral judgement and the interest involved [invoked] by a dramatic personality are two entirely different things. Now Mussolini struck me as a masterful personality. [He seems not only to have strength of determination, but a quick instinct for realising his opportunities which has enabled him to obtain such perfect mastery over a whole people. His great dramatic personality brought to my vision a man riding upon a wild horse who by his marvellous strength checked insane people and controlled them.] I felt that he must have great strength to obtain such perfect control over a whole people. But this does not necessarily justify his activities.

SALVADORI: He has not gained real mastery over the people. He represents their collective weakness. He is like a cancer which is ever growing in size out of the illness of the whole people, a people so sick that they have no strength left to resist.

TAGORE: The people with whom I came into contact in Italy were
              almost unanimous in assuring me that Mussolini had saved
              Italy from anarchy and utter ruin. I was much impressed
              when I was told the same thing by foreigners, notably by pri-
              vate English individuals who praised him as a saviour of Italy.
SALVADORI: It is not true. This is the opinion of people who are in favour
              of Fascism. Foreigners who are not friendly to Fascism cannot
              give free expression to their opinion in Italy. People who hold
              contrary views were not allowed to see you.
TAGORE: I have realised that I had no occasion to come into touch
              with any individual holding a contrary opinion. This was not
              wholesome.
SALVADORI: It is not true that Mussolini has saved Italy from financial ruin.
              The financial position of Italy was better before Mussolini
              came into power. Look at the lira: it was 70 to the pound,
              and now it is 130. There was great unrest in Italy certainly
              after the war, but this unrest was not Bolshevism. Foreigners
              do not know and they merely repeat conventional tales. Italy
              was actually on the way to recovering from the unrest when
              Mussolini started his campaign. The workers had realised the
              failure of their experiment, and even without Mussolini, a
              stable and orderly condition would have been reached in a
              short time. Foreigners who have no opportunities to under-
              stand, believe the conventional lie that Mussolini saved Italy.
              But what makes us unhappy is that you have unintentionally
              helped to support Fascism. We know it is unintentional, for
              you are too good to do so.
TAGORE: I did not support Fascism. I have expressed my admiration for
              Mussolini, but only as an artist. I was careful to make this dis-
              tinction, that I was only speaking as an artist. About Fascism
              the only thing about which I was assured by almost everyone
              I met was that it had saved Italy from economic ruin.
SALVADORI: It is not true.
TAGORE: Even had it been true it would not affect my position.
              Material success is not everything. As we say in India [*Tatha
              Kim*]—What then? Even if Italy is prosperous and is wal-
              lowing in money. Even if this is true, although you deny this
              very fact—it is of no avail. As an outsider I must claim some-
              thing more. If Italy does not contribute something which is

great, which is for everybody and for all time, we cannot be satisfied—I said the same thing in my speech at the University of Rome and also in an interview which I gave just before my departure from Rome. ['I am not really competent to judge what the Italian people think and wish. I hope they will realise that further pursuit of material wealth will never make them great. They will be a great world power only when they give the world permanent gifts of the spirit. Otherwise, national prosperity and political power dies with them. These are consumed in the process of enjoyment; but products of the spirit are for all time and countries.']

Your Garibaldi did not fight merely for the prosperity of his own country. He fought for freedom, for an ideal, and so he belongs to the whole of humanity. Before leaving Mussolini I expressed my hope that the painful period of tuning should be made final, that he will leave behind in the life of his people a tuned harp for the music of freedom.

SALVADORI: I fully understand. Material prosperity is irrelevant.

TAGORE: Yes, this I actually said. And about Mussolini also I did not say anything except as an artist. From an artist's point of view, he appeared to me as a great dramatic personality—like one riding upon a wild horse, who by his marvellous strength checked a wild, and almost insane people and controlled them.

SALVADORI: I understand you were interested in his character. I understood you from the beginning. He is certainly interesting, but he did not actually achieve all this by his own strength. The socialists had already realised their failure even before Mussolini came into power. He is maintaining his power through violent terrorism and by crushing the freedom of speech.

TAGORE: I have explained my own position. I should now like to hear what you have got to tell me, your experience.

[I can quite understand how even foreigners—for example, Englishmen residing in Italy—could condone acts of violence committed in the name of political necessity. That has become possible because of the callousness which possesses the world today. The world has, since the war, become accustomed to violence. This is why the English people could take part in and tolerate the atrocities committed in Ireland during the 'Black and Tan' madness. In Europe people nowadays do not seem to feel keenly about outrages committed by the men in power. I cannot but think that such deeds of ferocity as you speak of would have shocked the moral sense of Europe before the war.]

SALVADORI: But nothing appears in the papers in Italy. They dare not publish anything. In Florence 18 people were shot in one night. A father in bed was attacked, and while the children were shouting: 'Don't kill our father,' they shot him in bed. You don't know what we have suffered. I myself heard the screams of a woman whose husband was killed before her eyes. But nothing in the papers—never!

TAGORE: I wish I had known for certain the dark deeds that were being done in Italy, then I would not have come to that country—I certainly would not. I had not met any of the people who suffered. But now that I have seen you I realise my own responsibility.

SALVADORI: We have no means, we are helpless, we have no money, and we cannot do anything. We do not know how to inform other people. I hope you will help us. Italy is now buried in lies everywhere. It is so bad for the young generation—this teaching them love for Fascism and for morbid patriotism.

Of course there are few honest Fascists who do not know the violent side, and who not knowing, sincerely believe in Fascism. But most people are terrorised into acquiescing in it. We have suffered [and] know what it is in reality.

TAGORE: Let me tell you before we part that I have a genuine love for the Italian people, and I fervently hope that this great period of pain through which they are passing will not coerce them into accepting an ambition for fatness of prosperity in place of spiritual greatness. Once Italy was the luminous centre of the West. In the art galleries of Rome and Florence the evidence of her marvellous creative power, both in its variety of perfection, has been overwhelming in its effect on a visitor like myself who comes for the first time to witness it. This exuberant impulse of creation which once overflowed the Western continent must still be lying in suspense in her being, and I hope it will not be smothered into a stillness of

death by any reign of terror and lure of greed, that once more
it will find its true work and rescue Europe from the dominion of the machine.[12]

The conversation ended here. Tagore became conscious of his
responsibilities. While bidding goodbye, the poet said, 'I'm so sorry!
Now I shall do what I ought to. I hope my influence will not be
interpreted as "the devil in disguise".'

Signora Salvadori left the hotel leaving Tagore in a state of
dismay and disturbed. His mental state was comparable only to the
trauma he had experienced during the Jallianwala Bagh massacre
seven years ago! In the first instance, he wanted to publish this
dialogue. So, without further delay, a draft of this conversation was
sent to Salvadori for his approval. On 10 July, the poet left Zurich
for Vienna via Lucerne.

Vienna

On 14 July 1926, Angelica Balabanoff and the advocate Signor
Modigliani came to see Tagore at the Hotel Bristol in Vienna.
Balabanoff's association with Mussolini has already been discussed
in an earlier chapter. Modigliani was the attorney in the Matteotti
trial; both were living in exile in Vienna.

Tagore initially was not very responsive during this meeting.
After his discussion with Signora Salvadori, Tagore had already
decided his future course of action and was reluctant to listen to
anything new. Welcoming them half-heartedly, the poet said, 'You
may not tell me in detail what's happening in Italy. I have been
there and I can't do anything about it nor do I have anything to
say.' But when he heard that Balabanoff had given an interview
about Mussolini in a journal, the atmosphere changed. He sat for
a discussion. We shall again refer to Mahalanobis's diary for this
conversation:

TAGORE: Your interpretation of Mussolini's character coincides with
            the impression he made upon me—a coward and an actor.
            When I asked the English ambassador if he thought the

impression was correct, he said, it was not—Mussolini was a great courageous man. However, he was not convincing and I was glad to have a confirmation in your interview of my impression. I should like you to tell me more.

BALABANOFF: I shall have to begin by saying that the Italian people who have attempted more than any other people, to apply your own attitude towards war, do not deserve that you should accept the hospitality of a man who came to power through violence and assassination.

TAGORE: Please do not misunderstand me. When I came to Italy I knew nothing about the situation nor could I get in touch with reality. You are [only the] second person who has given me any idea of what Fascism is. The first one I met after [I] had left Italy. You may be sure that I will make a statement of what I think about the Fascist regime.[13]

Tagore's article 'Uber den Fascismus' was published in *Neue Freier Presse* in Vienna in August. The article ends thus: 'To be ruled by a tyrant is a great misfortune for any country. But to know that one has worshipped an individual who owes his success only to his negative quality is a tragedy.' Angelica Balabanoff remembered this comment for many years. The essential reason for the misfortunes of Italy is embedded in this comment.

Meanwhile, a long reply from Salvadori came with his comments on the write-up of the meeting Tagore sent for his approval. He obviously did not like the poet's noticeable admiration for Mussolini. He wrote:

[...] I believe that if public opinion everywhere was made to realise the true state of things in Italy, a feeling and a cry of horror would run over all civilised, and even tortured, nations. If you wished to have documents, I would suggest to you a book or pamphlet written by the poor martyr Matteotti: *Un anno di dominio fascista* (One year of Fascist dominion). In it you would find a long list, which fills about forty big 8vo pages (44–81), of hundreds and hundreds of crimes of every kind committed by Fascists from November 1922 to November 1923, and left unpunished. And these represent only a part; for many remain unknown. [...] Will you allow me to say that your remarks about Mussolini's 'striking' and 'masterful' personality spoil the whole of the interview and, if published, will greatly damage our Cause? At least it would be necessary to explain and define what you mean by personality. In a certain sense even criminals and lunatics (like the Roman emperor Nero and Cesar Borgia, the Prince of Machiavelli) may present the appearance of strong personalities, but only the appearances. In fact these individuals never possess, or can possess, a real strength of will and of character; on the contrary they live under the complete dominion of the worst instincts of human nature, and act according to the caprice of the moment on the influence of their surroundings.

Concluding the letter, the professor wrote:

I hope you will forgive me if I suggest that it would be a great and beautiful action on your part, if you sent back to the ignoble donator [sic] his gift of books. As soon as Italy has recovered her liberty and her place among civilised nations, I promise to you, in the name of all true Italians, to make a new gift of the same books and works of art for your school.[14]

The dialogue between Tagore and Signora Salvadori was published almost verbatim in *The Manchester Guardian* in Britain on 7 August 1926. *The Times of India* also reprinted this conversation from *The Manchester Guardian* in its 3 September 1926 issue.

Despite this, Salvadori wished to send his son Max to Santiniketan, but since Tucci was still teaching there, Tagore did not encourage the idea to avoid further complications.

Tagore never got a chance to meet Gaetano Salvemini. The professor had lost his Italian citizenship in 1926 and the government had confiscated his property. He moved to London and remained there ever since. Though the poet could not meet the professor, while returning from Vienna, he did meet his wife in Paris for a brief while.[15] Mrs Salvemini remarked later about this meeting in a letter to the professor:

[...] Tagore appeared to be less angry about the incident and rather more annoyed for being forced to protest against it. [...] Since he did not know Italian, he was completely dependent on the interpreters. His friend had noticed certain changes in his statements published in the newspapers.

For example, when the poet wished Italy well, the newspaper twisted the statement as the poet wished 'Fascist Italy' well! Tagore commented with regret, 'This is not true'. He loves Italy and its people and can feel the sincerity and warmth of their reception.[16]

Later, Salvemini contacted Elmhirst for references about Tagore's trip to Italy during the writing of his article '*Tagore e Mussolini*'. The Elmhirst–Salvemini letters are still preserved at the Elmhirst Archive at Dartington.

After his meeting with Salvadori, Balabanoff, and Modilliagni, Tagore was convinced that his Italian tour was a blunder. The next day, 15 July, he wrote to Rolland, '[…] In Zurich I had an interview with Madam Salvadori, the result of which you will see later on. I have to pass through a purification ceremony for the defilement to which I submitted myself in Italy. […]'[17]

Amid unrest, Tagore wrote a long letter to Andrews in India expressing his changed views on Italy. He condemned fascism severely despite maintaining his poet-like dignity and courtesy. He expressed to Andrews his wish to publish this letter in the Indian press. A copy of that letter along with a separate note was sent also to Formichi and Rolland on 21 July 1926. He wrote to Formichi:

Hotel Bristol   21 July, 1926
Vienna

Dear Friend

I send you a copy of the letter which I have sent to Andrews. This will give you my idea about my attitude towards Fascism. I have been forced to give my explanation because, not only in Europe, but [also] in India the rumour has been circulated that I have advocated the doctrine of Fascism and I have taken up the mission of defending it when I go to India.

In the meanwhile the evidence from the other side is pouring down upon me—and some of the facts are of a disturbing character. I cannot tell you what a great suffering it has caused me—for I have a deep love for your people. Also I realise that my expressed opinion of this political movement will hurt you and this thought is constantly oppressing my mind. Our cause of Visva-Bharati will receive a setback in Italy which is a matter of great regret for me. And yet I cannot help taking the step I have taken for I do

Facsimile of Salvadori's letter to Tagore, 10 July 1926
Source: Rabindra Bhavan.

represent certain ideals for which I had faced unpopularity in my own country and division in some parts of the West. The report which appeared in the Indian newspapers last year after my return from Italy contained extracts from the Fascists' papers fiercely attacking me for my humanitarian ideals. I feel certain that my espousing the cause of Fascism could be a kind of moral suicide. But exactly that is being widely believed by peoples of all shades of opinion in Europe and other continents. I find it absolutely impossible to let it go uncontradicted and with a great feeling of pain I have allowed myself to express my opinion about my position with regards to this movement.

I fervently hope that you will understand the situation and forgive me and still consider me as one of your best friends.
With love
Rabindranath Tagore[18]

Finally, he sent a copy to Elmhirst expressing his wish to publish the letter in the British newspapers. He added:

Accompanying this you will find a letter which I am sending to Andrews in Santiniketan. I hope in this letter I have clearly been able to explain my opinion about Fascism and that you will agree with me that it should be published in some of the papers in England as well as in India. [...] Of course my opinion is based upon inadequate data and my mind may still be obsessed with some bias in favour of Mussolini for what he has done for Visva-Bharati. Possibly some day I shall come to the conclusion that it was a sinister design on the part of my evil fate to have brought me into my relation with this man who may be altogether a fraud and no real personality. Somehow I have the unenviable knack of getting myself entangled in responsibilities that should have been avoided and I regret that I have allowed myself to pay this last visit to Italy [...].[19]

Formichi's response arrived on 30 July 1926. It was bitter and quite understandably he took the side of Mussolini. He wrote:

Gurudev—
Thanks for the copy of the letter you have sent to Mr. Andrews. Of course it is destined to have the widest possible publicity. You have said the worst you could against Fascism, and at the touch of a magic wand of something

Rome (21). Via Marghera 43.
30, VII, 1926

Gurudev,

thanks for the copy
of the letter you have sent
to Mr Andrews. Of course
it is destined to the widest
possible publicity. You have
said the worst you could
against Fascism, and at the
touch of the magic wand of
something that you believe
sheer truth you have allowed
not even a single of your impressions, convictions and promises,
to survive.
Last year my countrymen waged
war against you, as they were
deluded into the belief that
your visit had a political aim.
It was an offensive war that
I was lucky enough to smother
soon after its birth owing to
Mussolini's equanimity and to
your over and over again repeated
statement that you wanted to
keep aloof from Politics and to
be considered only as a Poet.
And my countrymen knew how
to show you their admiration,
love, nay, worship, as soon as
you came again to Italy as a

Facsimile of Formichi's letter written to Tagore, 30 July 1926
Source: Rabindra Bhavan.

that you believe to be sheer truth you have allowed not even a single one of your impressions, convictions and promises to survive.

Last year my countrymen waged war [tour in Italy in January 1925] against you as they were deluded in the belief that your visit had a political aim. It was an offensive war that I was lucky enough to smother soon after its birth owing to Mussolini's equanimity and to your over and over again repeated statement that you wanted to keep aloof from politics and to be considered only as a poet. And my countrymen knew how to show you their admiration, love, nay, worship, as soon as you came again to Italy as a poet determined to keep the strictest neutrality in the field of politics. You have deemed now necessary to come out of this neutrality and you have written an article which is a declaration of war. This time it is a defensive war that is forced upon my countrymen, and as you can easily imagine, I shall side with them with all my heart and have my place in the very first ranks. My situation will be that of Arjuna constrained by fate to fight against his relatives, friends and spiritual guides. Arjuna, however, was reluctant at the outset and wanted the lesson of Srikrishna to know where his duty was: I know already Krishna's lesson, and therefore my duty fills me with enthusiasm. You try to demonstrate to me in your last letter that you could not help taking the step you have taken because the rumour has been circulated that you have espoused the cause of Fascism. Let us imagine that Mr. Smith has been taken for Mr. Arnold. Will it not be sufficient for him to say: 'no, I am Mr. Arnold', and in order to defend his identity will it really be necessary for him to say: 'no, I am not that rascal of Mr. Arnold!'?
With infinite sadness
Carlo Formichi[20]

Rolland was not quite pleased with the letter written to Andrews. He thought that the letter was still written too cautiously. He disliked the mild tone of the letter indicating the poet's obligation to Mussolini. Rolland selected the more powerful and significant sentences of the letter and prepared a statement. This edited statement was sent to *Europa* for publication in August. It was also sent to other socialist journals like the *Lumanie*. It has been mentioned earlier that Balabanoff was impressed by the statement published under the title '*Uber den Fascismus*' in the Vienna daily *Neue Freier Presse*.

In Britain, the letter to Andrews was published in *The Manchester Guardian* on 5 August 1926. The entire text of the letter is given here:

Philosophy of Fascism
A Letter from Tagore
Refusal of Support

(The following is the text of a letter which Rabindranath Tagore has sent to Mr. C. F. Andrews.)

My mind is passing through a conflict. I have my love and gratitude for the people of Italy. I deeply appreciate their feeling of admiration for me, which is so genuine and generous. On the other hand, the Italy revealed in Fascism alienates itself from the ideal picture of that great country which I should love to cherish in my heart.

You know I had my first introduction to Italy when I was invited to Milan last year. It takes a long time to study the mind of a people, but not long to feel their heart when that heart opens itself. I was in the city only for a very few days, and in that time I realised that the people loved me. Rightly or wrongly, one can claim praise as one's desert, but love is a surprise every time it comes. I was strongly moved by that surprise when I found loving friends and not merely kind hosts in the people of Italy. It grieved me deeply, and I felt almost ashamed when I suddenly fell ill and had to sail back home before I could fulfil my engagements in all the other towns.

Then followed the magnificent gift from Mussolini, an almost complete library of Italian literature, for my institution. It was a great surprise to me. In this greeting I felt the touch of a personality which could express itself in this direct manner in an appropriate action of unstinted magnificence. This helped me to make up my mind to visit Italy once again, in spite of the misgivings created by the reports reaching us in India about the character of the Fascist movement.

I had neither the qualifications nor any inclination to dabble in the internal political issues of the European countries. For this reason I wanted to keep my mind neutral when I came to Italy. But we live in a whirlwind of talk today, and an individual like myself is compelled to contribute to that universal noise, dragged by the chain of *Karma*, as we say in our country. I allowed myself to fall a victim to this relentless *Karma*, with its ever lengthening coil of consequence, when I succumbed to the importunity of the interviewers in Italy.

The Interviews in Italy

The interview is a dangerous trap in which our unwary opinions are not only captured but mutilated. Words that come out of a moment's mood are meant to be forgotten; but when they are snapshotted, most often our thoughts are presented in a grotesque posture which is chance's irony. The camera in this case being also a living mind, the picture becomes a composite one in which two dissimilar features of mentality have made a misalliance that is likely to be unhappy and undignified. My interviews in Italy were the products of three personalities—the reporter's, the interpreter's, and my own. Over and above that, there evidently was a hum in the atmosphere of another insistent and universal whisper, which, without our knowing it, mingled in all our talks. Being ignorant of Italian I had no means of checking the result of this concoction. The only precaution which I could take was to repeat emphatically to all my listeners that I had as yet no opportunity to study the history and character of Fascism.

Since then I have had the opportunity of learning the contents of some of these interviews from the newspaper cuttings that my friends have gathered and translated for me. And I was not surprised to find in them what was, perhaps, inevitable. Through misunderstanding, wrong emphasis, natural defects in the medium of communication, and the pre-occupation of the national mind, some of these writings have been made to convey that I have given my deliberate opinion on Fascism, expressing my unqualified admiration.

This time it was not directly the people of Italy whose hospitality I enjoyed, but that of Mussolini himself as the head of the Government. This was, no doubt, an act of kindness, but somewhat unfortunate for me. For always and everywhere official vehicles, though comfortable, move only along a chalked path of programme too restricted to lead to any places of significance, or persons of daring individuality, providing the visitors with specially selected morsels of experience.

The only opinions I could gather in such an atmosphere of distraction were enthusiastically unanimous in praise of Mussolini for having rescued Italy in a most critical moment of her history, from the brink of ruin.

'Absurd to Imagine That I Could Support It'

In Rome I came to know a Professor, a genuinely spiritual character, a seeker of peace who was strongly convinced not only of the necessity but of the philosophy of Fascism. About the necessity I am not competent to discuss, but about the philosophy I am doubtful. For it costs very little to fashion a suitable philosophy in order to mitigate the rudeness of facts that secretly hurt one's conscience. One statement which particularly surprised me, coming from the mouths of fervent patriots, was that the Italian people owing to their unreasoning impulsive nature, had proved their incapacity to govern themselves, and that, therefore, in the inevitable logic of things, they lent themselves to government from outside by strong hands.

However, these are facts that immediately and exclusively concern Italy herself, though their validity has sometimes been challenged by European critics. But whatever may be the case as to that, the methods and the principles of Fascism concern all humanity, and it is absurd to imagine that I could ever support a movement which ruthlessly suppresses freedom of expression, enforces observances that are against individual conscience, and walks through a bloodstained path of violence and stealthy crime. I have said over and over again that the aggressive spirit of Nationalism and Imperialism, religiously cultivated by most of the nations of the West, is a menace to the whole world. The demoralisation which it produces in European politics is sure to have disastrous effects, especially upon the peoples of the East who are helpless to resist the Western methods of exploitation. It would be most foolish, if it were not almost criminal, for me to express my admiration for a political ideal which openly declares its loyalty to brute force as the motive power of civilisation. (That barbarism is not altogether incompatible with material prosperity may be taken for granted but the cost is terribly great; indeed it is fatal.) The worship of unscrupulous force as the vehicle of Nationalism keeps ignited the fire of international jealousy, and makes for universal incendiarism, for a fearful orgy of devastation. The mischief of the infection of this moral aberration is great because today the races of humanity have come close together, and any process of destruction does its work on an enormously vast scale. Knowing all this, could it be believed that I should have played my fiddle while an unholy fire was being fed with human sacrifice?

Fascism an American Infection?

I was greatly amused when reading a Fascist organ to find a writer vehemently decrying the pantheistic philosophy of the passive and the meditative East, and contrasting it with the vigorous self-assertion and fury of efficiency which he acknowledges to have been borrowed by his people from their modern schoolmasters in America. This has suggested to my mind the possibility of the idea of Fascism being actually an infection from across the Atlantic.

The unconscious irony in the article I refer to lies in the fact of the writer's using with unction the name of Christianity in this context—a religion which had its origin in the East. He evidently does not realise that if Christ had been born again in this world he would have been forcibly turned back from New York had he come there from abroad—if for no other reason, then certainly for the want of the necessary amount of dollars to be shown to the gatekeeper. Or if he had been born in that country, the Ku Klux Klan would have beaten him to death or lynched him. For did he not give utterance to that political blasphemy, 'Blessed are the meek', thus insulting the Nordic right to rule the world, and to that economic heresy, 'Blessed are the poor?' Would he not have been put in prison for twenty or more years for saying that it was as easy for the prosperous to reach the Kingdom of Heaven as for the camel to pass through the eye of a needle?

Christianity and European Political Thought

The Fascist Professor deals a pen thrust against what he calls our pantheism; but that is a word that has no synonym in our language, nor has the doctrine any place in our philosophy. He does not seem to have realised that the idea of Christian theology, that God remains essentially what he is while manifesting himself in the Son's being, belongs to the same principle as our principle of immanence. According to this doctrine the divinity of God accepts humanity for its purpose of self-revelation and thus bridges the infinite gulf between the two. This idea has glorified all human beings, and has had the effect in the Christian West of emancipating individuals from the thraldom of absolute power. It has trained that attitude of mind which is the origin of the best internal politics of the Western peoples. It has helped to distribute the power of government all over the country, and thus has given it a permanent foundation which cannot be tampered with or destroyed by the will of one individual or the whim of a group. This consciousness of the dignity of the individual has encouraged in the West the freedom of conscience and thought. We in the East come to Europe for this inspiration. We are also dreaming of the time when the individuals belonging to the people of India will have courage to think for themselves and express their thoughts, feel their strength, know their rights, and take charge of their own government.

Aggrandisement of the Slave State: A Lesson from India

The Fascist writer I have quoted is evidently fascinated by the prospect of the economic self-aggrandisement of the nation at the cost of the moral self-respect of the people. But it is the killing of the goose for the sake of golden eggs. In the olden civilisations the slavery of the people did build up for the time being powers of stupendous splendour. But this spirit of slavishness constantly weakened the foundations till the towers came down into the dust, offering as their contribution to humanity ruins haunted by venerable ghosts.

In bygone days in India the State was only a part of the people. The mass of the population had its own self-government in the village community. Dynasties changed, but the people always possessed the power to manage all that was vital to them. This saved them from sinking into barbarism, this has given our country a continuity through centuries of political vicissitudes.

Our Western rulers have destroyed this fundamental structure of our civilisation, the civilisation based upon the obligations on intimate human relationship. And therefore nothing today has been left for the people through which they can express their collective mind, their creative will, or realise the dignity of their soul, except the political instrument, the foreign model of which is always present before their envious gaze. We come to Europe for our lesson in the mastery of this instrument, as Japan has done and has been successful in her purpose. But must our friend the Fascist philosopher come to us to copy our political impotence, the result of the surrender of freedom for centuries to the authority of some exclusive reservoir of concentrated power, while rejecting our great ideal of spiritual freedom, which has its basis in the philosophy that infinite truth is everywhere, that it is for everyone to reach it by removing the obstruction of the self that obscures light!

Impression of Mussolini

I am sure you will be interested to know what was the impression that I have carried away from my interview with Mussolini. We met only twice, and our meetings were extremely brief, owing very likely to our difficulty of communication through the slow and interrupted medium of an interpreter.

In a hall of which the great size is accentuated by an unusual bareness of furniture, Mussolini has his seat in a distant corner. I believe this gives him the time and space to observe visitors who approach him, and makes him ready to deal with them. I was not sure of his identity while he was walking towards me to receive me, for he was not tall in proportion to his fame that towers high. But when he came near me I was startled by the massive strength of his head. The lower part of the face, the lips, the smile, revealed a singular contradiction to the upper part, and I have often wondered since then if there was not a secret hesitation in his nature, a timid doubt which was human. Such an admixture of vacillation in a masterful personality makes his power of determination all the more vigilant and strong because of the internecine fight in its own character. But this is a mere surmise.

For an artist it is a great chance to be able to meet a man of personality who walks solitary among those who are mere fragments of a crowd which is always on the move, pressed from behind. He is fully visible in his integrity above the lower horizon obstructed by the dense human undergrowth. Such men are the masters of history, and one cannot but feel anxious least they miss their eternity by using all their force in taking the present by the throat, leaving it dead for all time. Men have not altogether been rare who furiously created their world by trampling human materials into the shape of their megalomaniac dreams, to burden history at last with the bleached bones of their short-lived glory; while there were others, the serene souls, who with the light of truth and magic of love have made deserts fruitful along endless stretches of grateful years.

Suspended Appraisement

But to be honest, I must confess that I cannot fully trust my own impression, caught from a momentary glimpse of Mussolini in which mingled the emphasis of the surroundings in which I was placed. There have been times when history has played tricks with man and through a combination of accidents has magnified the features of essentially small persons into a parody of greatness. Such a distortion of truth often finds its chance not because these men have an extraordinary weakness of those whom they lead. This produced a mirage that falsifies the real and startles our imagination into a feeling of awe and exaggerated expectation.

To be tortured by tyranny is tolerable; but to be deluded into the worship of a wrong ideal is humiliating for the whole age which has blundered into submission to it. If Italy has made even a temporary gain through ruthless politics she may be excused for such an obsession, but for us, if we believe an [sic] idealism, there can be no such excuse.

And therefore it would be wise for us to wait before we bring our homage to a person who has suddenly been forced upon our attention by a catastrophe, till through the process of time all the veils are removed that are woven round him by the vivid sensations of the moment.

My letter has run to a great length. But I hope you will bear with it, knowing that it has helped me in making my thoughts clear about my experience in Italy and also in explaining the situation in which I have been placed. This letter which I write to you I shall make use of in removing the misunderstanding that has unfortunately been created in the minds of those who are in harmony with my ideals about the problems of the present age.

Rabindranath Tagore.[21]

In reply to Tagore's letter in *The Manchester Guardian*, Formichi wrote a long letter to the editor of the newspaper stating the other side of the story. That letter was published on 25 August 1926. The complete letter follows:

Dr. Tagore in Italy
His Two Interviews with Signor Mussolini

To the Editor of the Manchester Guardian.

Sir,—My attention has been called to the statements published in your paper by the Indian poet Rabindranath Tagore concerning Italy and Fascism, and as it was I who made the arrangements for the poet's two visits to Italy, accompanied him during his stay in this country, and acted as his interpreter both in public and in private, I feel that I must make certain points clear in connection with his visits to Italy and with the interviews that he accorded. There are perhaps some points on which my memory of the facts may help Dr. Rabindranath Tagore to reconstruct the story of his relations with Italy; that he needs my assistance for this purpose may be gathered from a letter which he wrote Mr. Andrews and which has already been published.

With regard to Dr. Tagore's first visit to Italy, it is necessary to add to his own account of it that it gave rise to a regrettable misunderstanding. Certain Fascists elements, in fact, had seen in that visit the result of the activities of their opponents, who were supposed to have invited the poet to Milan for political purposes; the Poet himself was accused of having made allusions disparaging to the Fascist movement in his speeches and in a short poem on Italy. National feeling was much aroused in consequence. I had been with him during the whole of his visit, and was well aware that neither in his words nor in his intentions had he ever thought of interfering in the politics of a country which he was visiting for the first time. No one better than I knew that he had come to Italy only to receive the homage of affection due to a great Poet, and I myself, being a Sanskrit scholar and wholly outside politics had invited him and arranged, together with other friends, for his reception. Naturally, I regretted the misunderstanding and was anxious for an opportunity to remove the cause of it. The chance was not long in presenting itself.

Dr. Tagore invited me to come to his institution at Santiniketan as visiting professor; every year, in fact, he invites some Western scholar in Indology to lecture to his advanced students in Sanskrit. My esteemed colleagues Sylvain Levi of Paris; Maurice Winternitz of Prague; and Sten Kono of Christiania, had preceded me, and all of them had done their best to contribute to the advancement of the institution through their scholarship and the gift of books to the library. I knew that the students regretted that Italian books were lacking, whereas there was abundance of English, French, and German books.

Before sailing for India I assured our Prime Minister that Dr. Tagore was far from being a political intriguer, and that on returning to Bombay from Italy he had expressed himself to the journalists who interviewed him in the most correct manner as far as the Fascist movement was concerned. I also asked Signor Mussolini to grant me a gift of Italian books for the library at Santiniketan, in order to promote cultural relations between the two countries. Signor Mussolini was quite convinced by my assurances as to the poet's attitude, and very generously presented me with an almost complete library of Italian classics to be conveyed to the Santiniketan library. I thereupon sailed for India, and on my arrival at Santiniketan Dr. Tagore was much touched by and very grateful for the gift, of which he recognised the disinterestedness and the noble aim which had inspired it—

namely, the desire to establish a channel for the exchange of ideas between Italy and India. The last words of his cable of acknowledgement to Signor Mussolini were:

> 'I assure you that such an expression of sympathy from you as representative of the Italian people will open up a channel of communication for exchange of culture between your country and ours, having every possibility of developing into an event of great historical significance.'

I spent four months at Santiniketan, and the Poet had every opportunity of knowing me: I was fortunate enough to deserve his esteem and affection. We seldom spoke of politics, and when he decided to come to Italy a second time he spontaneously said that in the lectures which he would deliver there he would avoid any subject connected with politics, because, he declared, 'politics always lead to controversy'.

Having to make the arrangements for his reception, I sent word from Santiniketan to the Italian Foreign Office that Tagore intended to visit Italy, and asked whether I should apply to private committees or whether the Government would prefer to provide for the comfort of the Poet. Signor Mussolini at once replied extending the hospitality of the Italian Government to him and his retinue. Dr. Tagore greatly appreciated this token of kindness on the part of the Italian Premier, his only anxiety being whether his health would permit him to perform the journey.

In the meanwhile I sailed for Italy, and on May 14 I received a cable from Dr. Tagore informing me that he and his party were about to sail for Naples. From the moment of his landing in that port I was always by his side, introducing people to him and acting as his interpreter. On May 31 the poet met Signor Mussolini for the first time. I was present at the interview. Signor Mussolini understands English fairly well, so that I had mainly to translate into English the premier's phrases in Italian. Although they met for the first time they had had so much sympathy for each other from afar that the interview was most cordial. The conversations ran chiefly on the cultural relations to be established between Italy and India and on the lecture which the Poet was to deliver in Rome. With almost paternal anxiety Signor Mussolini insisted that the Poet should not overstrain himself but take a real rest in Rome; he was extremely pleased when Dr. Tagore informed him that he would stay a whole fortnight in Rome instead of a week. Turning to me, he suggested the chief places of interest which Dr. Tagore should visit, adding: 'You have only to let me know whatever may be agreeable to you and I shall be only too happy to provide it for you.'

I escorted the poet back to his hotel and asked him his impressions. 'Without doubt', he said, 'a great personality. There is such a massive strength in that head that one cannot help being reminded of Michelangelo's chisel. And at the same time he is a simple man who makes one feel that it is impossible for him to be the cruel tyrant whom so many are pleased to depict'. A reporter who understood and spoke English was then admitted, and asked the poet for a short statement representing what he felt about modern Italy. Dr. Tagore at once penned the following words: 'Let me dream that from the fire bath the immortal soul of Italy will come out clothed in quenchless light'.

The poet's admiration for Mussolini went on increasing on account of the reports he heard from various authoritative quarters. On returning from a visit to a certain foreign personage, whose name I am not at liberty to mention, Dr. Tagore declared to me that he thenceforth entertained no doubt about the splendid future of Italy, that as long as Mussolini lived Italy was safe, that history had always been made by great men, that we were to be envied in having this great man, and that he knew at last how to answer our detractors as soon as he should cross the Italian frontier. This feeling of genuine admiration for Mussolini the Poet repeated to the reporters who swarmed around him, although it is true that to those who asked him his opinion of the Fascist movement he replied that he had had no opportunity of studying its history and character. I always took the greatest care to translate his words faithfully to those reporters who were ignorant of English. The majority, however, could communicate directly with him. I wish to emphasise the fact that I acted as his interpreter in nearly all these interviews and that only when I was unavoidably absent I allowed Dr. Assagioli to take my place.

The Poet's stay in Rome could not be the rest intended by Mussolini. But this was not in the least due to a 'chalked path of programme'. Official receptions were reduced to a minimum and limited to those which might be agreeable to Dr. Tagore, notably the visits to the King, to the Governor of Rome, and to the University. The crowd of reporters and admirers asking for autographs was a great strain, but in the afternoons he was able to drive out wherever he pleased, although he often preferred to remain in his room owing to heart trouble.

On the eve of his departure from Rome on June 14 Dr. Tagore was again received by Mussolini. This second interview was even more cordial than the first. The poet said to the Premier that there is a creative force lying dormant in the intimate nature of all things. It is the exclusive call of great personalities to set that force working. Science provides the materials, the personality takes possession of them and, waking up the soul which is in them, accomplishes the work of creation. Italy provided with a personality seemed to him the fittest medium for bringing the Asiatic and European civilisations close to each other, for allowing the dream and mission of this whole existence to become a living reality. 'You are, Excellency', he added, 'the most misrepresented man in the world'. 'I know it', Signor Mussolini answered smiling, 'but how can I help it!' The conversation then turned on the subject of the scholarships to be created in order to provide for an exchange of students between Italy and India. The poet further declared that he greatly wished to make the personal acquaintance of the great Italian philosopher Benedetto Croce, whose philosophy is so akin to that of India. Signor Mussolini asked me to arrange the interview, as Croce was absent from home. This I did by telegram, and the interview took place the following day. Dr. Tagore finally expressed the wish to possess a portrait of Mussolini. The request was immediately granted and the Premier sent him a beautiful handsomely framed photograph of himself, on which he wrote the words 'With deep admiration', followed by his signature.

I accompanied Dr. Tagore during the rest of his journey through Italy, which was a triumphal progress, until he crossed the frontier at Domodossola on June 22. A cordial letter from Dr. Tagore, then at Villeneuve, dated June 25, contained the following phrase: 'My mind is drinking copious draughts of peace and rest, and I feel gloriously happy'. There was no hint of the distortion which publicity sometimes inflicts on a poet 'whose chief value is not in his opinions, but in his creations'. I could not quite grasp the meaning of this hint at the time.

A second letter dated July 7 from Zurich then reached me. Dr. Tagore wrote that he felt very unhappy because since he had left Italy numerous facts had been brought to his notice about the methods of Fascism which challenged the judgement of humanity and prevented him from remaining silently neutral. Twenty days later a third letter reached me. It announced war and brought under my eyes the writing that has given rise to the present statement. 'The rest is silence'.—Yours, &c.

Carlo Formichi,
Professor of Sanskrit at the University of Rome.
Rome, August 14.[22]

In the first week of September, many of the Indian dailies published the poet's letter to Andrews. The Indian press was rather baffled by the sudden change in the poet's stand. Feelings were mixed. One section was happy to see that despite the royal reception by the host, the poet stood by his ideals and condemned fascism without hesitation, while another section was critical of his unpredictable attitude. They thought that the poet should not have criticized Mussolini so strongly. Notwithstanding his principles, Mussolini had apparently never expressed any unfavourable remarks about Tagore. On the contrary, he had treated the poet's associates quite royally. Another group thought that the poet should not have accepted the Italian invitation in the first place and held the poet's two secretaries responsible for this unfortunate outcome. *The Bengalee* wrote on 2 September 1926:

There can be no doubt that Rabindranath Tagore was disillusioned about the Fascists and Fascism if he had any illusions about them, as soon as he went to Central Europe and freely talked with leaders of Humanistic movements on the continent. The interview published by the *Manchester Guardian* does not differ [...] in essentials from a certain letter alleged to have been written by the poet to Mr. C.F. Andrews from Vienna which was published in a Calcutta daily through the courtesy of a foreign news-agency. The interview has been commented upon by the *Manchester Guardian* and by 'Kappa' in the *Nation* and *Atheneum*; and both those journals are glad that Tagore is not head over heels in love with Fascism, as he was made out to be by the Italian papers and does still look at things with a poet's broad vision as he was accustomed to do before. But the episode of denunciation of Fascism has come as such a surprise to some of the poet's friends and admirers that they are disputing the genuineness of the letter. Their sense of hospitality forbids them to assume that after having been feted so much by the Italian Government and the people, he ought not to have said these hard things about his hosts so soon after. But this is exactly the point which has appealed to others.

Tagore and Mussolini are almost antipodal to each other in their outlook on life. One is an aggressive and narrow-minded nationalist, and the other is an avowed pacifist and internationalist. In spite of that, Mussolini has, for a long time, been known to us as an admirer of Tagore and there was nothing to be wondered at in this. Human attachments often go by contraries of nature. So we have been unable to find how Mussolini's interviews with Tagore or the latter's acceptance of a royal invitation was exceptionable on that account. It was as much creditable to the dictator as it was a triumph for the poet that he was given almost royal honours. But the mystery gathers round the faked interviews with which the Fascist press was deluged in order to show the internationalist poet as a lover of narrowly nationalistic Fascism. Some inkling of what was happening in Italy was given to India through a London message to a local contemporary. We had our misgivings at that time about the soundness of the alleged views of the poet, but now we are told by the poet himself that he never supported Fascism. All that he laments now is that he did not come to know of the sufferings of the people at the hands of the Fascists to be in a position to condemn them for the oppression face to face. Contact with Romain Rolland and other humanists has awakened in the poet a sense of the reality. All the honours that have been showered upon him have not, as was to be expected, stood in the way of his speaking [out] his mind and we hope the Italian people will heed the words of one whom they love and who is their admirer and stop to search their own hearts in their mad career for power.[23]

The Italian press, especially the broadsheet dailies, did not publish the poet's letter to Andrews or its content in their papers, although journalists were not unaware of the letter. Some of the editors of the Italian newspapers became rather eloquent. The *Assalto*, published in Bologna (28 August 1926), did not hesitate to make rather savage and obscene comments about Tagore's tour:

That Tagore, who came to Italy twice and inflicted on us his very heavy poetic lucubration, is an old actor who is worthy of our highest contempt. [...] This guru is kept by various governments, he is paid so much at each lecture. [...] This viscid, insinuating individual, who is as honeyed as his words and poems, came to Italy as he was invited, paid and helped by the Government. He exalted Italy, glorified Fascism, and sang the praises of Mussolini. [...] As soon as he crossed the border, this old man with an unsound soul, who impressed the public with his long black tunic and his white beard, talked behind the back of Italy, Fascism and its great leader, who is endlessly greater than him. [...] He approximately behaved like prostitutes who always swear they are in love with their latest customer. Today we claim we do not like Tagore as a poet anymore because he is emasculated and without backbone. He disgusts us as a man because he is false, dishonest and shameless.[24]

The mouthpiece of Mussolini, *Il Popolo d'Italia*, spouted venom against Tagore. *The Manchester Guardian* published the English version of the editorial on 10 September 1926:

The Old Harpoon

When the unemployed hangers-on of certain so-called circles of culture decided to invite the celebrated Indian Poet Tagore to tour the country we were not enthusiastic for the idea. Italy, by good fortune for herself and the world, has plenty of literary schools and of art in general, and has nothing to learn from the Indians. Anyway, Mr. Rabindranath, Poet of Flowers, Stars, and Pounds Sterling, unbuttoned his tunic and preached in broken English to various provincial gatherings overcome by the imbecile attraction of the exotic and the international. After this experience Tagore returned a second time to Italy, accepted the homage of the Prime Minister, and flaunted his feathers in the principal towns of Italy. Again he failed to arouse our sympathy. A Poet who does not feel the tragedy of his own people is for us not a Poet but a pseudo-mystic. This dishonest Tartuffe (Santone), whom the idiocy of others has promoted to the stature of greatness, profited by Italy's traditional and lordly hospitality towards her guests. Italy saw in him the symbol of the great Indian people and its terrifying dilemmas. Tagore then recrossed the frontier and immediately began to spit poison against Italy. Who cares? Italy laughs at Tagore and those who brought this unctuous and insupportable fellow in our midst.[25]

Tagore went to Paris from Vienna. From Paris, the poet's team went to Dartington in England to spend a week with the Elmhirsts. From there, they went to visit the Scandinavian countries. Later on, they visited Belgium, Germany, and the Central European countries. Finally, they boarded the India-bound ship from Constanza around the middle of November. On 18 December 1926, the poet returned to Santiniketan.

Tucci had left Santiniketan by the end of November or early December, before Tagore's return. Probably he was directed by the Italian government to leave Santiniketan, though his tenure was almost over. From Rome, he elaborately wrote to Tagore, on

29 December 1926, a highly critical note of the poor administration and the failure of Santiniketan to reach its own ideals.
He wrote:

Gurudev
Coming back from Europe, you will have been astonished that I have left
Shantiniketan for good. But you know that there is no fault of mine, if
some hopeless misunderstanding compelled me to transfer myself some-
where else. I regret very much to have been deprived of the company of
so good and learned friends as Shastri and Sen are, and to have lost the
opportunity I had there to learn from you so many things, as I did in our
daily meetings. But I have no responsibility. Of all this only I regret that
my sudden departure did prevent me to speak to you frankly about many
things and especially about Shastries. Having come to your place full of
enthusiasm and having also written some very admirative [admirable]
articles on Shantiniketan, as soon as I went there I feel myself rather compelled to explain why, if I am again invited to write about it, I think that
I shall express myself in a quite different way. I do not like that you or
others may suppose that till [while] I was in Shantiniketan I kept myself
silent and when I went away I began my criticism. You know perhaps my
sincerity and therefore I hope that you will not have such a bad opinion
of my character; moreover any one of my friends in Shantiniketan knows
clearly my ideas because I did not avoid to say frankly what I felt—and
certainly not out of a spirit of mere criticism; but because Shantiniketan, as
an International Institution belongs to the world, and not to India only or
to a small group of men, and therefore all those who have some connection
with it or are inspired by the same ideals are morally compelled to say what
they think about it. Progress comes out from criticism of friends—moved
by this spiritual and intellectual interest. I had in my mind to point out to
you all that I had the opportunity to see there in about one year. Speaking
of your school you said recently that a poet is like a butterfly and those who
have to carry into practice his ideals are like silkworms. I wanted especially
for you to be aware about those silkworms and the defectiveness of their
work: it seems to me that they are unable to understand your ideals and are
chiefly responsible of variety of things that are not quite in accordance with
all that you had in your mind. The consequence is that there is something
in the atmosphere in Shantiniketan which does not agree with your main
ideal—to make of it a meeting place of the East and the West. But of course
I cannot entertain you on those things in a simple letter, especially since I
am unable to go into details. Moreover being too general my criticism could

seem the expression rather of personal grievance than of a sincere love for the institution. I hope that I shall meet you and have frank talk with you. On the eve of my leaving Shantiniketan I would have liked to receive a set of your books—which now I can understand quite well—not as a gift for the love that I may have as a mark of love. Nobody realised how such a gift could have been appreciated by me: and I myself did not ask for it remembering that what is asked is in fact bought.

I hope that you are in good health.

Yours truly

G. Tucci

c/o Rome University[26]

In reply, Tagore wrote on 31 December 1926:

Dear Friend

I felt very much relieved when I received your letter this morning, for I was assured that nothing has happened which could permanently alienate you from me. Though I was given to understand when I was in Europe, that your attitude towards the Ashram had become contemptuously hostile, I never allowed that fact to modify in the least my feeling for you as a friend and my admiration for you as a very richly gifted scholar. I am fully conscious that my own ideals find many obstacles in their realisation in my ashram, but the same thing would have happened in other parts of the world where the great multitude of men has failed in results that have the stamp of orthodox sanction and therefore are easy and useful. I have seen new educational experiments attempted in several institutions in Europe with big funds and efficient organisation, struggling with the same moral difficulties as ours which are inherent in the materials they most use and surroundings that they cannot alter. But the most unfortunate factor in our case which created the unfavourable impression in our mind [is] the scurrilous calumny repeatedly whispered to you behind our back against some of our important members who, at that moment, had no opportunity to defend themselves. However, this has been the usual fate of those who in the service of their cause not only trust their own ideas but also all sorts of men who are allowed to come close to their bosom upon which they can easily inflict cruel hurts.

I earnestly hope that we shall have occasion to meet again and in the meanwhile do not forget that I am

your affectionate friend

Rabindranath Tagore[27]

Tagore never had the opportunity to meet Tucci again. Visva-Bharati had awarded Tucci with its highest honour, Desikottama, in 1961, but he could not come to Santiniketan to receive it personally.

In 1930, Tagore arrived in America after his tour to Russia where he met Formichi in New York. Formichi was then the chair of Italian culture at the University of California at Berkeley. In the course of conversation, Tagore expressed his intention to patch up the bitterness and misunderstanding with Mussolini. The professor advised the poet to write a letter to Mussolini mitigating all misapprehensions. Tagore wrote a letter while still in America, but before sending it to Mussolini directly, he first sent it to his son Rathindranath in London with a note attached for his approval. The note read:

Prof Formichi came to see me. He still has a genuine love for us. I asked him whether my passing through the country [Italy] would be acceptable, and he suggested that simply writing a letter to Mussolini would clear all misunderstanding. [...] That letter is enclosed here. If you have no hesitation, send the letter to him. It is not desirable to keep the altercation with Italy alive.[28]

The letter to Mussolini read:

1172 Park Avenue,
New York (USA)
21 November 1930
Your Excellency
It often comes to my memory how we were startled by the magnanimous token of your sympathy reaching us through my very dear friend—Professor Formichi. The precious gift, the library of Italian literature, is a treasure to us highly prized by our institution and for which we are deeply grateful to Your Excellency.

I am also personally indebted to you for the lavish generosity you showed to me in your hospitality when I was your guest in Italy and I earnestly hope that the misunderstanding which has unfortunately caused a barrier between me and the great people you represent, the people for whom I have genuine love, will not remain permanent and that this expression of my gratitude to you and your nation will be accepted. The politics of a country is its own; its culture belongs to all humanity. My mission is to acknowledge all that has eternal value in the self-expression of any country. Your Excellency has nobly offered to our institution on behalf of Italy the opportunity of a festival of spirit which will remain inexhaustible and ever claim our homage of a cordial admiration.

I am, Your Excellency,

Gratefully yours,

Rabindranath Tagore[29]

Surprisingly, neither Rathindranath or Mahalanobis, nor anyone of Tagore's inner circle ever mentioned this letter in their memoirs. In fact, the existence of the letter was only first revealed in a book published in 1987.[30] For a long time, Tagore scholars were not sure if the letter had been sent to Mussolini. However, Mario Prayer tells us that the letter was actually sent, and Sofori, in his book *Gandhi in Italy*, mentions that he had seen the letter in the 'Political Affairs, India' section of the Italian External Affairs Department.[31] According to the postmark, the letter was received by the department on 10 December 1930—its document number was 13288.[32] Nonetheless, there is no evidence yet to confirm whether or not Mussolini had seen this letter.

It is true that Tagore never eulogized fascism, but there is no doubt that he was fascinated by Mussolini. It took a long time for him to overcome this fascination—perhaps not until the time when Mussolini attacked Abyssinia and other Mediterranean states.

Notes and References

1. Abantikumar Sanyal (tr.), *Prasanga: Romain Rolland* (Kolkata: Papyrus, 1991), p. 29.

2. Formichi File.

3. Sourindramohan Mitra (tr.), *Khyati Akhyatir Nepathey* (Kolkata: Ananda Publishers, 1977), p. 494.

4. *Daily News*, 11 June 1926, p7c7.

5. Newspaper clippings, 1926 folder, Rabindra Bhavan.

6. Mitra, *Khyati Akhyatir Nepathey*, p. 511.

7. Supriya Roy (ed.), 'Rabindranath Tagore's Tour in Europe in 1926', *Rabindra-Viksha*, vol. 38 (2000), pp. 41–4.

8. Romain Rolland, *Inde*, translated into Bengali, *Bharatbarsa*, from French by Abantikumar Sanyal (Kolkata: Radical Book Club, 1976), pp. 132–3. Retranslated into English by the author.

9. Salvadori File.

10. Guglielmo Salvadori, 'Fascism and the Coming Italian Elections', *The New Statesman* (1924), pp. 596–7.

11. The paper *Courriere degli Italiani* published from France was a representative paper of those Italians who were living in exile in Europe. A copy of this paper including an article *'Il Poeta e l'Assassimo'* (The Poet and the Murderer) was sent to Tagore beforehand. The article in the form of a letter was written by Signora Salvadori, but signed as 'One Italian Mother'. See the Appendix in this book.

12. Roy, 'Rabindranath Tagore's Tour in Europe in 1926', pp. 51–4.

13. Sisir Kumar Das (ed.), *The English Writings of Rabindranath Tagore*, vol. 3 (New Delhi: Sahitya Akademi, 1996), pp. 903–4.

14. The full text of the letter of Salvadori to Tagore is included in the Appendix.

15. Salvemini's first wife, Maria Minarvini, with her five children perished in an earthquake in 1908. Tagore met his second wife, Firnande Luceir, who knew English well.

16. Gaetano Salvemini, *'Tagore e Mussolini'*, *Esperienze e Studi Socialisti in Onore di U. G. Mondolfo* (Florence: La Nuova Italia, 1926), pp. 191–206.

17. Krishna Dutta and Andrew Robinson (eds), *Selected Letters of Rabindranath Tagore* (Cambridge: Cambridge University Press, 1997), p. 329.

18. Ibid., p. 337.

19. Krishna Dutta and Andrew Robinson (eds), 'The Tagore–Elmhirst Correspondence', *Purabi: A Miscellany in Memory of Rabindranath Tagore, 1941–1991*, Letter no. 46 (London: The Tagore Centre UK, 1991), p. 98.

20. Formichi File.

21. 'Philosophy of Fascism', *The Manchester Guardian*, 5 August 1926, p9c7, p10c1–2.

22. 'Dr. Tagore in Italy', *The Manchester Guardian*, 25 August 1926, p16c3.

23. Newspaper clippings, 1926 folder.

24. Salvemini, *'Tagore e Mussolini'*, pp. 191–206.

25. 'Fascist Way with Tagore', *The Manchester Guardian*, 15 September 1926, p6c1–2.

26. Tucci File.

27. Dutta and Robinson, *Selected Letters of Rabindranath Tagore*, p. 342.

28. Bikash Chakravarti, '*Mussolini-ke Rabindranath*: 21 November 1930', *Chaturanga* (2009), p. 105.

29. Dutta and Robinson, *Selected Letters of Rabindranath Tagore*, p. 394.

30. Nepal Mazumder, *Robindranath o Koekti Rajnaitic Prasanga* (Kolkata: Chirayata Prakashan, 1987), p. 65.

31. Mario Prayer, 'Italian Fascist Regime and Nationalist India, 1921–45', *International Studies*, vol. 28, no. 3 (1991), p. 253.

32. Chakravarti, '*Mussolini-ke Rabindranath*', pp. 105–18.

Epilogue

In his lifetime, Rabindranath Tagore received invitations from several governments to visit their countries. He mostly accepted the invitations, though sometimes he had to decline for logistical reasons. Of the countries that invited him, Italy, Peru, and Spain were passing through a disturbing state of internal political affairs.

When Tagore accepted the invitation to visit Peru in 1924, the Indians there were involved in the Aprista Movement. The Legua government was extremely harassed by this radical upsurge. Moreover, the final settlement of the long-standing Tacna–Arica dispute with Chile, by which Peru surrendered the province of Arica, angered the extreme nationalists, resulting in the emergence of a kind of despotism. This was the political situation in Peru when its government invited Tagore to attend its centenary celebration of independence. Romain Rolland apprehended that the reactionary government of Peru might exploit Tagore's image and warned Tagore about this in a letter, sent through Sardar Singhji Rana, describing the Peruvian political situation. It is not known for certain if Tagore ever received that letter. However, whether the letter reached him or not, Tagore could not afford the luxury of refusing the $50,000 offer from the Peruvian government during the severe financial crisis at Visva-Bharati and accepted the invitation. However, the poet did not reach Peru: He fell ill while he was passing through Argentina and returned to Europe after taking nearly two months to recuperate in Argentina in the care of Madam Ocampo. In the end, his Peru programme had to be called off.

Tagore was invited by the Spanish government in 1923. Between 1923 and 1930, the Spanish government was run by a military regime led by Primo de Rivera, a radical nationalist and a supporter of the 'anti-Catalan crusade'. His associates later attempted to form a separate party, the Patriotic Union, which was dissolved some time later. The invitation to Tagore was offered during this time of political turmoil, but was also cancelled for some unknown reason.

Nevertheless, Tagore's Italian tour materialized!

In a letter written to Elmhirst,[1] Tagore expressed his regret that his meeting with Mussolini and the events that followed were pre-ordained disasters. No doubt Tagore's Italian tour, especially the second one, was an ideological blunder for him. Yet now, after nine long decades, there are reasons to review Tagore's Italian episode in the light of new research.

After the First World War, most of the participating countries were devastated by economic depression, unemployment, sectarian violence, and all kinds of social ills. As a result, some extremist ideologies emerged in the search for resolution of these internal problems. Bolshevism, followed by communism in Russia, fascism in Italy, and Nazism in Germany, were the new political philosophies seeking to find drastic measures to overcome the socio-economic plight faced by the countries.

During the mid-1920s when the Indian nationalistic movement reached its height, some of these external political forces chose India as the ideal battleground in which to exert their influence on the movement. While the Soviet effort to 'Bolshevize' India failed miserably, India's state of affairs became almost a favourite with fascist propagandists. Thus, the failure of alleged Soviet plots behind the Indian rebellion provided a perfect pasture ground for the fascists.[2] In 1925, an authoritative journalist of the Italian regime, M. Appelius, visited India which culminated in a meeting with Mahatma Gandhi. Appelius regarded Gandhi as one of the 'three unsurpassed spirits of modern history' (the other two being Mussolini and Lenin). Appelius, however, hardly understood the spirit of satyagraha, the main political weapon of the Indian nationalist, assuming it held little interest for the fascist readership. During the same period, an influential member of the Hindusthan Gadar Party, Muhammad Iqbal Shedi, was also trying to gain support for the Indian cause from the fascist regime. He became an intimate of Mussolini's brother Arnaldo and persuaded him to become more positive towards the Indian revolt and Gandhi.[3] As a result of such currents and cross currents of external political influence, the Indian intelligentsia had formed a divided opinion of Mussolini and his regime. *The Modern Review* and *Prabasi*, the two leading Indian journals at that time, regularly reported disparate information on the political conditions of Italy and the news of Mussolini. Mussolini was seen by a section of the critics as a rising star, a saviour of Italy, equivalent to Mazzini and Garbaldi. The other section largely deplored the regime's totalitarianism and unrestrained despot.

As a regular reader of these journals and newspapers, it is difficult to believe that Tagore was not aware of Italian politics. He had at the least some basic information about Mussolini's government. But the political condition of Italy had hardly any influence on his decision to visit. He was never interested in a country's politics, but rather in the spiritual and cultural endeavour of its humanity. Italy, the land of the poets and artists, had been dear to his heart since his teenage years and was his first European experience. In spite of that, however, his proper visit was left so long due only to matters of timing.

Although Formichi did not meet Tagore before 1925, he had collected a great deal of information about him through his contact with one of the closest members of the Tagore circle—Kalidas Nag. He was not only aware of the poet's literary excellence but also some of his ideals. Tagore's avid conviction that global peace should be achieved through the meeting of the East and the West in a common fellowship and understanding impressed Formichi. Nag also informed Formichi about Visva-Bharati, the international institution founded by the poet, where he wanted to give his ideals concrete shape. While in his professorial role at the University of Rome, Formichi had been working simultaneously for the Ministry of Cultural Propaganda Abroad in Italy since 1917, before Mussolini's rise to power. Now, he became genuinely interested in establishing a cultural link between India and Italy using Tagore as a bridge. So, when Rathindranath wrote to Formichi of the possibility of Tagore visiting Italy in May 1921, he was eagerly waiting to meet him in Florence. However, in the end, the tour was abandoned.

In 1921, while Tagore was visiting countries in Europe as a 'one-man peace envoy', he was also searching for distinguished academics and scholars to join his proposed university as visiting fellows. Several European professors, namely, Sylvan Lêvi from France, Maurice Winternitz from Czechoslovakia, and Sten Kono from Norway, offered their services to Tagore's university. Formichi's name was also under consideration as a visiting fellow. On Tagore's side, the failure to meet Formichi was equally disappointing, as the poet was then passing through Lucerne (Switzerland), very close to Italy. Four years later, after an intensive persuasion from Nag, Irani, the two English visitors, and also from Formichi himself, the poet decided to visit Italy on his way back from Argentina.

Meanwhile, Mussolini's rise to power in 1922 and the political unrest within Italy led to despotism, murders, oppression, and deterioration of law and order in quick succession. The dictator issued a stark warning to his citizens, 'If necessary, we shall use the bludgeon and also steel. A rising faith must needs be intolerant. Either my faith is true, or yours; either yours or mine. If I think that mine is true, I cannot suffer secret murmurings, petty ambushes, skulking calumny, base slander. All these must be put down, overthrown, buried.'[4]

Initially, Mussolini claimed success in creating employment and improving roads, railways, and transport systems. He earned some credibility among the working class by introducing various welfare benefits for them such as sickness benefits, compensation,

and pension (though some claims were ambiguous). After visiting
Italy, praise for Mussolini came from several Bengali quarters
such as Suniti Chatterjee, a distinguished scholar and polyglot;
Shyamaprasad Mukherjee, leader of Hindu Mahasabha; Binoy
Kumar Sircar, an economist; and Ramananda Chatterjee, editor
of *The Modern Review*. Even Gandhi, who visited Mussolini in
1930, four years after Tagore's visit, was impressed with some of
Mussolini's economic and social reforms. Gandhi wrote in a letter
to Rolland:

> Mussolini is a riddle to me. Many of his reforms attract me. He seems to
> have done much for the peasant class. I admit an iron hand is there. But
> as violence is the basis of Western society, Mussolini's reforms deserve an
> impartial study.... [Mussolini's] care of the poor, his opposition to super-
> urbanization, his efforts to bring about co-ordination between capital and
> labour, seem to me to demand special attention. [...] What strikes me is
> that behind Mussolini's implacability is a desire to serve his people. Even
> behind his emphatic speeches there is a nucleus of sincerity and of pas-
> sionate love for his people. It also seems to me that the majority of Italian
> people love the iron government of Mussolini.[5]

However, this initial success was bought at a high price. Middle-
class intellectual liberals, though initially supportive of Mussolini,
became increasingly sceptical and disillusioned with the fascist
movement. These patriotic Italians, who refused to accept the total-
itarian government, faced dire consequences in their professional
and social lives. The price for open criticism of the government was
torture and even death. Amendola, Matteotti, and many more were
the victims of the fascist regime. Hence, for survival, the people
generally had three options open to them.

Firstly, they could refuse to compromise with the government and silently leave Italy to take refuge in another country.
It was not an easy decision to leave one's homeland, abandoning
one's establishment, and giving up professional income. However,
Salvemini, Salvadori, Balabanoff, Modigliani, and others chose this
option because they were not ready to compromise their principles.
Salvemini wrote this in his resignation letter:

The Fascist dictatorship has now totally suppressed in our country those conditions of freedom, in the absence of which the University teaching of history—as I understand it—loses all trace of dignity, because it clashes necessarily with free civil education and is reduced either to servile adulation of the dominating party or to a mere exercise of erudition, both foreigners alike to the moral consciences of the teacher and of the taught.

Therefore I am compelled to part from my young listeners and from my colleagues with deep sorrow, but certain that I am discharging towards them a duty of straightforwardness even more than a duty of consistency and respect towards myself.

I shall return to the country to serve in education when we shall have regained a civil government.[6]

Salvemini emigrated to England, while his property was confiscated by the government.

Secondly, citizens could live within Italy, but detached from the government, remaining neutral with eyes and ears closed, like Benedetto Croce, Duke Scotti, and other intellectuals who were the silent minority. It was not easy to maintain this neutral stance.

Thirdly, they could strike a compromise with the government for the sake of maintaining a safe existence, with or without having faith in fascism. Formichi, Tucci, professors and directors of several universities, middle-class intellectuals, civil servants, and people who welcomed the poet were amongst this majority group.

As an ex-journalist, Mussolini was conscious of the effective handling of the media in his favour. He knew that in order to consolidate his control over public opinion and fulfil his own aims by continuing the propaganda, he must exercise complete control over the press. Hence, on achieving power, he immediately and steadily started amending the rules of journalism. Soon the editors of the daily newspapers lost their rights to free expression and denigrating the government in print meant losing their jobs. Even readers of these dailies were threatened with physical assault. Vettori, the editor of *Giornale d'Italia*, was threatened by the police, later losing his job. Frassati, the editor of *La Stampa*, and Giordana, the editor of *La Tribuna*, were sacked and replaced by people chosen by Mussolini. *Il Resto del Carlino*, a newspaper known for its liberal views, was bribed and transformed overnight into a pro-fascist daily. Fascist magazines mushroomed under the patronage of the government, which invested and siphoned taxpayers' money. These publications had the single agenda of glorifying the Duce and his fascist strategy. When the readership of Mussolini's mouthpiece *Il Popolo d'Italia* fell drastically and that of *Corriere della Sera* went up, it indicated that a silent majority of the readers did not accept fascist policies.[7] As a remedial measure, Mussolini's brother Arnaldo was made the editor of *Il Popolo d'Italia*. The newspaper *Corriere della Sera* suffered the worst consequences. Its editor, Albertini, was once a supporter of fascism, but later withdrew his support. As a consequence, the office of this newspaper in Milan was burnt down. *The New Statesman*, a British weekly magazine, published Salvadori's eyewitness account:

An incident has just taken place at the station in Florence which […] I will cite as an example. The *Corriere della Sera*, the gravest and most widely circulated newspaper in Italy, published in Milan, was waited for at the station by some thirty Fascisti, all armed. As the bundles of newspapers were unloaded, at 2 o'clock in the early afternoon, the Fascisti seized upon them, carried them out, and on the piazza before the station made a bonfire of them under the eyes of a gaping crowd that knew better than to interfere, since the Fascisti shoot on sight. The police made a feint of protesting, but knew that to arrive late would please the Government, and in any case the arrests they might make would not be maintained.[8]

Often, the first pages of the national newspapers were scrutinized and approved by the prime minister's office before giving clearance for printing. All the newspapers were directed to send one copy to the prime minister's residence every morning.

Such was the political backdrop in Italy in 1925 when, in January, the poet arrived at Genoa. While travelling by train from Genoa to Milan, he casually asked Formichi to update him about the political situation in the country. As it was their initial meeting, Formichi exercised restraint. However, Tagore was more interested in the people than the politics of the country and did not discuss politics during the rest of his tour.

In 1924, the poet was invited to Italy by an academic society of Milan, not by the Italian government. Through Guido Cagnola, Formichi persuaded Circolo Filologico Milanese, a prestigious association of philological and literary studies to organize Tagore's trip to Italy that year. Duke Scotti, the president of the society, was an influential and aristocratic personality and an anti-fascist intellectual. Because of his high position in the society, he escaped assault by the fascist militants. Formichi was also an old-time aristocrat in spirit, if not by birth. Though Formichi was not a political person, he had an allegiance towards fascism—a fact that he never attempted to hide. In fact, many Italian orientalists and theosophists tended towards fascism and anti-Semitism in those years.[9] Initially, Formichi was not aware of Scotti's anti-fascist standing. Scotti knew that Tagore's intellect and principles would place him in opposition to fascism. He wanted the Philological Circle's programme to have a political nuance so that an anti-fascist atmosphere might be created.[10] Later on, Scotti mentioned this in a letter to Salvemini. Tagore's speech was perceived as an indirect rebellion, especially by the young fascist activists and, as a consequence, his connection to an anti-fascist personality easily aroused the suspicion of the government's followers. One would not be surprised if they had put the poet under surveillance. Although during his first trip Tagore had no contact with Mussolini, the latter was well aware of the poet's presence in Milan. According to the Rome correspondent of *The New York Times*, Tagore was under pressure to visit Rome.[11] Only 15 days before Tagore's arrival, there was an unsuccessful coup d'état to overthrow the prime minister. Mussolini was going through a period of severe political crisis and inviting Tagore to Rome could have diverted people's attention, an idea not in the Duce's mind at that time. Although Formichi had suggested to the poet that his Italian trip would be incomplete without a visit to Rome, whether the suggestion was to visit the university or meet Mussolini is not clear. Formichi was quite aware of the psyche of his fellow countrymen, and he did his best to prevent Tagore from getting entangled in any kind of political debate: Italy was not the ideal country conducive to free thinking at that time. Formichi was cautious from the moment since Tagore asked him to give a political brief of Italy during his train journey to Milan. Moreover, since he was the primary organizer of the poet's trip, he took upon himself the responsibility of ensuring the comfort of Tagore and his entourage. This was probably the reason why Formichi guarded the poet more than was necessary, and this gave the impression to the other members of Tagore's entourage that Formichi was trying to use him for political gain.

With the revelation of Scotti's anti-fascist stance, a silent ideological clash developed between him and Formichi. However, Tagore was not aware of this tension. There is no contemporary document available to throw light on the relationship between Scotti and Formichi. Tagore's son Rathindranath was also not aware of such complications as his primary concern was for his father's health. On the other hand, there was an undercurrent of tension in the interpersonal relationship between Formichi and Elmhirst—the latter suspected that there were secret preparations to woo Tagore politically under Formichi's directions. Elmhirst had expressed these views in some of his correspondence,[12] but these suspicions were probably not true. The major cost of Tagore's trip was met by Milan's Philological Society, though the people of Turin and Florence also contributed their small share. These organizations were expecting the poet not only to visit but also lecture, which presumably Formichi had assured. It is expected that Elmhirst, as Tagore's secretary, was aware of this. Even if he was not, the poet himself knew this. One can never be sure whether the meetings arranged by these organizations were politically motivated as Tagore had accepted these invitations in the following year, that is, 1926, when he revisited Italy. Formichi was in an uncertain position with the organizers when Tagore's tour programme had to be abruptly cut short owing to illness. Unknown to Tagore, there were heated exchanges between Formichi and Elmhirst regarding the cancellation of his trip to Turin. Probably this was the reason why there was a strain in the relationship between Elmhirst and Formichi. Was it due to the inherent, subconscious disdain of the British for the Italians? Did the complex psychology, suspicions, and misunderstandings lead to the poet's entourage identifying Formichi as an accomplice in Mussolini's plot? Suspicions about Formichi were further strengthened after the unfounded rumour of the presence of a woman spy at the Hotel Cavour, where Tagore and his party were staying. Tagore, however, was not aware of any such underlying stress between Elmhirst, Scotti, and Formichi during the tour.

Tagore's lecture in Milan had upset a section of the fascist audience. From the very beginning, Formichi had doubts that Tagore's humanitarian message would be acceptable to the audience in the political atmosphere of the time, which was why he wanted to have some idea of the text of Tagore's speech at the outset. However, Tagore could not oblige Formichi. Later on, Formichi uncharitably commented:

[…] A poet may be understood and forgiven when he feeds on humanitarian chimeras, precincts from historical necessity and follows his day-dreams in order to form vague, yet high-sounding sentences which can secure him longed-for applause. This, in fact, may prove amusing, especially to those who struggle against the huge difficulties of this tangible and real world, and perfectly realise the absolute uselessness of cheap sermons of love and peace. Rabindranath preached that humanitarian sermon not knowing that it was absolutely out of place, for it was made in an environment filled with impassioned national sentiment that was ready to suspect, get angry and react violently.[13]

A harsh comment from Formichi indeed! Formichi probably expected Tagore's first lecture to be above criticism. He was disappointed with the outcome and his reaction was abrupt.

In an article published in *Il Popolo d'Italia* in 1921, Mussolini had predicted that the Moplah Rebellion would be the reason for the end of British rule in India. Other than this single article, there is not much evidence of Mussolini's interest in India until the mid-1920s.[14] Nonetheless, Mussolini's assessment of India was very clear. According to him, Italy and India should have a clear understanding since both countries were anti-British. A common foe would bind both nations in friendship, or so Mussolini believed. However, one point of difference was that, during that period, many English journals and newspapers both in Italy and abroad were praising Mussolini and his governance. There were several

English and American communities in Florence, and many English dailies were regularly published there. Most of these newspapers praised Mussolini's government for bringing about peace, stability, and prosperity for Italy as well as for securing the lives of foreign nationals there. The British ambassador in Rome gave Tagore a similar impression. Salvadori, however, concluded in an article:

> [...] Strangers who come abroad see that the country seems quiet, but order imposed outside the law cannot be durable. When the image of order, with feet of clay, falls suddenly, as fall it must, those countries who have not taken the trouble to look below the surface will have done Italy an ill service in encouraging the kind of infatuation for Mussolini which has come over many people, even among the Italians; and chief of these countries is England, whose Press and whose subjects abroad hail Mussolini as the Saviour of his country.[15]

Tagore remarked to Signora Salvadori that the British overlooked Mussolini's violent atrocities because post-War Britain had become used to violence; the inhuman Black and Tan policy of the British against the Irish proved that. Therefore, the British were not critical of the atrocities committed by powerful men. However, British diplomatic policy was more complex. It is possible that in order to allow further deterioration of Italy's interior, the British in Italy continued to follow a campaign of false praise. The British and French funded Italy in many ways to bring Italy into their alliance during the War. Mussolini's newspaper *Il Popolo d'Italia* was financed by both the British and the French.

Mussolini knew well that in order to gain the confidence of his people in fascist policy, a positive publicity campaign would be an effective tool. The premier would, therefore, invite the foreign press and distinguished foreign visitors from all walks of life, showcasing the accomplishments of his government. Undoubtedly, he was to a large extent successful in this strategy. In fact, between 1925 and 1935, until Italy attacked Abyssinia (now known as Ethiopia), numerous famous foreigners besides Tagore visited Italy and were full of praise for its apparent prosperity. They were people such as W.B. Yeats, George Bernard Shaw, Mahatma Gandhi,

Ezra Pound, and even Hollywood actor Douglas Fairbanks, and many more.

In 1926, Mussolini was struggling with a difficult time in his political career. Despite the state-controlled press, the news of Amendola's and Matteotti's assassinations filtered out of the country, and the socialist press all over Europe capitalized on it to condemn fascist policies. Mussolini's own assassination was attempted several times, and his image deteriorated rapidly in the international stage. At this juncture, an appeal for economic aid for Tagore's school came to him through Formichi. While Formichi was trying to open direct cultural links between Italy and India, Mussolini had other plans. He seized the opportunity to fulfil his responsibilities in the field of international culture and decided to utilize Tagore's presence in Italy to accomplish his earlier plan. At that time, Tagore was an international icon of peace and liberty. If he endorsed fascism and its role in rejuvenating a nation that had lost its glory, the entire world would take a different view of Italy—this was the idea that formed in Mussolini's mind. He unhesitatingly accepted Formichi's proposal with unusual munificence. He could subject Tagore easily to his plan since Tagore was neither knowledgeable of deeper Italian politics nor of the Italian language. Mussolini considered Tagore an ideal prey.

What followed is quite well known. Impressed by Mussolini's generosity, Tagore decided to return to Italy to express his gratitude. His return to Italy in the following spring was already on Tagore's agenda. Before leaving Italy in 1925, he assured his return in a beautiful poem which was circulated in the Italian press. Consequently, Formichi and Tucci did not have to work hard to convince Tagore to return to Italy for the second time. From now on, it seems that Formichi had to play a dual and antithetical role— that of the intellectual with deep respect for Tagore, on the one hand, while simultaneously in the role of Mussolini's 'yes-man', on the other. Events that followed showed some kind of duality in Formichi's action.

According to Formichi, after Tagore decided to visit Italy for the second time, he contacted the Foreign Office to find out if the government would extend a state invitation or if a private organization would make all the arrangements. Formichi received Mussolini's message sanctioning the state invitation to Tagore on 20 January 1926. This establishes the fact that having Tagore as a state guest had already been decided by Mussolini. However, no official letter of invitation has yet been traced, which is rather unusual. Perhaps the Italian government was too cautious about not creating a controversy prior to Tagore's trip. Even the Italian embassy in Calcutta was kept in the dark about the state invitation or, probably, the embassy was told to keep silent. Tagore, however, knew that he was visiting Italy as a state guest from the very beginning; his intimate circle was aware of it too. Even the international press knew it. But before boarding the ship from Bombay, Tagore told the press that he had never received any invitation from Mussolini: So there was obviously no written invitation. On 15 May 1926, Tagore maintained that his second visit was due to the promise he had made to his friends in Italy. This led to the idea that Tagore was invited by the Italian government after his arrival in Italy, the possibility of which, again, remains unfounded. This ambiguity is confusing. Was Tagore conscious of the controversial aspects of Mussolini's invitation? Did he exercise caution from the beginning?

The presence of the two Italian professors, Formichi and Tucci, in Visva-Bharati had created repeated controversy. The article 'Fascism in India' published in the *The Modern Review* is remarkable. The news item quoted a source in the American press and alleged that Indian fascists were becoming a source of concern for Britain, that Italian professors were doubling up as fascist agents and in close contact with Indian princes, and that a number of fascist clubs were appearing in Calcutta and Bombay. Based on these reports, the *The Modern Review* observed:

We are not aware of any activity of Fascists in India. [...] We know of the visits of only two Italian professors to India, viz., Prof. Formichi and Prof. Tucci. The former has left India after lecturing on subjects relating to ancient Indian scholarship, philosophy and religion, mostly at Santiniketan, and also at Dacca, Benaras and Calcutta Universities. [...] It was not part

of his business, public or private, to see Indian princes. Prof. Tucci is still
in Santiniketan. He is an indologist and sinologist combined and is doing
professional work, he also has neither the leisure nor the inclination to go
about seeing princes.[16]

The Mahalanobis couple also felt that the presence of the two
Italian professors was not entirely without motive, though they
did not show any reason or proof to support their hunch.[17] They
could not be accommodated in the ship with Tagore's party during
the 1926 tour because their request for berth reservations came
at the last moment. According to Rapicavoli, the captain of the
king's army, Tucci, had warned the foreign office in advance against
Mahalanobis. His presence could create problems because he was
close to the poet who consulted him and valued his opinion. Was
this the reason why their berths were cancelled at the last moment?
In a letter written by Tucci (possibly to Andrews), he mentioned
that initially there were directions from Tagore's secretary to book
the passage for four people.[18] These four persons were the poet,
his son Rathindranath, his daughter-in-law, and his secretary. The
rest of Tagore's party decided to join later, and at the last moment
it was difficult to have berths reserved. Could this be a reason why
the Mahalanobis couple were dropped, in order to accommodate
others? After such a long time, today it is only a matter of speculation. But it was evident that even before the visit to Italy, Formichi
and Mahalanobis had some clashes of personality, which surfaced
every now and then during the trip. From his experience of the
poet's first visit, Formichi realized that in order to maintain a
respectable balance between the two antithetical duties of showing Tagore his due respect and working according to the wishes of
his master Mussolini, he needed to have complete control over the
entire situation. The presence of Elmhirst or Mahalanobis could
have worked against him. This could be a possible rationale if we
look for corroboration in Formichi's actions during the trip.

There is no denying the fact that Tagore's artistic self saw an
attractive personality in Mussolini. He had repeatedly mentioned
this and never withdrew the statement, even under pressure. In his
letter to Andrews, he described Mussolini thus: 'He was not tall in

proportion to his fame that towers high. But when he came near me I was startled by the massive strength of his head. The lower part of the face, the lips, the smile, revealed a singular contradiction to the upper part.'[19] He had commented to Signora Salvadori, 'he did interest me as an artist. [...] Mussolini struck me as a masterful personality [...] his great dramatic personality brought to my vision a man riding upon a wild horse who by his marvellous strength checked insane people and controlled them.'[20] After meeting Mussolini for the first time, he had remarked to Formichi, 'Without any doubt his is a great personality. There is such a massive vigour in that head, that it reminds one of Michelangelo's chisel.'[21] This last comment was widely publicized in the newspapers. Physically, Mussolini was not attractive in the conventional sense of the term. He was short, his head was disproportionately large compared to his body, and below his broad shoulders, the lower part of his body was similarly disproportionate—in fact, an ideal subject for the cartoonist! According to Mussolini's biographers, he had a dramatic personality beneath a deceptive mask. He could change his personality according to the situation, like a chameleon. In particular, he always had a pleasing and deeply impressive effect on people during their first meeting. Obviously, Romain Rolland did not like Tagore's over-appreciation of Mussolini, which also annoyed Salvadori. However, the German historian Emil Ludvig, who critically analysed Mussolini's character, had commented, 'I am content with the artistic observation of a remarkable personality.'[22] This comment is significant.

The Italian press had widely published all the praise that Tagore had expressed in his poetic language out of courtesy for Mussolini's generosity and impressive words. This is common in the media and the Italian press was no exception, especially when publicity was a primary objective. But it is also true that Tagore never supported fascism in his statements at any time. He had reiterated that he desisted from commenting on political issues as he was not sufficiently aware of the details of Italian politics. Still, Mussolini being synonymous with fascism, it was widely publicized that Tagore supported fascism. Moreover, Tagore had commented that the state policies of one country might not be relevant to another country. Even Mussolini had said that his state policy was not for export! Equally, it was true that there was little publicity of Tagore's wide humanistic views, international cooperation between the countries of the East and the West, and so on, which he expressed in his interviews and in the course of conversation with Italian intellectuals. He had mentioned in many of his interviews that the Italian people should realize that the mere pursuit of material wealth would never make them great; they would be a great world-power only when they give the world permanent gifts of the spirit. Otherwise, national prosperity and political power died with them. These were consumed in the process of enjoyment: But products of the spirit were for all time and countries.[23]

But none of these comments was published in the newspapers that the present author has accessed. This might be explained in several ways. The first and the most popular view is that Formichi understood the psyche of the Italian people. He did not want the Milan event to be repeated. He did not want Tagore to be the source of another controversy and, therefore, carefully edited his statements before translating and handing them over to the press. Another possibility is that Formichi had translated Tagore's words quite faithfully. The press, having the prime minister's office in mind, took it upon itself to edit out portions that were not in tune with fascist ideology, as a precautionary measure.

During his second tour, Tagore gave a lecture in every city he visited. These lectures did not contain any anti-fascist elements. Reports of the speeches were published in the press according to the understanding of the reporters. These were truthful and harmless reports of the welcomes extended to the poet and the places he visited. With strong state censorship, most newspapers carried more or less similar monotonous reports as none were allowed to express their own views. However, the articles on Tagore, though inadequately researched, were apparently published without being censored.

Another allegation against Mussolini's government was that it had planned a tour of Italy for Tagore which would only highlight the positive aspects of fascism. The poet himself admitted that since he never had a chance to meet the common people or those belonging to the opposition, it was impossible for him to form an idea of the negative aspects of fascism. This claim needs to be scrutinized. Tagore's itinerary reveals that he was shown around the places that any common tourist would visit in Florence and Rome, for example, the Capitol, the Colosseum, the Roman Baths, the University of Rome, the Florence museums, and the Fiat factory in Turin. These places were certainly not the flagships of fascism. As the poet was also an educator and his love for children was well known, he was shown institutions like Orti di Pace or Casa del Sole and other non-governmental and semi-governmental organizations: Neither of these were examples of the achievements of the fascist government. One thing has baffled Tagore scholars—in his 36-hour stay in Rome, Gandhi, who was not a significant connoisseur of art, had been shown the Sistine Chapel, whereas during his fortnight stay, Tagore did not express an intention to visit this extraordinary work of art, despite the fact that Mussolini's relationship with the Vatican during this period was fairly cordial.

During the interview with Signora Salvadori, Tagore mentioned that he had on no occasion had contact with anybody opposed to the fascist regime as he was always surrounded by people of fascist allegiance. It is true that the political climate in Italy was not conducive for the public to speak out against the government. But on the poet's side, there is no evidence to suggest his eagerness to meet contemporary writers and artistes, or to discover their literary and artistic attainments and output during this crucial period in Italy. The only person he was keen to meet was Benedetto Croce and the meeting took place in rather extraordinary circumstances. Even during his long and secret meeting with Croce, Italian politics were not the subject of discussion. This silence of Croce puzzled Rolland. Croce later explained in his diary, '[...] since Tagore had requested Mussolini's permission to see me, I could not give vent to the bad opinion I had of Fascism and Mussolini, and had to remain silent. It was a question of good taste.'[24]

Tagore's trip to Italy did not have any political significance within Italy. In a way, Mussolini's plans did not yield the expected results. The letters written by Tagore after his trip to Italy did not help lessen the extreme tragedy of the Italians. On the contrary, these communications had disappointed people like Rolland and Salvadori.

Tagore had received an unprecedented reception from the Italian public. The letters from his Italian admirers are preserved in the Italy file of the Rabindra Bhavan Archive in Santiniketan. Some of these letters were written as early as 1921, when exploratory letters were being exchanged between Formichi and Rathindranath regarding Tagore's possible Italian trip! Like many other European countries, this mass worship of Tagore in Italy was not solely because of his literary achievements. The children of Milan were told that one of the 'Three Wise Men' from the Bible had appeared before them! Barring a handful of intellectuals, Tagore's image of the 'Wise Man from the East' was most popular among the common people of Europe between the two World Wars. Brecht aptly described this unprecedented euphoria about Tagore in Germany:

What a strange contrast! From the stormy symphony of our times, from the roaring, brazen rhythm of battle comes forth the sweet melodies of this man from the East. They sing and celebrate love and happiness, which seem insignificant, even unreal to us at the present time. They lament and bemoan a sorrow which to us appears too trivial, too personal to grieve for.

And yet, how strange and wonderful it is that we after all are compelled by these strains to celebrate and to lament; we forget how sombre are our times; we forget strife and misery and, led by the Poet's hand, are impelled to wander into a sunny land of peace. It is proof of this Indian poet philosopher's great mastery that he succeeds in captivating us even at this time.[25]

Italy too had a similarly euphoric response to Tagore.

Whatever motives Mussolini had for Tagore, during his regime, probably no other state guest received such an unprecedented welcome as did Tagore and his retinue. The Italian treasury had opened its coffers quite generously to play host to this Indian poet. Quite naturally, any uncharitable discourse against such a generous host seemed quite discourteous to the poet at first. Tagore's sensibility, propriety, and gratitude were misinterpreted by Salvadori, Salvemini, Duhamel, and others as sycophancy. Even his letter condemning fascism was expressed in the language of a poet. It was polite and reserved. For obvious reasons, the courteous tone of his letter was not appreciated by the tortured and exiled individuals. Consequently, the letters they wrote to the poet and the articles they wrote about him carried a note of ridicule and satirical chiding!

An interesting comment by Amartya Sen came out during an interview for the Italian newspaper *La Voce Republicana*. He remarked:

I remember well his confused relationship with Italy during Fascism. Given his keen interest in freedom, one might expect he would be a staunch antifascist. At the same time, however, and for the very same reason, he was extremely critical towards British Imperialism. For a short time, hence, he allowed himself to be impressed by the Fascist propaganda. He believed that in Italian Fascism there could have been the seeds of a new 'anti-imperialism'. Dimmed by that illusion, he accepted to be 'exhibited' by the regime during a brief official visit in Italy.[26]

Whether this remark is justified or not, Tagore's esteem for Mussolini was untarnished for a few years more. Probably after Italy invaded Abyssinia, Tagore completely changed his opinion about Mussolini. But even before that, on 23 February 1927, Romain Rolland and Henri Barbusse held an anti-fascist conference in Paris to stop the monstrous cruelty of the fascists and appealed to all right-thinking people of the world to unite. Barbusse had written to Tagore with the same appeal, to which the poet expressed his support thus: 'Therefore I rejoice at the fact that there are individuals who still believe in a higher destiny of man, proving in their suffering the deathless life of the human soul ever ready to fight its own aberration.'[27] On 17 March 1935, Tagore drew a sketch of Mussolini. Perhaps the news of the impending Italian invasion of Abyssinia triggered him to draw the cartoon. Nearly two and half thousand paintings and drawings of Tagore were mostly untitled, whereas this particular cartoon was distinctly titled as *Mussolini*.

Mussolini, a cartoon drawn by Tagore, 17 March 1935
Source: Rabindra Bhavan.

At the end of his life, Tagore wanted to make up for his earlier
neutral attitude by issuing a call to fight the fascist monster:

The she-serpents hiss everywhere, exhaling poison-breaths.
Soft words of peace will sound like hollow jests.
Before I take my leave
let me invoke
those who, in human homes, are preparing themselves
to wage war against the monsters.[28]

At the end of his life, the humanist, pacifist poet even supported armed struggle and wished the Anglo-French camp to win as 'the tarnishing of the history of mankind by the Fascists and Nazis has become intolerable'.[29] Fortunately, for the poet, he did not live to see the horror and cataclysm of another devastating World War.

On the other hand, even after experiencing complex psychological tensions within themselves, Formichi and Tucci could not quite rid themselves of the regard they had for Tagore. Thirty-five years after the poet's Italian tour, Giuseppe Tucci reminisced, '[…] I still consider the time I spent with the Poet one of the richest in my life; those years in which the inspiration of the *Rishi* [sage] helped to germinate in my soul some seeds which perhaps were to give later their fruit.'[30]

Even after exchanging bitter correspondence, five years later, Carlo Formichi wrote with reverence, 'That the world should know and love renunciation and action, East and West, a poet, made of light and of music, sang and is still singing luminous and melodious songs. Rabindranath Tagore—let humanity bless him.'[31]

Notes and References

1. Krishna Dutta and Andrew Robinson (eds), 'The Tagore–Elmhirst Correspondence', *Purabi: A Miscellany in Memory of Rabindranath Tagore, 1941–1991*, Letter no. 46 (London: The Tagore Centre UK, 1991), p. 98. It reads:

> Possibly some day I shall come to the conclusion that it was sinister design on the part of my evil fate to have brought me into my relation with this man who may be altogether a fraud and no real personality. Somehow I have the unenviable knack of getting myself entangled in responsibilities that should have been avoided and I regret that I have allowed myself to pay this last visit to Italy.

2. Mario Prayer, 'Italian Fascist Regime and Nationalist India, 1921–45', *International Studies*, vol. 28 (1991), p. 250.

3. Ibid., pp. 251–2.

4. Gaetano Salvemini, 'The Terror in Florence', *Review of Reviews* (November–December 1926), sourced from newspaper clippings, Visva-Bharati.

5. Palash Ghosh, 'Mussolini and Gandhi: Strange Bedfellows', www.ibtimes.com/mussolini-gandhi-strange-bedfellows-214200, accessed 1 April 2015.

6. G. Salvemini, *Reviews of Reviews*, cited from *The Modern Review* (January 1926), p. 72.

7. Denis Mack Smith, *Mussolini* (London: Granada, 1983), p. 79.

8. Guglielmo Salvadori, 'Fascism and the Coming Italian Elections', *The New Statesman*, 1 March 1924, pp. 596–7.

9. Giuseppe Flora, 'Rabindranath Tagore and Italy: Facing History and Politics', *Reclaiming a Cultural Icon* (Calcutta: Visva-Bharati, 2005), p. 284.

10. G. Salvemini, *'Tagore e Mussolini'*, in *Esperienze e studi socialisti in onore di U.G. Mondelfo'* (Florence: La Nuova Italia Editrice, 1957), p. 191.

11. *The New York Times*, 23 January 1925, p12c1.

12. Elmhirst Archive, Dartington.

13. Mario Prayer, 'On Tagore', *Rabindra-Viksha*, vol. 39 (2001), p. 39; translated from Carlo Formichi, *India e Indiani* (Milan: Edizioni Alpes, 1929).

14. Prayer, 'Italian Fascist Regime and Nationalist India', p. 249.

15. Salvadori, 'Fascism and the Coming Italian Election', pp. 596–7.

16. 'Fascism in India', *The Modern Review* (May 1926), p. 600.

17. Nirmal Kumari Mahalanobis, *Kobir sange Europey* (Kolkata: Mitra and Ghosh, 1969), pp. 39–40.

18. Tucci File, Rabindra Bhavan. This is an eight-page letter written by Tucci addressing 'My Friend' [written to whom—Andrews?]. The relevant part of the letter is quoted here:

> [...] You know that we succeeded in securing four berths in the steamer for the Poet, Rathi, his wife and one Secretary and this was in accordance with a written request sent to me through Morris by Mr. Rathi. Just the day before the departure the Consul received a letter in which they requested a formal invitation from our Government and asked for six berths. The letter was written in such a way that it appeared to me and to the Consul very impolite, especially considering all that we had done to obtain from the Government the best facilities. I went from Calcutta back to Santiniketan in order to show the letter to the poet and he was very disappointed and told me that he knew nothing about that very unkind letter. It is useless that I tell you what Rathi said to me and the Consul when we met him. Only I remember that when he told us that the berths were asked for Mr. Lal and for the secretary he forgot that for Lal at least the berth was already fixed for the next steamer. Of course the government was informed about this and you can easily fancy the bad light that these shenanigans have thrown onto the entourage of the poet and perhaps onto the poet himself.

19. Rabindranath Tagore, 'Philosophy of Fascism', *The Manchester Guardian*, 5 August 1926, p9c7, p10c1–2.

20. Swapan Mazumder (ed.), 'Rabindranath Tagore's Tour in Europe in 1926', *Rabindra-Viksha*, vol. 38 (2000), pp. 51–4.

21. Carlo Formichi, 'On Tagore', tr. Mario Prayer, *Rabindra-Viksha*, vol. 40 (2001), p. 25.

22. Sourindramohan Mitra (tr.), *Khyati Akhyatir Nepathey* (Kolkata: Ananda Publishers, 1977), p. 525.

23. Mazumder, 'Rabindranath Tagore's Tour in Europe in 1926', p. 53.

24. Benedetto Croce's *Taccuini*, note dated '1951', cited from Mario Prayer, 'Tagore's Meeting with Benedetto Croce in 1926', *Rabindranath Tagore: A Timeless Mind* (London: The Tagore Centre UK, 2011), p. 269.

25. Martin Kämpchen, *Rabindranath Tagore in Germany: A Documentation* (Kolkata: Goethe-Institut, 1991), p. 25.

26. Giuseppe Flora, 'Rabindranath Tagore and Italy', p. 281.

27. Nepal Mazumder, *Rabindranath: Koekti Rajnaitic Prasanga* (Kolkata: Chirayata Prakhan, 1987), p. 53.

28. Rabindranath Tagore, *Prantik*, verse no. 18, tr. Ketaki Kushari Dyson, *I Won't Let You Go* (Newcastle upon Tyne, England: Bloodaxe Books, 1996), p. 211. This is reproduced with the kind permission of the translator.

29. Mazumder, *Rabindranath*, p. 25.

30. Giuseppe Tucci, 'Recollection of Tagore', *Rabindranath Tagore—Centenary Volume* (New Delhi: Sahitya Akademi, 1961), p. 60.

31. Carlo Formichi, *The Golden Book of Tagore*, ed. Ramananda Chatterjee (Kolkata: The Golden Book of Tagore Committee, 1931), p. 81.

Appendix

In Milan, the poet was under the weather, confined to the hotel, and not allowed to see any visitors other than some of his very close friends. Duke Scotti was one of those who regularly visited him. Even in his weak state of health, the poet discussed a variety of subjects, one of which was on death, transcribed by Elmhirst and reproduced here. This conversation was like beads of thought not strung into a lace as a written text.

On Death

DUKE: I liked very much, the translation I read of your play 'The Post Office'. From it I received the impression that you felt about death as though it was a kind of revelation of the Divine.

POET: I have had so many experiences of loved ones who have died, that I think I have come to know something about death, something perhaps of its deeper meaning. Every moment

that I have spent at the death bed of some dear friend, I have
known this, yet it is very difficult to describe how for me
that great ocean of truth, of existence, of life, from which life
itself springs and to which all life returns, can never suffer
diminution by death. It is this ocean of life that I feel it most
difficult to describe in words. I see how the individual life
comes back into the bosom of this ocean at the moment of
death. I have felt too how great and fathomless this ocean is,
yet how full it is of personality. For personality is ever flowing into it. Ever receiving into its bosom, it becomes instilled
with personality. Yet this ocean seems as nothing, as neither
light nor darkness, but one great extension of the universe, an
eternity of peace and life. It is very difficult to say how I have
come to feel this, but I could see how easily and naturally life
flowed back into this ocean, how our own personal self found
entry, was received and accepted. I felt this, and now I know
that nothing of personality can be lost.

Science recognises atoms, all of which can be weighed and
measured, but never recognises personality, the one thing that
lies at the basis of reality. All creation is that, for apart from
personality, there is no meaning in creation. Water is water
to me because I am I, and so I have felt that in this great
infinite, in this ocean of personality from which my own little
personal self has sprung, lies completion of the cycle, like
those jets of water from the fountain which rise and fall and
come back home again. It is thus that we are received into
the heart and the bosom of the Infinite Personality. This is
what I myself have felt. It has been an experience for me
which cannot be described.

Everyday we see a continuation of this process of death,
like metre in a poem. At every point metre is a restriction.
An indefinite flow of words can never become a poem, but
must have this curtailing of liberty we call metre at every
step to prevent indefiniteness and vagueness. So life is always
being curtailed into its rhythm, its metre. Every day is a death,
every moment even. If not there would be a vast desert of
deathlessness. Life itself is demonstrated to us through death,
for death gives to the world that rhythm which is creation.
I have often felt this, and now science has shown us the fact
that the difference between one element and another is only

that of rhythm. The substance is the same, the rhythm is different. Rhythm in fact makes all the difference. So the whole of creation is nothing but the play of rhythm. We are each put into a different rhythm and all different individuals have their own rhythms. There is at the same time a fundamental unity, as in a poem in which each line possesses its own unity.

Possibly there is no such thing as substance. Science now says that matter is not matter, but electric force, and that substance does not exist. But there is rhythm, and the continual play of rhythm through which variety comes. I find that this is true of the poem. The words are the material. So long as they remain in their prose form they don't give a feeling of the eternal. The moment they are taken and put into rhythmical form they find their own soul, they shatter the boundaries of rhythm. It is the same with the rose. In the pulp of its petals you may find everything of the material that went to make the rose, but the rose is lost, for the boundaries that gave the rose rhythm are lost and with them is also lost the finality which had in it the touch of the Infinite.

Again, the rose appears to me to be still. Yet, because of its particular form and shape and harmony, it has an eternity of movement within that stillness, it is ever going round and round; it is always active, it is possessed of a dynamic quality; it has the quality of a picture that possesses perfect harmony. You can go on looking at such a picture forever, for it gives a swing to your own consciousness which makes your own mind active. If the picture was a mere patch of colour on the canvas, it would have no movement. It would be dead. But the moment that colour is placed within rhythmic boundaries, it always speaks. It is never still. It gets a dynamic quality which constantly speaks to our consciousness. Through such active movement eddies are formed. So long as the water spreads itself over the countryside you may have nothing but a swamp. The moment you set up a bank, the current is checked and goes round and round. So in perfect rhythm, form is always moving, as with the stars, and like the planets which seem to us so still, but which are never still. A great picture is always speaking to our consciousness. It is never still, and for that reason you never grow tired of it. But news from a newspaper of some tragic happening is still-born. We read the paragraph whilst we take out our tea and forget it. Put the facts for us in rhythmic form and they may speak, eternally, they may never cease to speak. The news may be mere commonplace from some journal and lack any dynamic quality, but give it rhythm and it can move for all time. That is art.

You must know that the materials of the rose and the rose tree are everywhere, but they have to be brought together and confined in rhythmic form in order to live. So the rose is created out of the great vague vastness. We don't know how it has been collected and put into rhythmic form, how from the indeterminate it finds everlasting being and becomes an eternal fact. So long as it is all merged in the vague it is nothing to me, yet it must have been everywhere. Somehow from this vast everywhere it has been put into perfect rhythmical form and has formed an eddy in our consciousness, so that, when we see it, it gives us a shock of delight. 'Ah!' we say, 'I know you. You are, as I am, a great fact. Because of this great fact in you, you are.'

Creative love imposes that rhythm, as a poet, who finds joy in his own creation, imposes a rhythm round his thoughts and words that gives them perfect shape. It is my joy that takes hope through rhythm, and as in the Upanishads it is infinite joy, that takes varied shapes and expresses itself in an eternity of creation, so around my own thoughts in my poems this impulse of joy impresses its rhythm. For the artist, lines are infinite in number and in shape, curved or rectangular. By gathering these lines into his own person and by imposing upon them his own rhythm, he directly imprisons certain of them in the chain of his love and joy. Thereby they become a creation. He has limited the unlimited.

The thoughts and the dreams of my mind are indefinite. Directly I define them. I become a creator. It is this limiting process which is the work of a genius. When a man is possessed of this power of control, when he can gather together and put the indefinite under the law of his own genius, his work is a work of creation. He limits the unlimited, he defines the indefinite.

Source: The Dartington Hall Trust.

The exiled Italians who took refuge in France, for a while, regularly published a paper titled *Corriere degli Italiani* from Paris where '*Il Poeta e l'Assassino*' (The Poet and the Murderer) was published in its 16 June issue in 1926. Although the writer at the end of the article was anonymously mentioned as 'An Italian Mother', she was Signora Salvadori. A copy of this paper was sent to Tagore at the care of Romain Rolland. Tagore received the paper, but failed to understand it as it was written in Italian. The present author received a photocopy of the article with its English translation by courtesy of Salvadori's granddaughter Clara Muzzarelli.

The Poet and the Murderer

I do not know whether, before sitting down opposite each other, they embraced: He, the mild singer of all things good, and the other the incarnation of violence, of falsehood and of cowardice.

No. I do not think they embraced. The thing is not possible, not even imaginable. There is a natural instinctive invincible repugnance which no effort of the human will can overcome, there are contacts against which soul and body rebel with all their moral and physical energy. It is true that in periods of great crises and of intellectual and social upheaval, the most atrocious offence against human and divine laws, and monstrous unions, and reversals of inviolable rules and of fundamental principles, may come to pass, without the world dulled by a too tragic experience, seeming to realise what happens.

But you, oh! the gentle poet of nature and human fraternity, why have you left the quiet haven of Santiniketan, where one learns to love and to nourish the spirit with all that is holy and beautiful, to come to a land where for years God is insulted at every moment and where His holy laws are trampled upon, and hate, vengeance and fratricide are daily taught and practised?

Have you come for a brotherly conversation with the insane 'Emperor' of the new Italy? What is there in common between you and he; between you, the great hearted apostle of peace and liberty, and he, who has dedicated all his ill-omened existence to an insane dream of nationalistic dominance and the conquest of material benefits?

Perhaps you did not know. Had you not heard the stories of horrid deeds that happened in my dear country; in the land of St. Frances of Assisi? He too was an apostle like you of universal charity. Had no one told you of the strife, brother against brother, provoked and ordered by the insane 'Emperor' of murders, massacres, the nameless violence and endless persecutions?

How is it, oh righteous Tagore, that you have not understood all this with your wide intelligence and your deep intuition? How was it that your sagacious spirit failed to warn you that the gift of books, and the invitation to visit Italy, and the hospitality offered by that ignoble buffoon, could not derive from an inward impulse of the soul, incapable as the offerer is a spontaneous feeling, nor from a sincere admiration for your art and work, so far removed from his vulgar mind, nor from any communion of aims, impossible between he who lives on the highest peaks of the human spirit, and he who wallows in the mud of the lowest material passions? It was nought but a hoax and a pose, behind which some double end was hidden, some political aim both foolish and puerile!

Indeed it is not improbable that the insane 'Emperor', absorbed in raving after grandeur, which makes him dream the undoing of the British Empire, thought, in his measureless ignorance, to have found in the great poet of India, now awakened to a new life and a new consciousness, a useful tool for his secret aims, of his megalomaniac intrigues, of his tortuous machinations.

In no other way can his interest for your school at Santiniketan be explained, a centre of universal brotherhood, and the negation of that false patriotism, of that frantic nationalism, which form the characteristic of the new State and the new education installed in Italy, and which for you instead, are the greatest danger for the peace of humanity, the greatest hindrance to disarmament and the reconciliation of people.

You wrote in your famous letter of 2nd March 1921: 'We have not even a term to indicate "Nation" in our tongue. That word does not suit us. We try to conquer, not for ourselves, but for the Kingdom of God. We believe in the power of the immortal spirit. We struggle, not for our independence, but for the liberty of the whole human race. This is the meaning of "Swaraj", our ideal of spiritual independence.'

And did you believe, you misguided poet, that these your magic words, these your holy aims, these thoughts so high and pure, might find an echo, be it ever so far and indistinct, in the dark recesses of a mind obscured by moral perversity?

What an abyss, what antithesis between the verses and discourses of the poet, noble, measured, expressing high ideas and guileless feeling and deep meditation, and the vulgar harangues shouted by the 'Emperor' through the piazzas of Italy.

But most certainly you, oh sage Tagore, when you found yourself face to face with the unworthy comedian, and could for a moment fix your deep dark eyes, grave and thoughtful, in the shifty and restless ones of the grim mandate, you must have understood your error.

Certainly in that instant, when your intuition tore aside the veil of falsehood and the full light beat upon your mind, your thought will have flown to the quiet haven of Santiniketan, haven of peace and goodness and beauty, and a bitter regret must have troubled your soul, the regret of having cherished a gift which you should never have accepted, because the hands which offered it were soiled with fraternal blood.

Return, return, gentle poet, to your old, silent India, venerated of us all. Return to your inaccessible mountains, to your majestic rivers, to your impenetrable jungles.

Hasten to leave, gentle poet of infinite love and eternal beauty. Oh! I know well that you live too far above the mud of this unhappy Europe, this luckless Italy, to have the candour of your pure soul stained by it, and may well repeat the sublime words of Beatrice:

'I have been made by God, thanks to His mercy, in such a way
That your misery doesn't touch me,
Nor flame of this fire assails me.'

Hasten to return to the land where you were born and where your disciples wait for you impatiently. This is not your place. The unclean snake that has corrupted a whole people and a whole generation of children and youths, preaching them to violence and falsehood, extinguishing in their yet unconscious souls every light of brotherliness and human pity. The snake winds its poisonous spires round you, and, if it cannot touch your incorruptible soul, yet it makes of you a tool for its oblique aims, for its lies and evil-doing.

Hasten away as soon as possible; return to your country, but do not wake her from her age-long slumber to the sad knowledge of the incurable ills of a civilisation doomed to dissolve and disappear in the agony of a comfortless, hopeless death. And, after having immersed and purified your limbs in the holy waters of the divine Ganges, source of physical health and moral purity, sing again in your melodious measures of all that is beautiful and holy and high and pure and continue to be the blessed apostle of peace, fraternity and love.

An Italian mother
June, 1926

Source: Archivio Salvadori Paleotti, Fermo, Italy.

The following lecture is a draft marked 'In Venice' and is still pre-served in the Dartington Hall Trust archive dated 1 February 1925. The poet was supposed to deliver this lecture at the University of Venice, but failed to do so due to his illness. The lecture was eventually published with an Italian summary in the university's journal, *Rivista dell'Ateneo Veneto* (January–June 1925).

There was a time when Italy opened her gates for contact between the East and the West and I hope that road to communication may be revived again, for the sake of an exchange, not merely of material wealth from East to West, but of those spiritual and intellectual treasures which are still left in the East. This interchange must not be one-sided, and those intellectual treasures which Europe has bequeathed to posterity must also find their way to the great Continent of Asia, so that there may be a real exchange of thought, an intermingling of minds and hearts between the two hemispheres.

We have often been told that the East and West are too different to meet together, that the difficulties are too great for such a combination and meeting. But I am sure that through such a gap the force of gravitation does work, that through this very difference a force of attraction is set up, and that because of this difference there must be a meeting in order for each to find its respective fulfilment.

Therefore though a poet has said, 'East is East and West is West and therefore the twain must never meet', we all know how in the past there have been meteorological currents in the atmosphere of sentiment circulating from East to West and West to East, and no one can prevent this circulation from travelling across the sea and from bringing human souls together.

The present age is dominated by the spirit of greed, and even though it brings men together physically, in reality it separates them. Through science all the human races have come closer to one another but because the great idyll of sympathy and cooperation is lacking, because greed and the use of force predominate, therefore, in spite of the eternal fact of the meeting of the races, we have not really met.

In the days when travelling was difficult, messengers who went from one country to another and who were willing to overcome the difficulties of the way, were able to reach the heart and spirit of a strange land and of its people much more easily than now, when communication is simple and travel so well provided with comforts. For we are not, all of us, gifted with those qualifications which give us the right to travel in a strange country and until we are ready with sympathy and adaptation of mind our travel may be an insult. If we cannot cultivate a respect for all humanity, if we are obsessed with the spirit of our own separateness which makes us contemptuous of that to which we are not accustomed, then we have no right to travel across our own boundaries. Because travel has become so easy, a kind of picnic in fact, because it is not hard to rush from one country to another, a great deal of misunderstanding has accumulated about people who are different from ourselves. Through the accumulation all kinds of difficulties arise. It is for instance difficult to do justice to a people that you do not truly know, and this case of communication has made it much more easy to be unjust to foreign races. You remember what respect your citizen Marco Polo had for China, how he travelled all that distances from his own mother country to the Far East, with immense difficulty. He had never made the study of geography that is easy for you. Yet, in spite of the shock, through his in-born sympathy for humanity, his adaptation of mind made it possible for him to feel a real respect for Chinese people, and for them to accept him as a friend. How few travellers there are today who enter into the spirit of a people with feelings of respect and awe. How many are possessed of that natural vulgarity of mind which is unable to penetrate beyond the veil of strangeness, into the sanctuary of the heart. The consequence is a world-wide mischief for which we are suffering. Europe can make her voice heard today, but Asia has not this power and must suffer mutely injustice and indignity from those adventurers who comfortably travel across her continent. This is the reason why it is possible for a poet to say, 'never the twain shall meet.' The twain did meet when there were physical barriers of all kinds. Haven't you had your gift of great spiritual treasure from the East? Wasn't it once possible for the Greeks to travel to India, to dwell there and to admire the religious and intellectual gifts that they received, and others after them? But what a vast difference today, not because East and the West have changed radically, but through the change of external circumstances, through an ease of communication, that makes it easy to put up at the hotel but no longer easy to enter the home, where alone it is possible to know the life of the people.

We are two great neighbours, East and the West, and it will be a great pity and a real shame for all humanity if we cannot come to know each other, if the barriers between us prove insurmountable. I have felt this pain of separation in my heart for long. Until we cross these boundary walls and shake hands in true fellowship we shall never have true peace in this world.

Our destiny is awaiting that great moment when East and West will be united in a spirit of love and co-operation.

This institute of which I want to speak is to represent this aspiration of man for the union of these two great continents, Asia and Europe. When we talk about the Orient or even about the Occident we are apt to generalise too much. I cannot say myself, however much I may wish it were true. Asia is a big continent, divided by great geographical barriers, by high mountains and by vast deserts, with climates of every variety. It is not therefore like the continent of Europe, which, if not altogether one from a geographical point of view, from that of human habitation is a true continent, possessing a real unity which is not sharply divided by physical barriers or by differences of climate. This has made it possible for the great peoples in Europe to come close in a real unity of culture, and to a certain extent also, of temperament, custom and habit. This similarity in all the different countries of Europe has been made possible because of the natural aspect of the continent, which is geographically almost like a single country compared to Asia, which with its different parts so violently, so brutally separated cannot truly be termed a continent. You all know how India has been segregated owing to the physical nature of its boundaries. Through the Himalayas in the North she has remained for long centuries a separate country in the heart of the world. This has enabled her to develop her own individual culture in unmixed purity, and therefore, because it had a true unity, she exercised an attraction to people who lived in distant lands. For centuries pilgrims came there from all parts of the world, Greeks, Muhammadans, Christians, Romans, Persians and Mongolians. All these people gravitated to India and formed a conglomeration of race, of civilisation, of religion and community which has taken on its own individuality, one that is not shared by the other countries of Asia. Semitic Asia for instance is fundamentally different from the part of Asia which India represents. Therefore, when we talk of the Orient as something which has unity, we must not generalise too vaguely; for Turks, Tartars, Arabs and Chinese each have their own peculiar features.

It is then difficult for me to speak for the whole of Asia, for so few there are who can find any comprehensive unity in all the Asiatic countries. Possibly there is some ideal of unity behind them all, but how few opportunities there are to study and realise this. Therefore I can only talk of India and I have come to your doors with the idea of bringing my mother country nearer to your heart. I never dreamt that this would be possible, but on my last visit to Europe I met with such a genuine feeling of love from the peoples of the different countries that I could not believe it to be true. So I set out to bring you word of this ideal India of the past, and India which today is materially poor, whose soul is asleep, but which still contains the seed of a great ideal, and thus to arouse your sympathy and respect for her, not that my own country may benefit but in order to bring about a unity of hearts between Asia, India and the West. For this reason I have founded Visva-Bharati. The word 'bharati' means that voice of India which is universal which is for all countries and for all time, and not peculiarly provincial, which transcends time and space, and adds to the wealth of all humanity. My intention was, however feeble my power, to make it possible to offer the best gifts of India to the world and especially to the West, and through this intellectual and spiritual hospitality in India to gain your gratitude and love. I know how poor from an external aspect this institution is, set up in an obscure corner of India, and how impossible it is for me to effect the great result of this communion of spirit between East and West, but we have a great saying in our scriptures that runs, 'only in action have you your right and not in the fruit.' That is, you must do what you can and never greedy of immediate result you have this right to do: but none to reap the harvest. That you must leave to the great Providence, and it may come or it may not.

I believe in this ideal and I take my stand in your midst on behalf of this human right which is being ignored, this privilege of man to own for himself all that has been created in all time by great men, to discover the fundamental spirit of truth which dwells in all races. Wherever they were born, all great men have lived for every individual in every country. No great poet, scientist or hero has ignored this, or tried to set up barriers to prevent the communication of these immortal treasures. The moment we attempt to check their passage, storm centres of unrest are set up and our peace is menaced through the prevention of intercommunication. It is to proclaim this truth that this Institution has been set up, and however feeble it may be, I should feel proud to be remembered as a poet who believed in it and who tried to give shape to truth, the highest truth, and therefore the only truth which can give us abiding peace. We have spread a seat where this truth may find its place and welcome. For the great Spirit of this age calls for the Truth of sympathy and cooperation among all peoples and races. This Spirit has come to our doors and [has] raised his voice saying 'I am your guest, I have come to your door.' I have tried to open the gate of the heart of India to the great Spirit of the modern age. If I am remembered at all, let it be for this.

Source: Archivio Salvadori Paleotti, Fermo, Italy.

Before sending the Tagore–Salvadori (Signora) dialogue to the press for its publication, the script was sent to Salvadori for his approval and comment. The following letter was his response.

Gland,

(Vaud)
Switzerland
16-VII-1926

To Sir Rabindranath Tagore
Dear Sir

I have read your copy of my wife's interview with you, and since I am personally concerned with it, I hope you will allow me to make two or three remarks and correct some statements.

My wife has already corrected the account of the Fascist assault on myself. But I wish to insist on the fact that, however shaken I may have been afterwards, as a natural reaction even in a strong and physical and mental organism like myself, I have never fallen into a state of stupor! (Perhaps you misunderstood my wife, as she expressed herself badly. Stupor in Italian has a quite different meaning from the English stupor.) And never did I lose my presence of mind. I only fainted for a few minutes under the terrible blows on my head, while the executioners were branding my poor face with bloody marks, two on each of my forehead, one the cheek, one on the chin, thus:

Indeed a terrible bloody mark to look at! It was the sentence of death stamped on my face. Only the Almighty God, sending my boy and then an officer to my rescue, saved me from being menaced by the band of ruffians waiting in the street. My boy, while waiting for me, overheard three of them speaking about somebody who was to be killed!

I was very sorry not to meet you, and it would be to me a great joy to do so on your way back to India. By then I shall have finished some lectures which I am preparing to give next month for the Women's International League for Peace and Freedom.

I believe that if public opinion everywhere was made to realise the true state of things in Italy, a feeling and a cry of horror would run over all civilised, and even tortured, nations. If you wished to have documents, I would suggest to you a book or pamphlet written by the poor martyr Matteotti: *Un anno di dominio fascista* (One year of Fascist dominion). In it you would find a long list, which fills about forty big 8vo pages (44–81), of hundreds and hundreds of crimes of every kind committed by Fascists from November 1922 to November 1923, and left unpunished. And these represent only a part; for many remain unknown.

But even more horrible than all crimes committed against the bodies (of fellow-citizens!)[,] more horrible than murder and torture, are the crimes committed against the souls of those who oppose the new slavery established by Fascism. Not only has Fascism produced a moral havoc and devastation, the results of which will weigh heavily for a long time on the national consciousness; but it has actually introduced new devilish forms of punishment, the thought of which alone ought to make any human being shudder as something monstrous. I mean that people are driven on purpose to despair, to suicide, to insanity, by means of incessant and infernal persecutions, and so deprived of their reason. In my town a poor friend of mine has been reduced to a state of idiocy by continual terror and repeats incessantly: When will it finish? When will it finish?—Also in my town a shoemaker to whom it was signified by tolling the bells that his last hour had come, recently attempted suicide—In Milan, a judge who had lost his post was unable to earn his living because of Fascist machinations and committed suicide. The official explanation was that the unfortunate man suffered from an 'incurable illness.' But his doctor courageously revealed the truth, declaring that he had nothing the matter with him.

I could multiply cases almost indefinitely, but I have no more space, and I do not wish to detain you any longer. Suffice it to say that sometimes it was the government itself which gave formal orders to the authorities to make life impossible, 'render l'aria irrespirabile' (make the atmosphere unbearable), to its opponents. In some cases, like that of Gobetti, a young writer who recently died in Paris, their order was so well and literally executed that the poor victims die of it! When I think about this dreadful state of things to which my country is reduced, I really wonder how it had happened that Tagore has accepted Mussolini's hospitality, and that he has found his personality 'striking' and 'masterful'.

If you knew him better, I am sure you would change your opinion about him, and perhaps come to the conclusion that 'there is nothing in him', as the great historian Guglielmo Ferrero once said. And as to his moral character, you would probably be obliged to admit with Angelica Balabanoff (an honest and intelligent lady who knows him very well, and who assisted him in the direction of the socialist newspaper *Avanti*) that he is the greatest coward among cowards. (See an article by her published in the *People of Brussels* of 10th November 1925, and other article by her in the *Wiener Arbeiter Zeitung* of December 1925.) Whatever he may be, he is certainly a great criminal, and a man affected by syphilis and mega-lomania, a man unsound in body and mind and morally insane. As to his supposed strength of determination, you will find in the same articles by Mrs. Balabanoff facts which show all the country, i.e. that Mussolini has always been a most weak man, afraid of assuming responsibilities, incapable of any action when unassisted by other people, extremely subject to the influences of those around him (*unglaublich becinflussbar*). Indeed, this great criminal is simply a tool in other people's hands, an instrument of the reactionary forces tending towards slavery and intellectual and moral darkness against the forces of light and freedom.

Will you allow me to say that your remarks about Mussolini's 'strik-ing' and 'masterful' personality spoil the whole of the interview and, if published, will greatly damage our Cause? At least it would be necessary to explain and define what you mean by personality. In a certain sense even criminals and lunatics (like the Roman emperor Nero and Cesar Borgia, the Prince of Machiavelli) may present the appearance of strong personalities, but only the appearances. In fact these individuals never possess, or can possess, a real strength of will and of character; on the contrary they live under the complete dominion of the worst instincts of human nature, and act according to the caprice of the moment of the influence of their sur-roundings.

If you study deeply what you call the 'personality' of Mussolini; you will find that such is exactly the case with this abject product of the general social neurosis of which the Italian nation is presently suffering—simply an interesting 'case' from the pathological point of view. And this indeed is the only excuse, or extenuating circumstance, which we can allow him for all the incredible evil he has done to poor Italy and the unfortunate Italian people. (Competent medical authorities have formally declared that he is mentally unsound, with evident symptoms of progressive paralysis, the consequence of his syphilitic infection, indeed, a worthy regenerator of the Italian nation!)

You say that as a poet, it is the human element—even in politics— which touches you most deeply, and the expression of the personal man in his work. Well, try to go to the bottom of Mussolini's morbid nature, and you will find, not a person, but a brute—real humanity, but the semblance of humanity, humanity degenerated and corrupted and presented to the lowest degree.

I hope you will excuse me for these considerations which I felt it was my duty to submit to your high judgement and your honest heart, and believe me, with the greatest respect.

Yours truly.

Guglielmo Salvadori

P.S. I   I hope you will forgive me if I suggest that it would be a great and beautiful action on your part, if you sent back to the ignoble donator [sic] his gift of books. As soon as Italy has recovered her liberty and her place among civilised nations, I promise to you, in the name of all true Italians, to make a new gift of the same books and works of art for your school.

P.S. II My friend Professor Salvemini is presently in Paris where he will remain in France the whole month. If you wish for other addresses in London, I will send them to you. He is incredibly impressionable.

Source: Rabindra Bhavan.

Index

About the Author

Born in West Bengal in 1940, Kalyan Kundu graduated from Presidency College and received his Masters from the University of Calcutta. He obtained PhDs in Botany from both Calcutta and London. It was in London, while pursuing Biomedical Research on Muscular Dystrophy at the Institute of Neurology, that he became interested in the work, philosophy, and life of Rabindranath Tagore. This passion led him to form an archive of Tagore's work in the United Kingdom, specifically for an English-speaking audience. From this archive, The Tagore Centre UK was born in 1985.

Kalyan Kundu is now the chairperson of the Centre and has several publications, both in English and Bengali, to his credit. These include: *Rabindranath Tagore: A Timeless Mind*, co-edited with Amalendu Biswas and Christine Marsh (The Tagore Centre UK, 2011); *He*, a translation, with Anthony Loyens, of Tagore's fantasy writing *Sé* (The Tagore Centre UK, 2003); *Imagining Tagore: Rabindranath and the British Press (1912–1941)*, co-edited with

Sakti Bhattacharya and Kalyan Sircar (Sahitya Samsad, 2000); and *This World Is Beautiful*, an anthology for young Tagore readers co-edited with Sakti Bhattacharya, Jill Parvin, and Kalyan Sircar (The Tagore Centre UK, 1988). All of his publications have received critical acclaim in media. In addition, he has published important research papers on Rabindranath Tagore, which have been well received throughout the academic world.